The Future-Ready Brand

The Future-Ready Brand

How the World's **Most Influential CMOs** are Navigating **Societal Forces** and **Emerging Technologies**

Mitch Duckler

Forbes | Books

Published by Forbes Books, Charleston, South Carolina.
An imprint of Advantage Media Group.

Forbes Books is a registered trademark, and the Forbes Books colophon is a trademark of Forbes Media, LLC.

Printed in the United States of America.

10 9 8 7 6 5 4 3 2 1

ISBN: 979-8-88750-178-9 (Paperback)
ISBN: 979-8-88750-179-6 (eBook)

Library of Congress Control Number: 2024900954

Cover design by Matthew Morse.
Layout design by Ruthie Wood.

This custom publication is intended to provide accurate information and the opinions of the author in regard to the subject matter covered. It is sold with the understanding that the publisher, Forbes Books, is not engaged in rendering legal, financial, or professional services of any kind. If legal advice or other expert assistance is required, the reader is advised to seek the services of a competent professional.

Since 1917, Forbes has remained steadfast in its mission to serve as the defining voice of entrepreneurial capitalism. Forbes Books, launched in 2016 through a partnership with Advantage Media, furthers that aim by helping business and thought leaders bring their stories, passion, and knowledge to the forefront in custom books. Opinions expressed by Forbes Books authors are their own. To be considered for publication, please visit **books.Forbes.com**.

To Elaine and Drew, who will always remain at the core of every-thing important to me.

CONTENTS

PUBLISHER'S NOTE

In his 2019 book, *The Indispensable Brand*, Mitch Duckler took major brands to task for the "identity crisis" they faced with so many *indistinguishable* from one another, failing at arguably the most important job of brand management—*differentiation*. Then Mitch offered a best practices workflow for "becoming an *indispensable* brand and sustaining that brand excellence over time."

Now in *The Future-Ready Brand*, Mitch looks to a new set of challenges facing chief marketing officers (CMOs) and finds the solutions from the CMOs themselves. For the better part of a year, Mitch interviewed the CMOs of the world's leading brands not only to identify the real marketing challenges they're

Featuring in-depth interviews with CMOs of...	
Abbott	Kohler
Accenture	KPMG
Ally Financial	Lagunitas
American Eagle	Lexus
BMW	McDonald's
Boston Scientific	Moderna
Canva	New Balance
CapitalOne	PepsiCo
Caterpillar	Polar
Coca-Cola	Progressive
Coty	PwC
CVS Health	Salesforce
Danone	SEE
Deloitte	Sephora
Deutsche Telekom	Telefonica
H&R Block	Travelers
Herbalife	Unisys
Hilton	UPS
IBM	US Cellular
John Hancock	Wells Fargo
Juniper Networks	Yum Brands

facing but also to reveal how to best manage them. Mitch's qualitative research is thusly turned into a new best practices workflow for handling the *futurewaves* now cresting on every CMO's horizon.

The book is divided into three sections: positioning, personalizing, and promoting. Each chapter begins with a Global 2000 company case study and then spins out its learnings and discoveries.

The first section of *futurewaves* are the societal shifts that are forcing brands to **position** very differently to meet the values and expectations of an emerging consumer base. At the heart of this force is an ever-increasing emphasis consumers place on the resonance (or lack thereof) of a company's purpose. In addition, postpandemic attitudes have prompted a broader and more holistic view on wellness, which has profound implications for brands even outside the so-called healthcare industry. Finally, the emergence of a complex Gen Z as the dominant generational cohort will shape how brands are positioned in the marketplace for decades to come.

The second section is comprised of the emerging technological innovations that'll allow brands to **personalize** the product offer and customer experience with near-prescient precision. Artificial intelligence (AI) is hyper-personalizing the product offer and customer experience, and enabling brand marketers to approach the ever-elusive aspiration of one-to-one marketing. *XR technologies* and the Metaverse are creating omnichannel strategies that result in more fully immersive brand experiences. And Web3 has the potential to truly democratize the worldwide web and to provide marketers with unprecedented levels of direct access to consumers.

The third section details the marketing activation trends that—fueled by technological innovations—are rejiggering the methods companies are using to **promote** their brands profitably. Emerging technologies—most notably generative AI—are shifting the relationship between brands and audiences. The combination of AI and XR technologies is adding a powerful afterburner impact on gamification strategy and its ability to drive top-of-funnel activity. Finally, virtual Influencers are working their way into the marketing mix and are driving outsized return on investment (ROI) for brands in the process.

What differentiates *this book* is the way Mitch weaves the insights of the world's most influential CMOs into his own distilled views on what's been working, what will likely work in the future, and how to get there from here.

Mitch surely knows of what he speaks—having spent three decades in Fortune 500 brand management and marketing. The first ten were in-house at **Unilever** and **The Coca-Cola Company**. The next ten with the global branding consultancy, **Prophet**. There he became a partner in the Chicago office and co-led the firm's brand positioning practice. Then Mitch launched the consulting firm **FullSurge** and has led strategic brand-related consulting engagements for some of the most prestigious brands, including **ExxonMobil, Deloitte, Scotts Miracle-Gro, American Family Insurance, Hyatt Hotels, Novartis, Abbott, Blue Cross & Blue Shield, Cox Communications, ManpowerGroup, LexisNexis**, and **Caterpillar**.

And so, in these pages, Mitch brings out the best of the best looking forward. Every marketer aiming to remain relevant tomorrow will read this book today!

FOREWORD
by Guy Kawasaki

The dizzying pace of technological innovation and cultural change has placed today's marketing leaders in an arena where the eyes of the world watch as CMOs grapple with unprecedented trials. How can brands stay relevant, let alone thrive, in such a rapidly evolving landscape? Enter Mitch Duckler's extraordinary *The Future-Ready Brand*. Herein Duckler brings together the greatest minds currently at work in the marketing world at large. Duckler humbly foregrounds their insights while guiding the reader through today's most burning issues in branding with keen insight and infectious optimism.

At the heart of Duckler's exhilarating tour through the perspectives of our world's most powerful CMOs is a call to view change not as a threat but as a tremendous creative challenge. It's not enough to be reactive; brands must cultivate a proactive stance, constantly scanning the horizon for the next big shift, be it in technology, consumer behavior, or global trends. Duckler delves deeply into emerging technologies, from AI to Web3, not to overwhelm but to elucidate their massive potential for revolutionizing brand experiences. Yet the most profound revelation that shines through in the book is that technology alone is not enough. Truly future-ready brands must tap into powerful societal shifts, aligning with the values of rising generations like purpose-driven Gen Z.

More than a thought leadership book, *The Future-Ready Brand* is a symphony of marketing's most relevant voices today and a compass for the complex, evolving world of branding.

As we enter a new era, *The Future-Ready Brand* provides the resources and direction brands need to embrace the opportunities of tomorrow.

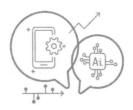

SECTION ONE: SOCIETAL FUTUREWAVES

How Brands Will Need to Be Positioned

In this first section, we'll look at the wholesale changes in societal and generational values that are prompting brands to *position* very differently to align with the values and expectations of a demanding new consumer base.

Chapter 1 shows how companies that *put purpose first* are invariably becoming industry standouts—manifest in their exemplary corporate cultures, publicly recognized competence, or as heralded champions of vital causes. Numerous benefits accrue to these purpose-driven companies, including a proven positive correlation between purpose and profit, outperforming the overall market, an ability to command premium pricing, enjoying greater brand loyalty with Millennials and Gen Z consumers, and winning the war for talent.

Chapter 2 looks at the bursting wellness economy and how a heightened *prioritization of health* impacts all brand marketers. Chief among these impacts is the need to reassess the brand promise in terms of a total health orientation, making the brand feel as "personal" as an individual's own wellness feels, finding ways to generate healthier in-store experiences, meeting consumers "where" and "why" they are shopping for solutions, and cultivating the brand's authentic community with a health orientation in mind.

Chapter 3 *parses the Gen Z cohort* into polar-opposite mind frames that marketers need to understand and align with. This means holding the company's public-facing actions to a higher level of accountability, pointedly meeting Gen Z where they're hanging out, integrating the brand/products organically into the action on gaming sites, and raising the brand's voice in both online and offline communities where values and interests are shared.

CHAPTER ONE
The Purpose of Brand Purpose

In October 2020, at the height of a global pandemic, most of Accenture's 624,000 employees gathered virtually and in offices across two hundred cities in forty-nine countries. Cameras in all the conference rooms leveraged state-of-the-art technology to make it feel like everyone was gathered in the same room. For the previous several weeks, a countdown clock on Accenture's intranet had ticked down the minutes to this event. Everyone anticipated a major announcement—one that would surely affect how the IT consulting company would do business for years to come.

The meeting kicked off with video messages from Accenture's senior leadership and line employees, as well. Each spoke enthusiastically about a big important announcement to come and about the role they'd played in bringing it to fruition. It culminated with a message from David Roland, then chairman of the board and interim CEO. Everyone listened in closely.

What was the big announcement? Was it the acquisition of a global multibillion-dollar company? Or perhaps a transformational shift in business model or strategic direction? No. It was to introduce the company's newly defined purpose. Ten words that would underpin everything Accenture stood for and that all of its employees would live by for years to come. Ten words, *"To Deliver on the Promise of Technology and Human Ingenuity."* So very much went into those words and then soon emerged from them.

The next day at every Accenture location, employees' computer screens lit up with the new ten-word company purpose and a corresponding brand repositioning, *"Let there be Change."* A new app let employees easily post this new purpose and brand strategy along with their profile photo on LinkedIn. The worldwide engagement from this one step was so tremendous that it prompted a board member to ask about the cost of such an impactful LinkedIn placement. The answer, of course, was "nothing" since the effort was entirely organic.

Of course, there was also a *paid* media effort to support the initiative. Three distinct TV ads were created to announce the new purpose and the *"Let there be Change"* branding to the world. Accenture bought up every single one of NBCUniversal media properties to simulcast its new ads around the world at precisely the same hour. Although somewhat commonplace now, this represented a first for NBCUniversal. At the same time, hundreds of thousands of employees were gathered on a Microsoft Teams video call to watch the ads run for the first time. It was truly a powerful moment for Accenture employees and for the brand.

The Purpose Dissected

Many months of hard work had gone into developing Accenture's new purpose. Hundreds of people within the organization, and outside as well, were interviewed for their perspectives on Accenture's true purpose for being. According to Jill Kramer, Accenture's chief marketing and communications officer, "There were two primary objectives driving the creation of the company's purpose. First, it had to represent an enduring North Star—something that was not merely fly-by-night. But the second was perhaps even more essential. Our purpose needed to be inextricably connected to the value we create as a business."[1]

Since Accenture creates value through its people, the purpose needed to both reflect and amplify the collective strengths of those people. Kramer saw it as "striking at the very heart of what the company is. People in vastly different roles within the company, and in vastly different countries around the world, should be able to *see themselves* in the purpose." So, Kramer broke down this new purpose into its component parts, to show how that objective was being met:

"The first component, 'To Deliver on the Promise,' is both a nod to Accenture's past and a foreshadowing of the future. Accenture has a history of *delivery* and executional excellence, represented in our (longtime) tagline, 'High Performance. Delivered.' Conversely, *promise* is an emotional and aspirational word that speaks to future potential, and it balances the more grounded and pragmatic notion of *delivery*."

In the second component of the purpose, "Technology and Human Ingenuity," Kramer noted the balancing act inherent in that. For while technology does help humans, it is humans who make technology better. There was considerable debate among Kramer's marketing team about which should come first, the technology bit or the human ingenuity bit. That is, is it more accurate to say that technology enables human ingenuity, or is it the other way around? At one point, Kramer decided that it really didn't matter. "Delivery and promise, technology and human ingenuity, they're essentially two opposite poles that are constantly pulling on one another while at the same time making one another better. It's what allows a company as complex and broad as ours to be all that we can be, but with a unifying principle at the core."

From Company Purpose to Brand Positioning

With Accenture's purpose solidified, Kramer turned her attention to the company's master brand. A brand's positioning should be the external manifestation of its business strategy—the promise it makes to all relevant stakeholders. When Kramer considered the "To Deliver on the Promise of Technology and Human Ingenuity" purpose, the relationship between it and the concept of *change* was clear. "There is one thing that is common across every client we serve," Kramer says. "They're all either trying to drive change or to cope better with it. So, we thought the simple statement 'Let there be Change' was profound because it acknowledges that change is good. It doesn't say it's easy, but it portrays change in a positive, tenacious, and optimistic light."

Most conspicuous to this idea of *change* in Accenture's brand positioning is the extent it goes to express a point of view. "We're not asking the world a question," Kramer points out. "We're putting a perspective out there that change is good, that value comes from change, so let there be change!" Like all strong brand positionings, this one speaks to both the heart and the mind—the "human desire to always be changing for the better and becoming the best version of yourself."

To be a robust brand platform, "Let there be Change" has to have staying power with the versatility to accommodate the marketplace's own changes over time. Kramer recognizes this and has planned for it. "If five years from now there's a pivot in the world and we start doing more things or different things, our brand platform may expand or morph. But we will still be anchored to our core purpose of technology and human ingenuity." So, the company's purpose statement can endure while the brand platform can, as needed, adapt to changing times to remain relevant.

Tying It All Together

This Accenture case study is especially compelling because it conflates three enterprise priorities: *business strategy* and *brand positioning* inextricably linked to *company purpose*. As Kramer puts it, "Our business strategy, company purpose, and brand positioning are all aligned around the notion of technology and human ingenuity inspiring positive change." In short, every business decision Accenture makes can align with its purpose. And so, this purpose and brand platform will surely serve as a bright motivational "North Star" for Accenture's many employees and marketplace offerings for years to come. In tandem, it should give Accenture a strategic advantage over its competitors that have not so clearly defined and executed on a meaningful corporate purpose.

What Is Driving This Interest in Purpose?

A big inflection point in purpose-driven thinking came with Simon Sinek's 2010 TED Talk, *How Great Leaders Inspire Action*, and his best-selling book the following year, *Start with Why*. It was rather bold and even revolutionary at the time to insist that businesses focus less on *what* they do and more on *why* they do it. And still, a good number of businesses "got Sinek." They did attempt to shift their thinking from *what* to *why*. At the same time, many more dismissed Sinek's ideas or only half bought in with an annual corporate social responsibility (CSR) project or a flight of billboards shouting out some feel-good slogan.

Sinek was among those who early on saw how then-esoteric concepts such as sustainability, social responsibility, and the fight against inequality would become "hot buttons" to consumers. He saw how those consumers would begin demanding more than just products and services from companies. They would demand that brands align with their values and make a positive impact on society while pursuing profit—summed up as "making a difference."

This public conversation about corporate purpose increased sharply in the mid-1990s and soon became a salient boardroom issue. An EY and Oxford University Saïd Business School study noted a fivefold increase in public interest in corporate purpose between 1995 and 2014.[2] In the decade since, there have been steadily growing demands for businesses to "do good."

Purpose has become paramount. It has led not only customers but also employees, investors, stakeholders, and civic groups to ask critical questions about the proper role of the corporation in society. So, what triggered this uprising of concern for corporate accountability? That EY/Oxford study identified six forces at work, and they are summarized here.

FORCE #1: LACK OF TRUST

Trust is the foundation of any successful business relationship. Yet big events, including the 2008 financial crisis, growing income inequality, and the pandemic, pushed the already teetering trust people had in corporations right over the cliff. This perceived failure of U.S. institutions was felt across the nation and was felt strongest by younger generations even as they were moving into their peak consumption years.

FORCE #2: INCREASING IMPORTANCE OF SUSTAINABILITY

Consumers now want products that do no harm to the environment and are produced in an ethical, responsible manner. They not only want it, but in ten minutes on the internet today, they can also easily discover which brands are authentically pursuing these high-minded goals and which are pretenders.

Companies are finding themselves fully scrutinized by the public and regulators as well on the stances they take on environmental, social, and governance issues. This pressure is compelling executives to question their operations and examine how they produce and deliver in a socially and environmentally sustainable way. And to question as well whether their product life cycles are being managed toward improving circularity—the newest effort to manage the earth's finite resources.

FORCE #3: SOCIAL INEQUALITY

Wealth inequality has hit historic highs, and it is often noted that 1 percent of the world's population controls at least 50 percent of global wealth. CEO-to-worker pay ratios are nearly 400 to 1, a 14× increase since 1978.[3] These coarse inequalities have led to a level of skepticism and distrust of elite companies that is unprecedented in U.S. history. It practically screams out for an open and transparent response from corporate leaders to make their good intentions crystal clear to all.

FORCE #4: IMPACT OF SOCIAL MEDIA

Consumers have more power than ever to impact a company's reputation through social media. Indeed, they've proven more than adept at harnessing social media to air a company's dirty laundry of unfulfilled brand promises faster and more effectively than even news organizations. A casual scroll through an X (formerly Twitter) feed now surfaces legions of disgruntled consumers posting their anger and frustration and tagging the company for all their followers to see. This has translated into a startling loss of control for companies and an urgent need to bridge the gap with genuinely transparent accountability measures.

FORCE #5: NEED FOR LONGER-TERM THINKING

As early as the mid-1990s, a large body of research aimed the spotlight on the planet's fast-multiplying crises that could endanger the environment and human life. This research enjoyed high-profile champions and public support. But only a few people were willing to pay an extra penny to mitigate the problems, even if they agreed the problems existed. That narrative has since changed and drastically.

A majority of consumers in all age groups now believe that companies have an obligation to not only implement sustainable practices but also drive innovative solutions for long-term environmental and social challenges. Seeking profit alone is no longer sufficient. Companies must consider the so-called triple bottom line of Profit + People + Planet. Unlike years past, consumers are now willing to pay a premium for products that align with their personal values.

FORCE #6: DIGITIZATION

Our wholesale leap into a data-driven world has completely altered how companies interact with customers. Instantaneous interconnectedness enables businesses to know and serve customers better. On the flip side, customers can quickly identify any discrepancies between a company's image and its actions. To benefit fully from digitization, companies are now obligated to embrace the transparency it requires.

The good news is that, when done well, the increased digitization of marketing can be a tremendous asset when looking to grow and connect with customers who align with the company's purpose. It can attract like-minded customers and foster a loyal community of passionate brand advocates.

Millennial and Gen Z Impact

Chapter 3 will focus on the emergence of "Gen Z" as the first confidently all-digital generation, but here it is worth highlighting Gen Z's views on corporate purpose. A 2020 study of eight thousand consumers and seventy-five companies/brands worldwide found a striking 92 percent of Gen Z saying they "would act in support of a purposeful brand."[4] Not far behind Gen Z are Millennials, with 90 percent of them indicating likewise. If these two generational cohorts are passionate about a cause or issue, they will purchase from companies that ally with their values.

This does not mean that younger people will refuse to use Amazon to buy cheap or questionably sourced products from China—only that they will make their brand preferences known when they have the opportunity to do so.

It is similar with Millennials' and Gen Z's choices of workplaces. These two cohorts came of age during financial crises, have been stuck with stagnant wages, witnessed the collapse of too-big-to-fail businesses, and endured a global pandemic. They see corporations as impermanent entities making unreliable promises. To them, the world is in constant flux. So, employment flexibility is not only desirable in their view, but it is also a means of survival. From this mindset, a job is not a job unless it offers more than just money. Gen Z will walk away from employment just as quickly as they'll forgo a purchase with a company that breaks their trust.

These views on the workplace reflect an equally important desire among Millennials and Gen Z to live their lives as individuals and not mere cogs in an ostensibly broken corporate machinery. Some will say there is a chicken and egg situation here—that corporations have turned away from employees and not the other way around. Either way, these generational views are very real. And savvy brand marketers will recognize their salience when aiming to connect with these audiences.

Three Types of Corporate Purpose

When most people think about corporate purpose, they tend to associate it with a cause—climate change, access to healthcare, and increased diversity being the most passionate concerns at present. So, they naturally assume that purpose-driven organizations will share in these concerns, as well. However, it's important to note that corporate purpose is not necessarily tied to these hot-button issues. In fact, a *Harvard Business Review* article "What Is the Purpose of Your Purpose?" found that companies derive purpose on three levels—culture, competence, and cause.[5] Here is a summary of the findings and some of the brands that are delivering on each type of purpose.

EXEMPLARY CULTURE

The distinct set of values, beliefs, behaviors, and day-to-day practices of a company define its corporate culture. All of these corporate modalities influence how employees interact with one another, with customers, and with the community. And it all manifests in a company personality and style, which, in turn, shapes the company's image and reputation, whether intentionally or not.

"What differentiates a purpose-driven brand from a transactional brand is *intention*—the underlying motivations," Peggy Ang explains. She's president and CMO as well as a board member of **Polar Electro**, the pioneer of wearable sports technology. "I consider corporate purpose to be how a company thinks about itself, and how it views its role in the marketplace and in the community. Your products and services are not going to differentiate you because they are easily replicated. What's going to define you is how you behave, and how you show up with customers and in the community. A strong purpose helps a brand move from transactional to authentic."[6]

This kind of thinking about a company's culture shaping its reputation is adeptly summarized in the purpose statement of another company, the confectionery manufacturer **Mars**. "The world we want tomorrow starts with how we do business today."[7]

EXHIBITING COMPETENCE

A company's unique set of skills, knowledge base, and expertise become the core competence they deliver to customers. By leveraging these strengths, the company becomes a purposeful leader in its industry.

Walmart exemplifies this with the purpose of "[s]aving people money so they can live better."[8] Walmart's supply chain mastery, coupled with cost undercutting and overall operational excellence, makes it uniquely qualified to claim this purpose.

Unisys relates its purpose to its long history of consistently delivering results and does it in two words: Experience Breakthroughs. Company senior vice president (SVP) and chief marketing officer Teresa Poggenpohl talks about the first word "experience" as a dynamic verb: "It is deliberate. We want to invite our clients and our people to experience breakthroughs with Unisys. That means helping them unlock a potential they couldn't reach before. As for 'breakthroughs,' they can be big or small. It could be something simple and elegant, like a new, more efficient process for one of our clients. Or it could be game-changing like a quantum computing solution that optimizes logistics management."[9]

And this company purpose is reflected in Unisys's brand positioning. Says Poggenpohl, "Our ad line is 'Keep Breaking Through,' and I think it captures the invitation and the aspiration we have in our purpose. It also captures the idea that it's not just one breakthrough, but continuous breakthroughs—that one leads to another and another. If you work with Unisys, this is how we think. We're always going to be experimenting with how to do something better, whether large or small, to help clients become industry leaders."

CHAMPIONING CAUSES

By shouldering the mantle of a social, environmental, or economic mission, a company demonstrates its commitment to making a difference. By becoming actively involved in larger societal initiatives, principally the Environment, Society, and Governance (ESG) and the Diversity, Equity, and Inclusion (DE&I) agendas, a company becomes a leader in advancing socially conscious policies and practices.

These agendas, and others like them, are only the most visible avenues companies can take to make a genuine difference in our world.

The people at **Abbott** recognize as much. "We went through a process where we learned that living life to the fullest was a human aspiration and something that we significantly contribute to," says Melissa Brotz, chief marketing and communications officer at Abbott—a leader in health technologies.[10] "In other words, good health is an enabler to living a full life. So that's how we arrived at our purpose: 'Life to the Fullest.' We turned 135 this year and we've been around because we've been living our purpose and delivering on it consistently for our stakeholders." Abbott's purpose of "Life to the Fullest" is being made apparent across the globe, such as in its "Real Madrid" football partnership that helps children at risk of malnutrition. This partnership is a tangible "expression of health through what the players are doing on the field, along with what good nutrition and good health can help you achieve," says Brotz.

Equally valuable societal contributions are being made by companies when they step up for communities in need. **Caterpillar**, the construction, mining, and engineering equipment manufacturer, is a leader in this regard. As told by the company's vice president (VP), head of marketing and brand, Yvette Morrison, "Your purpose has to be something more than just making a profit. And it has to be more than what you make or do. You need to go beyond mere product features and benefits and get to what difference you make in the world. It's the only way to distinguish yourself from the competition, because features and benefits are easily replicated."[11]

Yum Brands' **KFC** takes its cause advocacy right into the streets, literally. Nick Chavez, chief marketing officer of KFC, says the company's "goal is to serve joy to everyone with our original recipe. In 2022, we launched the KFC Sharemobile—a mobile food truck that delivered more than 70,000 meals to families in need during the holiday season."[12]

Progressive founded its insurance company by challenging the status quo and championing accessibility of insurance for people who were getting left behind. The company's chief marketing officer, Remi Kent, explains, "When we were founded, we didn't pursue premium customers. We wanted to insure people who had trouble getting insurance. We felt insurance should be democratized ... and that everyone should have access to it."[13]

Progressive recently introduced its new purpose. "We exist to help people move forward and live fully," says Kent. "Insurance is a promise that should stand behind you on your best days and stand up for you on your worst. We deliver on that promise by helping you recover from loss. However, our new purpose pushes us beyond that, to helping you generate the momentum to move forward with confidence so you can pursue the things in life that matter to you. By providing freedom from worry and proactive support, we enable you to make progress. By bringing our purpose to life, we want to protect the things that matter most to our customers and their communities. I'm hoping we will be recognized as the world's first purpose-led insurance company."

What Does It Mean to Be a Purpose-Driven Company?

To be clear, merely claiming a purpose doesn't necessarily make a company purpose-driven. It's easy to understand on face value that a purpose-driven company is committed to more than just making a profit. But in looking deeper into the machinery of establishing that company purpose, it becomes evident that a truly purpose-driven company has a crystal clear sense of its values, and it uses these values to drive its decisions and actions. It focuses on that focus, as it were. At every level of the company, it answers the coupled question: What problem are we solving, or how would the world be worse off if we did not exist?

These purpose-driven companies tend to hold three tenets very dear:

First, purpose drives not just its marketing and communications activities but also its overall business strategy. Purpose sets boundaries for what an organization will and will not do as part of its growth strategy. Purpose becomes the filter for evaluating strategic decisions, such as what markets to serve, where to make investments, how to hire employees, and, ultimately, why the business matters.

Second, purpose-driven companies effectively balance profit with purpose. They don't resort to choosing one over the other but instead balance profit and purpose by focusing on creating shared value. They find opportunities to create societal benefits that also drive financial returns.

And these purpose-driven companies tend to be more financially successful than non-purpose-driven counterparts in the long run, as we'll see. By creating value for *all* stakeholders, they effectively create a more resilient business model that is less vulnerable to short-term market fluctuations or changing consumer preferences. **IBM** epitomizes this with its purpose to "Make the world smarter" and its competency initiatives such as "Smarter Planet."[14] With technological solutions that make people's lives better, IBM, in turn, makes the planet better while driving consistently outsized ROI.

Third, purpose-driven companies embed purpose in the organizational culture. Just like DNA provides a body with the information it needs to develop, a strong purpose guides employees on how to act appropriately in accordance with the corporate purpose—all with the goal of maximizing positive impact.

With these three tenets—driving business strategy, balancing profit with purpose, and embedding in the company DNA—purpose-driven companies are backing beliefs with conscious action—not just paying lip service but also taking action.

Perhaps the biggest challenge for a company is to execute on these beliefs at every level of the organization. The Accenture case study at the outset touched on the work required to bring everyone on board. And, in fact, while 79 percent of business leaders profess that purpose is central to success, less than half of employees can verbalize the company's purpose in a coherent fashion.[15] To build a purpose-driven culture, a company must clearly define and communicate its purpose, align the culture to that purpose, and focus on hiring people who share those values and principles. As well, it is important to design employee rewards and incentives programs that reinforce or, at a minimum, are consistent with purpose.

Once again, a company can have a purpose yet not necessarily be purpose-driven. There is nothing wrong with simply having a stated purpose and supporting it with praiseworthy CSR initiatives. But only when a company effectively implements all three of the above tenets can it truly consider itself a purpose-driven company.

The Benefits of Being Purpose-Driven

Many benefits can be derived from being purpose-driven, and they tend to differ from company to company. However, the following benefits commonly accrue to companies that are purpose-driven:

STRATEGIC CLARITY

As demonstrated in the Accenture case study, purpose acts as a strategic North Star and allows key business decisions to be considered through a "purpose filter." Is this potential investment consistent with our purpose? Does this new product truly fit with our stated purpose? Is our purpose being advanced by entering this new market? When a company leads with purpose, decisions that are otherwise complex and challenging are often made with greater ease.

INCREASED PROFITABILITY

One of the six forces driving the rise of purpose (referenced earlier in this chapter) is the trend toward companies focusing on the triple bottom line: Profit + People + Planet. There is now substantial evidence that the first bottom line—that is, profit—is generally enhanced in purpose-driven companies over others. An EY study found that purpose-driven companies outperformed the S&P 500 by a factor of ten between 1996 and 2011.[16] More recent studies by the Harvard Business School, the Harris Poll, and the University of Oxford, all separate from one another, found a continuing positive correlation between purpose and profit.[17] Of course, a purpose-driven company is not necessarily going to be more profitable since a number of factors influence business outcomes. But the argument for adhering to the triple bottom line is persuasive.

PREMIUM PRICING

Complementing this increased profitability is the ability of purpose-driven brands to command premium prices more easily. This is the result of being able to engender a more loyal customer base—especially among Millennials and Gen Z who will pay a premium if the company's purpose resonates with them. This lift in loyalty is no small thing since these consumers have proven to be four to six times more likely to purchase from a purpose-driven company, creating a stronger floor under any premium pricing strategy.[18]

BUSINESS PERFORMANCE

A 2018 study done by DDI, the Conference Board, and EY found that purposeful companies outperformed the overall market by 42 percent, a remarkable figure. Additional research done by Deloitte analysts found these purposeful companies attaining 30 percent higher levels of innovation, 40 percent higher levels of workforce retention, and higher levels of customer loyalty, as well. UK-based multinational consumer packaged goods company **Unilever**, for example, saw its sustainable living brands including Dove, Vaseline, and Lipton growing 69 percent faster than the rest of its business lines.[19]

TALENT ACQUISITION

Purpose-driven companies are winning the war for talent since they are more likely to attract and retain the most valued job applicants. Two-thirds of Millennials take a company's social and environmental commitments into account when deciding where to work.[20] In addition, employees at purpose-driven companies are four times more engaged at work than their non-purpose-driven counterparts.[21]

What It Means to Be a Purpose-Driven **Brand**

Just because a company is purpose-driven, it doesn't necessarily mean that its brands are (or need to be) positioned around that specific purpose. A purpose-driven brand is one whose brand positioning is synonymous with its purpose—its strategic North Star. In other words, the purpose is not only the company's internal reason for being but also the market-facing manifestation of the brand that represents it. As such, just like with any brand positioning, it should inform marketing activation at every level.

 Whirlpool understands this well.

This century-old household appliance brand recently established itself as purpose-driven. It began with a series of candid conversations between Whirlpool management and its employees and customers about the brand's deep roots running into the present and on into the future. The company sought to move discussions beyond the mere selling of products to gaining a deeper understanding of how customers emotionally relate to their home appliances. This outreach and resulting analysis led to a humanistic expression of the brand's mission: to aid families in their well-being.

The brand's purpose centers around an aspirational vision that everyone deserves the chance to thrive, and the company can bring this vision to life through its innovative products and solutions that are also mindful of the planet. Says Jason Mathew, Whirlpool's senior director of Global Connected Strategy, "Every product we develop, every feature we create, and every collaboration we enter into is inspired by helping people care for the ones they love."[22]

Whirlpool has wrapped the very essence of its brand positioning around its purpose. Over a decade ago, the company launched its Every Day, Care™ campaign—purposefully shifting the conversation away from the old-time bells and whistles of its products to the very human concerns of daily caring for family. Whirlpool's senior director of Mass Brands and Channel Marketing, William Beck, says the multimedia campaign puts family and care first: "The campaign is about people, real modern families, and the impact of the care they give and receive every day. It's about proving how often-thankless tasks are so important—they are part of the emotional glue holding families together. It's a higher purpose driving our brand and a natural space for Whirlpool because we've been a part of these daily moments of care that have taken place in American homes for over one hundred years."[23]

The Every Day, Care™ ad campaign featured "Perceptions of Care" vignettes about the millions of Americans who care for children and aging adults in their homes. In showcasing the so-called sandwich generation, Whirlpool's ads brought three generations into the conversation: the younger generation unaware of the importance of caregiving, the middle generation wrestling with conflicting demands, and the older generation becoming dependent on daily care.

In 2022, Whirlpool refreshed its brand campaign with "Every Day, Care 2.0" while keeping to its purpose: to aid families in their well-being. In the refresh, the company extended its focus beyond cooking, cleaning, and washing to how Whirlpool helps consumers focus on what matters—the people they love. In a time when old-line consumer appliance companies are taking a beating, Whirlpool continues to remain relevant with purpose-driven branding.

A key point to be made here is that Whirlpool didn't necessarily have to align its corporate purpose (internal intention) with its master brand positioning and activation (external expression). The two can be, and often are, distinct. Yet when this alignment does occur, as we also saw with Accenture, the resulting marketplace impact can be profound.

Purpose-Branding across a Diverse Portfolio

For a multinational company with hundreds of diverse brands, the approach to purpose-driven branding becomes strategically complex and more challenging. An excellent study of this challenge is **Danone**, the French holding company with a portfolio of more than twenty-five brands in the yogurt, bottled water, and baby food categories.

Danone is actually one of the world's largest Certified B Corporations, organized to meet a high standard of social and environmental performance, transparency, and accountability. It is in the original DNA, in fact, going back fifty years to when the company's founder and CEO, Antoine Riboud, introduced a trailblazing concept in corporate responsibility. As shared by Linda Bethea, the current head of marketing at Danone, "Franck Riboud (son of Antoine who took the reins in 1996) essentially said that corporate responsibility doesn't end at the factory gates, that we should be responsible for the world we live in and the communities we serve. That truly is what led us down the path to becoming a B Corp, ensuring that everything we do is good for the people we serve and good for the planet."[24]

While Danone's larger corporate mission is to deliver health through food to as many people as possible, Bethea takes that to the granular executional level: "Every brand within the portfolio has a brand manifesto model, which outlines the brand's purpose, positioning, and individual contribution to corporate strategy and impact. Its purpose needs to be authentic to the brand, but also in service of our corporate mission."

To ensure that each brand delivers on this corporate mission, Danone has an entire team separate from Bethea's marketing team to focus on this very thing. Says Bethea, "The brands work very closely with my team to determine what is the role of that brand in delivering against the corporate mission." One of the examples of this is the Oikos yogurt brand: "Oikos' brand purpose is all about strength. It's the highest protein yogurt in the category, and its purpose is to power the strength that makes our customer unstoppable every day. So, the purpose is very much linked to the product's 'reason to believe' (protein), but also ladders up to the Danone purpose of delivering health through food to as many people as possible."

The Oikos brand purpose is suffused into its activation. Bethea explains, "Our Oikos 'Stronger Makes Everything Better' campaign is rooted in the protein inherent in the product, which gives you physical strength. But it also taps into what that strength enables you to accomplish every day. We have partnered with Deion Sanders in our advertising campaign, where he talks about what strength means to his entire family … and how it's different for him, versus his son, versus his mother, versus his sister." In speaking to the dietary needs of three generations, Bethea's marketing team extends the Oikos brand purpose longitudinally in service of the corporate bottom line.

Another Danone yogurt brand is Light and Fit, and its purpose is to enable women's economic empowerment. Says Bethea, "Women have cravings and they want things to taste delicious. So, we deliver flavors like strawberry cheesecake and key lime pie, so they can indulge all they want, but in a controlled way. This in turn gives them the confidence and security they need to thrive in other areas of their lives." And, again, this empowerment is brought to life through partnerships. "The Light and Fit brand partners with Dress for Success which demonstrates the link between the product benefit and the broader impact that we want to have with women's economic empowerment."

Bethea folds in brand purpose from the very beginning of the research cycle. "You have to start with insights. You have to understand who the consumer is and what they are struggling with. Because you ultimately want your brand purpose to solve a tension in their life or in society that they care about, because that gives your brand a true reason for being, a true purpose. And it has to be authentic. I mean, I work in food and beverage. Can yogurt save the world? Some people would say absolutely not. But we think if done the right way, we can absolutely have a positive impact, but it has to be done the right way. It would be disingenuous for us to say we care about food waste and food insecurity but then have a manufacturing practice that did the opposite. So, we think through not just what we say to consumers but what we do throughout the entire product development and marketing process."

So, for the Two Good yogurt brand, there is a "Meyer Lemon" flavor. It is manufactured using rescued fruit that would otherwise go to waste and go to landfills. Says Bethea, "We're reducing waste out of the food supply system because that's what we believe will help make the planet better. And then for every cup of Two Good yogurt you buy, we donate a meal to someone in need ... giving back to the communities and the people we serve."

Danone just keeps improving on its founder's goal of a purpose-driven company, extending that promise across many brands in many different countries, an impressive feat.

Articulating a Brand's Purpose

Earlier we outlined the three primary types of purpose-driven companies, as defined in a *Harvard Business Review* study. This can be a useful framework for identifying and framing company and brand purpose. The three types are exemplary culture, exhibiting competence, and championing causes. For each of these three, there are questions that should be asked to determine if the purpose is appropriate, credible, and resonant with the specific business/brand.

EXEMPLARY CULTURE?

A purpose that is based on culture is characterized by how a business operates internally and strives to treat its employees. So, it makes sense to look internally to explore the values and belief framework that guides the company's operations, including the type of work environment that is fostered.

- What behaviors and actions are expected from employees?

- How do employees feel about working for the company?

- How are employees expected to treat customers and behave externally?

- How do customers describe their interactions with the company?

EXHIBITING COMPETENCE?

If a company's purpose is based on competence, its unique contribution to society is the source of purpose. In this case, it makes sense to examine the impact that marketplace offerings have on customers and on society as whole.

- What are the company's core competencies, strengths, and advantages?

- What kind of problems does the company solve for?

- In what way is the world a better place because of the company?

- How is the company's product pipeline extending its competence?

CHAMPIONING CAUSES?

Just as with competence, a cause-based purpose is all about promoting social good and making the world a better place. However, the difference in championing a cause is that the "good" that results may or may not be attributed to superior competence and product offerings. Here, it helps once again to look internally.

- What social or environmental issues does the company champion?

- What specific positive change does the company want to bring about?

- What nonprofits or philanthropies does the company support?

- What is the company's involvement in Environment, Society, Governance (ESG) and Diversity, Equity, and Inclusion (DE&I)?

With the brand purpose articulated, next here are best practices for activating the brand purpose.

Best Practices for Activating Brand Purpose

Best practices in brand activation should not only drive short-term marketing performance but also build long-term brand equity.

LEAD WITH BRAND POSITIONING

As with any brand, the marketing of purpose-driven brands needs to be consistent with the brand positioning. This includes all marketing activation—campaigns, events, experiences, and communications. If the brand purpose is not woven into the marketing in a manner consistent with the brand positioning, the brand risks becoming diluted in the eyes of customers and other stakeholders.

ALLOW PURPOSE TO DRIVE PRODUCT DEVELOPMENT

Thinking about product/service development through the lens of purpose can drive innovation and sharpen a company's competitive edge, as shown in the Accenture and Danone cases. Purpose can spark original ideas and creativity in an organization. It can inspire employees to recast themselves into the roles of problem-solvers and value providers. A majority of executives in global companies (63 percent of them, based on an Economist Intelligence Unit and EY survey) agree that purpose makes them better able to disrupt, or respond to disruption, with their own transformational changes.[25]

BE READY TO TAKE A STAND

Companies with a strong purpose understand what they do and do not stand for. They are willing to take a stand—even on controversial issues—to create long-term value for customers and employees. To be sure, not everyone in the world will relate to or support the stand taken. Some may even find it off-putting and react negatively in a public manner. What's important is that the stakeholders who are most important—particularly the target customers—support it. Consistently lean into purpose. Never apologize for it, or waver in support of it, even when consumer sentiment temporarily shifts.

MEASURE RESULTS AND COURSE-CORRECT WHEN NECESSARY

Successful companies set metrics to track business strategy, tactics, and initiatives. This also should be the case for purpose—especially when that purpose serves as the brand's positioning. Consumer and customer sentiment should be consistently monitored to ensure that purpose remains relevant and that the brand continues to be associated with the purpose. If the brand is not getting credit for the purpose it espouses, then a review of all marketing activation needs to be conducted. If the purpose is losing relevance with target stakeholders, it may be time to reevaluate its appropriateness as a brand positioning—even if it continues to represent the company's purpose.

AVOID PURPOSE-WASHING

When a business claims to support a meaningful cause without backing it up with genuine action, that's "purpose-washing." And it can seriously harm a company's credibility fast in today's always-on world. As all marketers know, one of the key components of a brand's positioning are the "reasons to believe," or proof points. These proof points lend credibility to the promise being made. Identifying and clearly communicating these proof points are even more critical when the brand is steeped in purpose. A brand must be willing to back up its purpose with real action if it wishes to remain purpose-driven. Otherwise, it risks coming across as disingenuous at best and a fraud at worst.

Final Thoughts on Brand Purpose

The idea of being purpose-driven is certainly not new. It has been on the business radar for several decades. So, it's reasonable to wonder if the concept has already reached a tipping point, if it's a trend that will slowly lose steam until it all but disappears as a conscious endeavor.

The future is always unknown, of course. But the paths of generations can be mapped based on their activities in their formative years, and they rarely veer far off course. Millennial and Gen Z generations have made it clear that they expect greater transparency and accountability from companies before giving over their loyalty. They are demanding that companies have a purpose, and so, the concept is not likely to disappear in their lifetimes.

While Baby Boomers are still alive and kicking, they are primarily driving the agenda on retirement-oriented products and services. The bulk of today's buying decisions are being made by two new generational cohorts—Millennials and Gen Z—and likely will be for the twenty to forty years they will be ascendant financially.

Nonetheless, the value of purpose in brand strategy can only endure if it is also accompanied by value creation and financial performance. As shown with the triple bottom line, having a worthwhile purpose is critically important but not sufficient for success. As economic pressures and shareholder demands continue to increase, the most enduring purpose-driven companies will be those that find a way to stay true to purpose while also driving topline growth, profitability, and shareholder value.

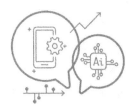

CHAPTER TWO
Beyond Health to Wellness

In chapter 1, we saw how at the height of the pandemic Accenture uniquely brought their global organization together to plan a new purpose-driven future. Some months earlier, another company was confronting the novel coronavirus in its own entirely novel way. That company, **Moderna**, would go on to save millions of lives in a Herculean mobilization that propelled the company from a near-nobody, even within the pharmaceutical industry, to a household name and the third-most positively recognized brand in America.[26]

"No one had heard of Moderna until we developed a Covid-19 vaccine," Moderna's CMO Kate Cronin recalls. "We became something very unusual in the pharmaceutical industry, a brand that everyone knew by name. When you think about a flu shot for example, you don't know who your flu shot manufacturer is; you don't even know the name of your flu vaccine. With Covid, you knew whether you got Moderna, Pfizer, or one of the other vaccines."[27]

Covid gave Moderna the triple-edged sword of a unique, new, and direct relationship with consumers, and sudden brand fame, but with no real branding apparatus in place to sustain that relationship. Prior to the pandemic, the company's primary focus had been on research and development across different diseases, explains Jason

Benagh, director of marketing operations at Moderna: "We had not planned on seeing our first vaccine in the market for a few more years. Much of what we needed to publish was at the request of local governments or public health authorities, so we focused on providers, vaccine program administrators, and even the public—putting health and the importance of vaccination above brand."[28]

Thus, Cronin's and Benagh's task was to capitalize on Moderna's new familiarity in an agreeable way. It was important to not be seen as exploiting the pain that many millions had suffered. Equally important was to *not* be cast into the unfavorable light of a big uncaring pharma company. Neither of these things were even close to true, but Cronin realized that public emotions had always run high around vaccines, none more so than Covid.

"There has been a lack of trust because the pharma industry as a whole has not been able to establish a real relationship with the patient," Cronin explains. "Generally, it's the physician who has the relationship with the patient, so there's always an intermediary. Now there's an opportunity to build a direct relationship and therefore build more trust with our consumer base."

In thinking through how to build this trust, Cronin sees parallels going back to Intel's 1991 rebranding campaign. "We are the experts in mRNA. So, it's almost like Intel inside; nobody really knows what a chip does, but they know that with Intel inside, it's faster and better, it must be good. So, you don't have to know how mRNA works as a consumer. You just have to know that it's pretty good, it worked really well with Covid, so I think it'll work in these other diseases. Oh, and Moderna is the best in mRNA."

Building up this trust and loyalty will be especially critical for Moderna, Cronin explains, "When we launch our next vaccine for RSV [Respiratory Syncytial Virus] or for the Flu. People will want to go in and say, 'I want the Moderna flu or the Moderna RSV vaccine.' And then eventually we'll have a triple combination vaccine—RSV, Flu, and Covid. So, you don't have to keep getting jabbed, you just get one shot that has three mRNAs in it … the ideal we need to think about in our customer relationships."

That ideal translates into Moderna's formal brand positioning as a platform technology company: "We act at the intersection of science, technology, and humanity—uniquely positioned to offer up solutions and be very agile across a number of different disease categories. Because our mRNA technology is an information molecule that teaches your body to fight disease, we are able to create customized products based on the needs of a person. mRNA is our hero."

And the brand messaging grows out of that legitimate hero product. In April 2023, Moderna launched a "Welcome to the mRNAge" advertising campaign with the tagline, "This changes everything."[29] The ninety-second branding ads were built around a giant red string symbolizing a strand of mRNA that can deliver messages to cells in the body to fight diseases. "One strand of mRNA could change life for the better—everywhere. And the company that's getting us there? Moderna. This changes everything," the ad trumpeted. In talking about the campaign, Cronin emphasizes, "*This changes everything* is not just a slogan; it's something we truly believe in. We believe that our mRNA technology platform is going to change everything when it comes to healthcare."

These twin notions of "change" and "everything being different" are the post-Covid themes that all health and wellness marketers are wrestling with and seeking to authentically embody in their brands now. Everything about healthcare has been turned upside down. Everyone is rethinking the concept of wellness.

It is making for interesting times.

Enormous Reach of the New Wellness Economy

Every effort to put a quantifiable dollar figure on the investment, pro-visioning, and commercializing of today's health and wellness markets is made difficult by the modern reach of healthcare itself. It runs so wide and deep that definitions blur.

- Is the global healthcare market now $60 trillion in size, and the U.S. portion $4.3 trillion, all in?

- Tucked under this massive healthcare umbrella, there's health and wellness. Is it now $4.5 trillion globally with the United States contributing a quarter of that, or $1.1 trillion a year?

- Will wellness tourism alone top $1.2 trillion globally, $231 billion in the United States, by 2027?

- Is the mindfulness movement the top growth sector, leaping to $52 billion a year now?

- Are sales of wellness wearables going to top $388 million in sales by 2025 with some 1.2 billion devices sold, 258 million of them smartwatches of which 40 percent are able to connect to monitoring and alert services, telehealth, doctors, the gamut?

- Has wellness actually become a higher top-of-mind issue than disease management to a majority of consumers?

These are, in fact, the findings from analysts at Accenture, PwC, McKinsey, the Global Wellness Institute, the U.S. government, and Statista.[30] They are credible findings and paint a clear picture of an industry expanding at a historic pace. Seeing compound annual growth rates (CAGRs) of 5–10 percent, companies are rushing to capitalize, and brands must be first and foremost *strategic* about how they choose to compete.

McKinsey offers help in this regard, suggesting in their "Future of Wellness" study that the six categories of most interest to consumers are better health, better fitness, better nutrition, better appearance, better sleep, and better mindfulness. To which a seventh should be added, better mental health. These categories will be discussed next. But first, let's look at the staying power of this interest in all health and wellness categories.

We know that in previous decades, consumers cut back on well-being spending when their finances were stretched thin, considering it discretionary spending. But a 2022 Accenture survey of eleven thousand consumers in sixteen countries found health and fitness has become "an essential" alongside groceries and household staples. Two-thirds of respondents said they were hurting financially, and yet, 80 percent of that group intended to hold steady or even increase their spending on health and fitness.[31]

"Despite hard times, it is clear that people have redefined health and well-being to be an essential good and plan to maintain or increase their spend in this area this year, regardless of income levels," says Oliver Wright of Accenture.[32] Fair to say, health and wellness have graduated from a "nice to have" with audiences worldwide to "a must have."

What are the underlying factors driving this interest?[33]

Why the Heightened Prioritization of Health and Wellness?

Interest in health and wellness can be attributed to eight principal factors:

- general awareness

- rising healthcare costs

- aging population

- employer wellness programs

- easy online research

- Covid's lasting impact

- long-term shift in attitudes

- technology accelerating everything

These factors have combined to drive individuals to prioritize their well-being and take proactive steps toward maintaining good health.

GENERAL AWARENESS

A sharp rise in chronic illnesses and diseases as well as contagions in recent decades, all fully reported and often sensationalized across every communications medium, has opened people's eyes and created a generalized anxiety about health. Conditions such as obesity, diabetes, heart disease, and mental health disorders have been linked indisputably to people's lifestyle choices. Inadequate nutrition, sedentary behavior, and a lack of self-care have been shown to impact health and prompted individuals to prioritize wellness and adopt healthier lifestyles.

RISING HEALTHCARE COSTS

Healthcare insurance costs for a middle-income household have almost tripled from 3.3 percent of income in 2010 to 11.6 percent in 2020, adding $8,070 a year in costs to the family budget.[34] This has created an obvious financial burden for many families. So, they have turned to preventive measures and self-care to reduce healthcare expenses. They are recognizing that investing in wellness can yield long-term cost savings even as it protects them from serious illnesses and diseases.

AN AGING POPULATION

People are living longer with the age sixty-five-plus population increasing from forty-three million in 2012 to sixty-five million by 2025, according to the Census Bureau.[35] This has triggered a "virtuous circle" effect, with advances in healthcare delivering longer life spans and those longer lives necessitating more—and more advanced—healthcare programs.

EMPLOYER WELLNESS PROGRAMS

Employers have seen the hard numbers: a healthy workforce is a more productive workforce with lower healthcare costs borne by the company. So, employers have added wellness programs to their benefits packages—including gym memberships, mental health support, and incentives for healthy behavior.

EASY ONLINE RESEARCH

The internet has changed everything, especially in healthcare, with nine in ten Americans feeling confident in the "facts" they find online.[36] There is also an increasing demand for health data right on a mobile device. Social media platforms and the Influencers on those platforms have taken health and wellness to millions who do not otherwise pay attention to traditional news outlets. Plus, it's so easy to purchase online, with 12 percent of all health and personal care sales now occurring there.[37]

COVID'S LASTING IMPACT

In the wake of the pandemic, two-thirds of Americans say wellness is more important to them than it was before.[38] Covid has united people in a shared global objective of protecting against the virus itself, strengthening people's immune systems, pursuing healthier lifestyles, practicing better hygiene, and caring actively about mental health conditions.

LONG-TERM SHIFT IN ATTITUDES

In the 1960s, there began a shift toward holistic health focusing on the combined physical, mental, and emotional concerns of the body—not just treating the symptoms of an illness but also addressing its root causes. Most popular early on were such practices as mindfulness, meditation, and yoga. More recently, this holistic movement has become an important part of a broader concept of "total wellness," which focuses on all aspects of staying healthy.

TECHNOLOGY ACCELERATES EVERYTHING

A steady stream of marvelous new medical devices, drugs, and treatments, and, of course, rapidly developed vaccines, have excited consumers and set the expectations for even more. Likewise, remote care technologies are becoming a preferred method of interaction for patients. People are receiving healthcare in their homes with the help of digital technologies. Remote patient monitoring devices and interfaces are enjoying wide adoption. This has sped up product cycles worldwide with some 180,000 products reformulated to meet the demands for healthier alternatives—that is a lot of products being adapted to a new marketplace.[39]

So how will these factors drive health and wellness forward?

How Health and Wellness Are Trending Forward

This interest in health and wellness is manifest in five trends that brand marketers are seeking to understand and align with:

- mental health ascendant

- total health orientation

- proactive self-care

- individualized wellness programs

- technology to the fore

MENTAL HEALTH ASCENDANT

Even before Covid focused a nation's attention on the fragility of health, many in the medical profession were deeply concerned about another potentially more devastating health crisis spreading from the heartland of America to the shores. A mental health crisis. Medical researchers were reporting that between 19 and 30 percent of the country—both adults and children—struggle with mental health conditions such as crippling anxiety and depression.

This issue of mental health has become a regular conversation between generations of family members at home, teachers and students in grade schools and up, employers and employees in the workplace, and public health officials and politicians in an official capacity.[40]

Companies are hearing from their employees that more needs to be done to support mental health, with nearly nine in ten of those employees saying mental health is a higher priority for them now.[41]

Though teens are notoriously difficult to assess with any accuracy, three in four say they struggled with their mental state during the pandemic and have enjoyed scant reprieve since. Teens are even advocating now for mental health days, like sick days, off from school.[42]

Venture and corporate investment in mental health and wellness has been fast rising. Industry reports estimate that the youth mental health market will top $26 billion in size by 2027 after a 1,500 percent increase in investment over the past four years.[43]

With an estimated forty-seven million Americans—1.5 million more than before the pandemic—reporting the telltale symptoms of mental illness, there is an urgency to deal with a no longer "emerging"—but now clearly apparent—public health crisis. Until very recently, the mentally ill were often the butt of jokes or dismissed as outliers, whiners, or inferiors. But that stigma has almost completely gone away in a sea change that will arguably impact health and wellness marketers more than any other issue for the foreseeable future.

While many specialty brands have moved aggressively into mental health, big savvy brands are there, as well. This concern for mental health is a natural extension of a growing holistic or total health orientation. Michelle Peluso, executive vice president and chief customer and experience officer at **CVS Health**, speaks to this: "While many specialty brands have moved aggressively into mental well-being, big savvy brands are there, as well. This concern for mental health is a natural extension of a growing holistic or total health orientation."

Peluso explains, "Whether it's about holistic skincare, whether it's vitamins and supplements, whether it's more natural beauty brands that have purpose attached to them … it's very important to think about what our brand voice is and how we respond to consumers. With the growth of vitamins and supplements, we offered a ground-breaking program in 2019 to require third-party testing, called 'Tested to be Trusted.' So, we took a position. Also, we're just celebrating our fifth-year anniversary of 'Beauty Mark,' which means we always show unaltered images in advertising because we don't want girls to have an unrealistic expectation of what beauty is."[44]

CVS went even deeper in 2022 with its "HERe for Her" campaign. Peluso says, "Women across this country feel like healthcare is not equal. There are places where the fact that you're a woman means your access to care, and your outcomes, are going to be different. One in four girls miss school on a regular basis because she can't get period products. We don't think it's right that in some states, the only essential healthcare product in our store that is subject to the luxury tax is women's period products. So, we back up our passion for women's health with bold actions."

Indeed, CVS reduced prices by 25 percent on its store brand period products, and it pays the state taxes on these products when possible, as well as working to help eliminate the tax nationwide.

Taking this position very seriously, Peluso notes that "women on average pay over $1,300 a year more than men simply because a product is pink, not blue. We firmly believe that you shouldn't have to pay more for a product because of its color, and we aim to ensure consumers don't experience that in our stores. You know, we go through every single SKU and when we occasionally find it, we eliminate the price disparity. I don't know how you can say you're a health company and then sell vaping products or cigarette products. Many others sell these products. But if we did, how could we possibly call ourselves CVS Health? Even though it's a big market opportunity, we do not sell these products because staying true to our purpose is important. Our purpose is to bring our heart to every moment of our consumers' health. It implies empathy, it implies innovation, it implies solutions, it implies understanding the local community and being there for *everybody*."

"Are we perfect? Of course not. But we are one of the only companies in health and wellness that is in every single community in America. According to the recent Axios Harris poll, we are the most trusted health and wellness company in this country. We're within 10 miles of 85 percent of every American. We're showing up in powerful ways."

"TOTAL HEALTH" ORIENTATION

Even as it has grabbed the headlines, it is fair to say that mental health is but one component of a "total health" orientation, which itself is emergent.

Those who've followed the holistic health movement since the 1970s know the paramount value of viewing wellness through a whole mind, body, and spirit lens. Indeed, holistic health practitioners would say they have always been concerned about the integration of mental, physical, and emotional well-being. Instead of simply treating symptoms, holistic health has sought to address the root causes of health issues and promote total wellness through modalities including mindfulness, meditation, yoga, breathwork, and alternative therapies.

But there is more than semantics involved in holistic health giving way to total health. Now, advances in neuroscience confirm on an actionable level the role that all five senses (sight, sound, smell, taste, touch) play in achieving wellness. This has effectively credentialed the old holistic movement, suggesting that it is not "quack science" but, in fact, an intelligent, and now proven, approach. This has led to the widespread acceptance of this total health orientation—with more than half of American adults ranking wellness as a top priority.

A company like **Danone** is at the forefront of this thinking. CMO Linda Bethea confirms that "conversation in recent years has expanded the definition of wellness to include total health—both physical and mental well-being. And I believe your mental health can have an impact on your physical health and your physical health can have an impact on your mental health."[45]

Danone, with its line of yogurts and other health products, was early to track market data exemplified by Google searches for "gut health" increasing 669 percent over five years. Bethea explains, "Activia Yogurt was one of the first probiotic yogurts on the market. It does a lot to bolster your gut health, which is really critical to your physical well-being." And, more recently, with the new yogurt product, Souvenaid: "This brand affects the synapses in the brain which improves long-term memory health over time—an increasingly important benefit for an aging population."[46]

This total health orientation is playing out across consumer markets in numerous ways. Some are faddish repackaging of old-fashioned ideas; however, they may become mainstream activities that substantial numbers of people care about.

- Springing up are social wellness clubs (Remedy Place, Six Senses Place, Peoplehood, Othership) that are actively fighting online loneliness by bringing people together in real life. These clubs are actually forging the genuine group connections that humans have always needed to thrive, calling it "social medicine."

- Among Millennials, self-care is becoming part of everyday life, and many are scheduling full-day spa visits into that life. All-day spa experiences with facial masks, waxing, workouts, and massage are not being viewed as indulgences but as self-care.

- Even though popular platforms like TikTok by their nature encourage an unhealthy, sedentary lifestyle, the platform feeds are bursting with new "micro workouts." These one-minute fitness challenges help people squeeze in healthy activity throughout the day.

- Intermittent fasting has become popular for protecting heart function, reducing the risk of disease, and lengthening life span. By 2018, the fasting app Zero had notched a million downloads and fifteen million fasts completed.[47]

- The mushroom mania that sprouted during the pandemic is only increasing. People are consuming mushrooms to improve health, reduce stress, boost immunity, and increase energy levels.

- Nighttime health hacks such as mouth taping (yes, taping your mouth shut while sleeping to breathe through your nose and humidify nasal passages) and sleep syncing (adjusting your sleep cycle to circadian rhythm to fall asleep quicker and reduce anxiety and tension) are becoming very popular.

- Women's healing circles have moved beyond the integrative spiritual wellness realm into common and widely practiced activities helping women support one another and connect on a deeper level.

This is by no means an exhaustive list of ways people are seeking total health and wellness today, but the depth and variety of activities shown previously are illustrative for brand marketers. And, of course, this discussion of trending health and wellness activities hasn't yet included individualized wellness programs, technology hacks, and proactive self-care.

PROACTIVE SELF-CARE

As noted, people of all ages, especially younger generations, now consider self-care something to be scheduled into their day-to-day lifestyle to enhance health and wellness over the long term. Whether it is wearing an Apple Watch to monitor vitals, increasing time for exercise, keeping a balanced diet, gauging body fat composition, or dozens of other programs, self-care has become a popular expression of self. Indeed, Google searches for "self-care" increased 107 percent over the last five years, led by Millennials who spend more than twice as much on self-care as Baby Boomers.[48]

Moderna's CMO Kate Cronin sees this as a movement to preventative care: "If you're not mentally well or you're under a lot of stress, it causes inflammation in the body and exacerbations of other underlying conditions. You're more likely to get infections because it reduces your immune system's strength. So, are you maintaining your health? Are you practicing preventative care? Are you doing all these things to keep your overall wellness in check?"

Another healthcare company that operates further behind the scenes, **Boston Scientific**, sees this self-care movement beginning rightly with their own employees who extend the company's brand through the products they develop.

"Our mission and vision is advancing science for life, which is very much about health and wellness," explains Jeff Mirviss, president of Boston Scientific. "And we think about how it plays out both internally and externally. On the employee side, we're doing a lot to improve our culture and our benefits, with a particular focus on health- and wellness-related benefits. For example, we offer free screenings for employees, Friday afternoons off, no meetings on Fridays, and a lot of education and awareness programs. This drives how we think about our product brands and our corporate brand externally. We don't do a lot of direct-to-patient marketing, but we do sponsor a lot of patient education and awareness efforts.[49]

"We have a device that allows patients to come off blood thinners, another that's an implantable pacemaker, and many more that patients wouldn't even know as Boston Scientific. We build the brand around quality, reliability, safety, and efficacy, so the patient has all the answers to any questions they or their loved ones might have. Healthcare decisions are usually made in partnership with a loved one. So, if a grandparent needs a pacemaker, the daughter might say, 'I've done the research and it looks like Boston Scientific has the greatest battery longevity, that really is the best choice.' The patient gets it!"

INDIVIDUALIZED WELLNESS PROGRAMS

For some years now, people have sought to attain wellness on their own terms, eager for a bespoke experience that considers their individual body type and wellness goals within their current environment instead of an impersonal, standardized approach. Two in five Americans have sought customized advice and plans for their health and wellness.[50] What has changed most recently is the ability of technology to deliver these personalized plans at scale.

And this has created a teeter-totter of tension between personalization and data privacy. On the one side, 71 percent of consumers do expect companies to deliver a fully personalized experience, with 76 percent of that group expressing frustration if it does not happen.[51] But on the other side, only a third of these consumers trust companies to handle their data responsibly, and 85 percent of them want to know a company's data privacy policies before making a purchase.[52] And a company can only deliver these personalized interactions if consumers turn over troves of personal data. So, how do company marketers reconcile this apparent dichotomy? Especially when they see reports from McKinsey that companies using data-driven personalization strategies experience up to 60 percent decreases in customer churn?[53]

These are the questions brand marketers must navigate in providing the individualized wellness programs consumers increasingly value.

TECHNOLOGY TO THE FORE

Advances in science and technology are altering the way health and wellness are thought about, delivered to the consumer, used continuously in an always-on fashion, and expected to enhance our lives in the years ahead.

Technologies, large and small, are seeping into every experience of wellness and health outcomes, from managing serious diseases to preventing debilitating diseases from occurring in the first place. They're already a prevalent factor in routine disease screening, genetic testing, meditation apps, dieting apps, and home diagnostics.

"One example of this is in continuous glucose monitoring," explains Melissa Brotz, CMO of **Abbott**. "If you know your glucose levels and how various foods affect those levels—and you see that information on your phone whenever you look at it—that is going to lead to positive behavioral change."[54]

The wearable healthcare device market, worth $16 billion worldwide in 2021, is expected to reach $30 billion by 2026 for a CAGR of 13.2 percent. It encompasses every kind of device for diagnosing problems in real-time, monitoring the body's physiology around the clock, and predicting medical conditions such as Covid infections three days in advance, with remarkable accuracy.[55] And with the adoption of AI in the healthcare sector, all of these technologies will only become more and more important to consumers.

So, with that, we have the five most pervasive health- and wellness-related trends marketers are dealing with today. Conspicuously absent from this list is the emergence of a new "Big 4" in the health and wellness world and the impact they are having.

Health Tech and the New Big Four

Four trillion-dollar technology giants—**Alphabet, Apple, Amazon**, and **Microsoft**—have been moving with aggressive and strategic finesse into the healthcare market. In so doing, they are dramatically reshaping the future of health and wellness and positioning to dominate in the sector.

By leveraging their impressive core business expertise in data capture, storage, computing, and communications, these four are reinventing the very nature of the wellness experience for consumers. And by introducing new monitoring and diagnosing modules built right into consumer-friendly wearable and embeddable devices, they are giving consumers far greater control over their personal health data, leading to a democratization of wellness.

These forays into healthcare have placed the four technology giants in a disruptive face-off with incumbent providers from hospitals to insurers and pharmaceutical companies as well as health technology firms.

ALPHABET

Alphabet, parent company to Google, is actively developing AI applications aimed at streamlining clinical research (Calico), speeding up medical diagnoses (DeepMind), and driving precision medicine that lowers hospital care costs (Verily). Direct-to-consumer products include Google Fit and FitBit, which link people directly to the Alphabet health and wellness ecosystem.

In effect, Alphabet is executing a pincer movement on the market: going after strategic partnerships with hospitals that embed the company's computing infrastructure in the hospitals and create a long-term dependency—and offering useful health tracking tools to consumers at low prices to generate valuable data that enables medical intervention. It's a strategic adaptation of a closed-loop system that ties both institutions and consumers into the Alphabet platform.

APPLE

Apple CEO Tim Cook has a vision of the company making its "greatest contribution to mankind" by revolutionizing how consumers manage their health for the better.[56] By turning its line of products into "portable patient health hubs," the company can monitor people's health, alert them to problems, call in medical help, and then assist in diagnosis and treatment later along each point of patient care. These health features can turn their already popular Apple Watch and iPhone into lifesaving products—a powerful branding promise.

Apple's key differentiator is a strong partnership with Stanford Medicine and sponsorship of the Apple Heart Study, which provides the scientific rigor to validate all of their health data collection.[57] The various Apple products will be able to collect irregular heartbeat data and alert medical teams, track and prevent diseases, offer hearing tests and vision tests, detect speech impediments as a result of a stroke, and even conduct genetic testing of users.

Apple uses this data to forge partnerships with providers throughout the healthcare system and, like Alphabet, is becoming indispensable to the provisioning of healthcare in the future.

AMAZON

Amazon's entry into the pharmacy space began by acquiring the online pharmacy PillPack and rebranding it as Amazon Pharmacy in 2020. This gave the company the ability to deliver medications to customers' doors nationwide. As of mid-2023, the company has yet to gain a significant foothold. However, a new Amazon Prime service for generic drugs at a low flat fee is expected to steal market share away from CVS, Walgreens, and Cigna, which together control more than half the market.[58]

Amazon's foray into telehealth, with Amazon Care, began as a service for its own employees with high hopes. They faced a number of regulatory compliance issues and privacy concerns, as well as competition from established primary care providers. After considerable investment, Amazon mothballed the service and resurfaced with Amazon Clinic—a virtual marketplace for third-party telehealth consultants. As of mid-2023, the service was available in only thirty-three states, dealt with only twenty common health conditions, and was not accepting insurance.

Recognizing the challenges it faced in trying to disrupt the traditional doctor visit, Amazon next purchased One Medical, a primary care provider with twenty-five locations nationwide. Amazon is expected to integrate One Medical into its Prime offerings, making it a more valuable proposition to younger audiences.

Of the Big 4, Amazon is facing the strongest headwinds in its relentless drive to capture share in health and wellness, but the vast size of the market and Amazon's deep pockets suggest much more news ahead.

MICROSOFT

Microsoft's Azure platform lets healthcare organizations store, manage, and analyze vast amounts of healthcare data securely. With an AI integration, Microsoft gives its large-scale customers the most advanced predictive analytics and applications for automating tasks, improving diagnostic accuracy, and enhancing patient engagement. Specific to that, the Microsoft Health Bot is a virtual health assistant that can check patient symptoms, run emergency room triage, and educate patients at each step of their hospital stay.

Through its collaborations, Microsoft also aims to address the complex challenges in healthcare, improve patient outcomes, and become an essential operating unit in hospitals and clinics. Microsoft's strategy is most similar to Alphabet's and puts it in direct competition for the prize of digitally transforming healthcare delivery worldwide. As well, Microsoft is in a race with Amazon to control the healthcare cloud market.

This battle of the four tech giants is altering every aspect of healthcare as they collide with legacy healthcare providers—from big hospitals and medical device manufacturers to neighborhood health and wellness providers. It is forcing providers to reassess their own brand positioning to remain competitive and relevant in the years ahead.

Wellness Directives for Brand Marketers

In the wake of a public health crisis unlike anything America has seen in a century, the entire health and wellness industry has been locked in a struggle to right the nation's ship of health again. Every company's marketing team has been called to deliver strategic performance results in the "new normal" where concern for health has become paramount.

And with the pandemic fading into history, hopefully, there are a number of directives for brand marketers.

ASSESS THE BRAND IN TERMS OF A TOTAL HEALTH ORIENTATION

Marketing professionals know that branding can be a difficult undertaking because it requires the answering of four questions: Who are we? What do we do? How do we do it? Why does it matter? The first three questions are fairly easy. It's the fourth that is always the taskmaster and more so for health and wellness companies in a time when the *individual's* health and *society's* health have become interwoven at a quality-of-life level.

So why does a company's brand matter? Or put differently, why is the brand making a difference in the target audience's lives? How does it make such a difference that it can be seen, tasted, toucheed, and felt deep in the gut of individuals, felt so viscerally that it practically bubbles up and out into our new shared health community?

In comparing a company's brand to that of its competitors, it's crucial to measure in terms of differentiation (How is it unique?), collaboration (Which forces have been aligned behind it?), innovation (What is it leaning toward?), validation (Why is it credible or believable?), and cultivation (How is it being cared for?).

If these questions are answered earnestly, they'll paint a true picture of the impact a brand is making on its target audience.

- Is the target audience still properly defined, or does it need to be reconsidered?

- Are the brand positioning and value proposition compelling and aligned with a new total wellness orientation?

- Is the brand promise differentiated by **what** it does, **how** it does it, **why** it does it, or **for whom** it does it (i.e., the four bases for brand differentiation)?

- Is the brand promise supported by proof points that are increasingly more holistic, self-directed, and technology-based?

A total health orientation is quite simply the process of thinking about the individual as a whole person. Not as a consumer of health products but as a person with a twenty-four-hour-a-day arc of needs and aspirations. And how does the brand matter in that full arc? How do the value proposition and product/service offering address the mental, physical, emotional, and spiritual components of an individual's life in a larger society?

For some brands accustomed to offering a point solution, this total health orientation can be daunting to contemplate. But certainly not for the alcohol and beverage marketer **Lagunitas**, a subsidiary of Heineken. It may seem a stretch for an alcohol marketer to be talking about total health, but Lagunitas CMO Paige Guzman took a recent conversation in that direction:

"I could envision one day our beverage product portfolio giving you wellness benefits throughout your day. Maybe there's a non-alcoholic product that has caffeine in it—some kind of a citrus spritzy mimosa type product—that you drink in the morning and it's a bit uplifting. In the afternoon, maybe there's a low-alcohol product that pairs well with food and aids with digestion. Later in the afternoon, there could be an espresso-type product that helps you through that mid-afternoon slump. And then in the evening, there is a drink with melatonin in it to help you achieve deeper sleep."[59]

This total health orientation may also seem less relevant to a life insurance company such as **John Hancock**. But John Hancock

CMO Kate Ardini explains, "We were the first life insurance carrier to bring Vitality to the US. Vitality is a science-based behavior change organization out of South Africa. They work with insurance carriers worldwide, combining data analytics with rewards and incentives to help people live better lives. It's all about shared value. You are going to hopefully live a longer, healthier, better life … plus you're going to get discounts on your premiums. And of course, the longer you live, the more premiums we collect. So, it's a win-win, and it's consistent with our overarching mission: Decisions made easier, lives made better."[60]

MAKE THE BRAND AS PERSONALIZED AS WELLNESS ITSELF

When it comes to wellness, there is nothing more personal. Consumers now expect wellness products and services to be customized to their unique needs. As a precept, that is understandable. The challenge comes in trying to continually increase the personalization of a company's offerings so as to give consumers greater control over their health and vitality.

Meeting that challenge begins by recognizing that wellness is not really about people, but it's about their emotions and passions. So, connecting with them requires an *emotionally intelligent* execution across the full set of marketing touchpoints. In this sense, it is rarely about a specific transaction but, instead, more about bringing out the emotions and passions that are dear to people, bringing them out as part of the brand experience. When brands can tap into people's intrinsic motivations to pursue wellness in ways that are resonant with the brand's attributes and positioning, that will spark the interest, attention, desire, and action that're hoped for.

While humans and data sit at near polar-opposite positions—one warm-blooded and the other coldly unfeeling—ironically it is data that is making marketing more human-focused. And this is certainly true when it comes to health and wellness. Marshaling data through digital platforms, mobile apps, and wearables allows marketers to create the most genuinely personalized nutritional, fitness, health, and wellness programs for individuals, allowing them to take fuller control of their physical and mental well-being.

Under Armour has executed brilliantly on this human-data interplay by investing in both its product lines and its database technology in order to innovate across its brand portfolio. Aiming to position the company as not merely a clothing innovator but also a future-looking total health solution, Under Armour has made key acquisitions and built a social fitness community across four mobile platforms: MapMyFitness, Endomondo, MyFitnessPal, and UA Record (since retired). A single dashboard gives customers a personalized experience across the spectrum of health—from workouts to activity tracking to nutrition.

This attention to a personalized digital experience for customers has helped Under Armour grow a global community of more than two hundred million users.[61] Their attention to the detail of how data drives custom experiences has rewarded the company with impressive organic growth and enviable brand loyalty.

MEET CONSUMERS "WHERE" AND "WHY" THEY ARE

To meet consumers where they are (using the right channel strategies) and why they are (tapping into their intrinsic motivations), today's future-ready marketers need to consider the strategies that will best make the brand experience more multisensory, engaging, convenient, and relevant—all the things that contextualize a total health orientation.

As with personalization, data is the key to unlocking those brand insights that may yet be hidden just beyond view: insights such as whether the product could be made more relevant by creating a wearable version or an app complement; whether the company's support tools are really as sharp as management likes to think or if customers feel left out in the cold oftentimes; whether the customers are even hearing the company's messages at all.

It's well known that digitally native Gen Z audiences tune out most channel communications while practically living on TikTok. Is the social media messaging of the company speaking a language that's being understood? Kate Cronin of Moderna talks about this on a familial level:

"My daughter went in for a head-to-toe dermatology appointment. She's twenty-five. And I said, wow, I didn't start doing that until I was well into my thirties. She said there's a TikTok'er who 'discovered' melanoma and shared it on TikTok and then inspired her to go get tested or screened. Interesting that she would listen to this Influencer over her own mother, right?"[62]

In this case, the subject matter was not fashion or music or makeup; it was cancer prevention. And yet a young woman obtained valuable information on it from TikTok. How many brand marketers feel confident that they are truly optimizing their messaging on TikTok and similar platforms?

Conjoined with social media marketing is Influencer marketing—for one could hardly exist without the other. And again, while brands are familiar with Influencers, and with all the "crazy" that often goes along with them, many brands remain reluctant to use Influencers—especially in health and wellness where these Influencers are seen (often correctly) as inauthentic or misaligned with the brand. The key to understanding the younger generation is as follows: the older generation's credentializers are automatically suspect—no matter their quality or veracity; the younger generation's Influencers are accepted as earnest truth if the recipient shares a similar worldview.

That there may be a logic breakdown in this trust schema is entirely beside the point; it is what it is. And in using Influencers, companies can maintain an ongoing organic social conversation, build out the company's video content library, cultivate relationships with the target audience, and even expand that audience through the auspices of a powerful storytelling medium.

We'll talk in-depth about Influencers in later chapters, but for here, they have evolved into a channel of their own to be leveraged to the brand's and consumer's shared benefit.

Through all of the marketing channels—brand communications, advertising, content marketing, website development, digital marketing, internal comms, public relations, and social media and Influencers—the messaging that meets consumers in both the "where" and the "why" can be powerful in today's total health orientation marketplace.

GENERATE A HEALTHY IN-STORE EXPERIENCE

Even before Covid froze retail store foot traffic at a standstill, the health and wellness store experience had changed dramatically, as had most segments in retail. With Covid receding, consumers are returning to stores but with a high expectation of *discovery*—whether through unique services, informational classes, gamified experiences, or just well-curated product displays.

Online shopping, curbside pick-up, and home delivery became new norms for retailers during the pandemic and continue afterward but at a nontrivial loss to the shopping experience. Having customers in the store lets health and wellness retailers connect on a personal level, which can drive loyalty and sales. So, retailers are focusing again on offering new and exciting experiences.

Skincare and cosmetics retailers are offering 3D camera views of customers' faces as they apply products, and then the customer simply hits a button for the purchase to be delivered to their home at a specified time and date.

Shopping is being reframed as a healthy activity, so consumers actually leave the store healthier than when they entered. Customers are being given discounts for walking to the store rather than validating for parking. Folks are encouraged to take the stairs rather than the escalator. Instead of complimentary coffee and water, health supplements are being offered. Store designs are featuring more daylight, plants, and fresh air to promote health and lower stress levels.

CVS Health has responded with innovative design formats that bring health and wellness to the forefront of the store. As explained by company marketing chief Michelle Peluso, "CVS has doubled down on MinuteClinics, Health Hubs, and similar services in more convenient positions in the store." And the thinking extends to virtual health. "We're finding that virtual care for mental well-being coupled with occasional physical care actually produces great outcomes, so we're making them more convenient. So, whether it's buying products and services, or picking up your pharmacy prescription, or actual medical care, CVS is aiming for an omnichannel level of personalization and convenience that is critical to the consumer's future."[63]

CULTIVATE THE BRAND'S AUTHENTIC COMMUNITY

Covid lockdowns forced people to isolate from their communities, and as they've emerged, they're looking for more connection and social interaction. So, wellness brands are revisiting their community-building strategies and looking to build even more compellingly authentic communities around their goods and services.

One of the most powerful forms of community building is hosting in-person events and classes and encouraging interaction among participants, such as inviting young parents into the store or public forums for weekly discussions on childhood nutrition and easy family meals.

At the same time, live online events will continue and can be effective at fostering connections though certainly less so. When the audience is naturally dispersed, creating groups on LinkedIn and Facebook and hubs like Mighty Networks can connect audiences and allow them to share experiences related to the company's offerings and messages.

SoulCycle and **Peloton** are well-known examples of fitness brands that are tapping into consumers' desire for social connection. However, smaller organizations can benefit from executing the community models. **Rapha Cycle Club** is a bike shop that has created a bicyclist community and retail dream destination for enthusiasts. Hosting chapters in clubhouses around the world, Rapha has created the ultimate brand feeling: being part of something bigger, "a global riding community with a friendly local spirit," as the website trumpets. Of course, members also get price discounts, limited runs of exclusive products, group rides, weekend specials, and clubhouse events—all easily accessible with the Rapha app. It's a complete community experience.

Boutique fitness chains are seeking to foster a greater sense of community. **TruFusion**'s members visit three to four times a week, above the industry average, because "people are using it as a social space; we have an unusual amount of people who come with friends," says CMO Steve Rockman.[64] TruFusion has even partnered with

OKCupid to host speed-dating workouts with live musicians for the entertainment value of it.

Similarly, office workspaces are becoming more focused on wellness. **Werklab**, for one, started as a coworking space for young professionals and then brought in total health programming to drive loyalty among members. "We aim to give members access to multiple modalities for caring for themselves," explains Christina Disler, founder of Werklab. "This involves everything from quiet corners and meditation cushions to daily movement classes and in-house reiki practitioners, expert-led workshops in neuroscience to mediumship and channeling, and a whole lot of things in between."[65] Werklab finds that this healthy community emphasis keeps members hanging around well after they've closed down their laptops.

Brands like these are taking the health and wellness of their customers very seriously and reaping the reward of a healthy, sustainable business model.

CHAPTER THREE
The Emergence of Gen Z

Gen Z, as those born between 1995 and 2010 are known, have already been put under the microscope by marketers and dissected, analyzed, and form-fit into a thousand explanations of "who they are." Yet, few know this generation as well as the companies that live or die by judging these microscopic findings *correctly*—companies such as cosmetics giant Coty with $5.5 billion in 2023 earnings. Coty has to be continually improving its understanding of Gen Z since that cohort is the biggest spender on beauty products.[66]

"Gen Zers are two different kinds of people really—quite opposites," Coty chief brands officer Stefano Curti says. "It's a bit like in society with so much polarization. We see it in Gen Z and even try to quantify it. We believe that approximately 35 percent of Gen Z is WE, and 65 percent is ME." [67]

"Gen Z ME tends to live in the metaverse, in the digital world. They tend to be content Creators running up the number of 'likes.' They spend half their day in front of their phones. They have a digital addiction. Gen Z WE, on the contrary, prefer authentic interaction. They rebel against the number of 'likes.' They are snobs about Instagram, are not on TikTok, and care instead about the bigger offline world, where they want to make a difference."

A look at these groups highlights a dualism:

- Gen Z ME is into escapism, self-empowerment, and style; they are fashion-driven and reactive.

- Gen Z WE is optimistic and unfiltered, driven by purpose and beliefs; they take action.

This recognition of opposites drives Coty's product development—and, indeed, the entire corporate positioning of the company. "We have looked at all our brands to ramp up their purpose. If you think about it, brands are really going back to their roots. There is no entrepreneur that has ever invented any product with money in mind first. It's always 'purpose first.' Always about making a difference in people's lives, making a difference in the industry. Gen Z is effectively going back to those values, requiring brands to be activists, to be on purpose. They have to align with the brand vision and mission in the world to fall in love with the brand. For Coty, our purpose is to unleash every vision of beauty, together."

For Gen Z ME, Curti notes that CoverGirl was created sixty years ago as the first healthy makeup. "There was concern that makeup could clog your pores, cause breakouts, allergies. Coty was the first brand in the U.S. that established a healthy makeup line that is good for your skin, actually makes your skin better while you wear it … then the first brand to launch 'clean foundation' in the early '90s. Putting a cleansing agent into a product was a contradiction then. Three years ago, when I joined Coty, we reconnected CoverGirl to its clean heritage. We launched the first clean mascara." Importantly, there is no legal definition of clean, but Coty turned it into a defining attribute of the brand, "what it wanted to stand for."

Continuing this "good for you" theme in their brand positioning, Coty made a decision to not formulate with over five hundred unhealthy ingredients commonly used in cosmetics. "We decided to take a stand, and recently launched the second clean mascara, called Lash Blast Cleantopia, that takes 'clean' to the next level and takes 'volume' to the next level. We launched a new range of powders and facial products called Clean Invisible. We brought 'clean' to eyeshadows. We strategically reconnected the brand to its original values that have purpose for Gen Z."

Curti emphasizes that this campaign was co-developed with Gen Z and Influencers. Curti's team began by hiring Influencers through TikTok and then turning them into employees who continued to hire more Gen Z Influencers to participate in product development. "Co-creation is very important for Gen Z ME. They want to have a say, they want self-empowerment. They're the ones who tell you, 'Understand me, don't define me.' So, we co-developed with them in our own TikTok studio, producing organic content for our TikTok handle."

Selecting the right kind of Influencers was a key to the success that would follow. "We don't go just with big Influencers. We go with small and up-and-coming Influencers. We connect them to our brand and the brand becomes a stage for them to increase their followership. Better to have a thousand micro-Influencers with five thousand followers than having macro-Influencers with fifty million followers. It's about creating a real connection. Gen Z doesn't like staged content. It needs to be genuine. Sometimes rough is better than polished."

Part and parcel of co-developing with the Gen Z audience was the discovery of how personalized digital-first marketing can be, must be. Curti says, "When you develop a plan that is digital first, you start with the tribes. People that are into nightclubs, people gravitating to culture and art, etcetera. And you fine-tune your messaging, your visuals, and your claims to the psychographics of these tribes. So, we didn't do a bunch of thirty-second TV commercials like we used to. We did two thousand different 'ads' so the company was no longer speaking one-to-many but instead one-to-one to each different customer." That's marketing to Gen Z ME.

As for the polar-opposite Gen Z WE, Coty partnered with Adidas on an "Active Skin & Mind" line of shower gels and deodorants that come with a larger message. Curti says, "We relaunched in September 2022 with 100 percent recyclable and refillable bottles, plastic-free formats and a 98 percent biodegradable formula ... attaching the brand to a purpose through sustainability."

At the company level, Coty is also speaking to Gen Z WE by choosing to "undefine beauty." To sharpen that point, Coty called out the major English dictionaries. "You know how dictionaries use words in context?" Curti asks. "One example is, 'She was a beauty in her youth.' But there are so many things wrong with this statement. Beauty has been connected historically to the stereotype of a woman. A woman needs to be beautiful and young. A man doesn't have to be beautiful and young. So, we called a couple of dictionaries. We wrote letters to them. Then we launched a public campaign featuring a petition—it's called #UndefineBeauty. Petitioning for dictionaries to update their definition of beauty."

This "reconnected" company purpose runs through every decision Coty makes now. As CEO Sue Nabi puts it, "[W]e are united by fearless kindness to push the boundaries of what's comfortable and expected, finding new ways to operate. This is how we prefaced Coty's 2022 sustainability report on progress toward reducing greenhouse gas emissions, reducing product packaging materials, and paying employees equitably regardless of gender."[68]

This commitment to the values of Gen Z WE has been good for business, with Coty's share of the global cosmetics market increasing significantly. Curti reports, "We track the penetration of the brand by age group, and we've seen penetration significantly increasing in the last two years among Gen Z and Hispanics in the U.S. We have posted twelve consolidated quarters of EBITDA growth, and eighteen months of market share growth. When I joined, the company stock value was $3.50 per share; today we're trading at around $12. Yet, it's always purpose FIRST."

Through the Generations

Generational change has long been the engine driving societal change. And major-scale events have usually shaped each new generation's views. The Progressive Era tried to unite a country through the Civil War and into Reconstruction. The Missionary Generation followed with a Protestant sweep across the plains. The Lost Generation fell under the disillusionment of World War I and Prohibition. The Greatest Generation was famously named for their heroic sacrifices in World War II. Baby Boomers born around 1940–1960 were influenced by the Vietnam War and social upheaval. Gen X born around 1961–1980 garnered a reputation for cynicism amid continuing upheavals that snuffed out idealism. Millennials born around 1981–1995 had their worldview shaped by 9/11 and the internet. And now Gen Z exhibits a ME-WE orientation that both reflects and refracts the deep schisms in society as manifest in financial uncertainty, climate anxiety, pandemic fears, and social inequality. (Of course, there is already a Gen Alpha in the making. But still young, they do not require as much attention from most brand marketers as yet.)

Fair to say that any attempt to characterize an entire generation in a few pages—especially a generation with such a fascinatingly dualistic nature—is going to be rife with oversimplifications. Fortunately, for marketers, it is now far easier to assess a generation in all its facets with data analytics tools.

Gen Z ME Snapshot

By 2026, 82 million Gen Zers will turn the country into a majority "other than white" tableau of races. This diversity is further delineated by traditional metrics (25 percent of Gen Zers *are* Hispanic) and emergent metrics (50 percent of Gen Z *identify as* BIPOC—Black, Indigenous, People of Color).[69]

As with race, the sexual preferences of Gen Z are shifting. Only 48 percent say they are "completely heterosexual," and 48 percent value brands that do not classify their products as male or female.[70]

A concern for one's personal health—in both its physical and mental aspects—may be the standout differentiator of this generation. Self-care within a total health orientation is leading Gen Z ME to make healthier food choices, sample more health products, and cut back on alcohol or replace it with other drugs believed (correctly, and incorrectly) to be less harmful.[71]

A second standout differentiator of Gen Z ME is a passion for gaming, with 90 percent of them identifying as gamers or game enthusiasts and spending almost twice as much time with friends online than off. If the choice is between going to a fun party and playing a game on a computer screen, they choose the latter. As a result, the esports and gaming market is now worth almost $200 billion. But this love of games is so ubiquitous that it carries over into the product marketing decisions of almost every company—not just gaming companies, as we'll see.[72]

Gen Z is also the most educated of generations—at least based on acceptance into college (59 percent have attended versus 52 percent of Millennials). Gen Z is also more likely than previous generations to finish a four-year college, go on to higher education, and jump into the workforce. This includes having multiple jobs. Nearly half of Gen Z over the age of eighteen are working a side hustle—many just to make ends meet as well as with the long-term objective of retiring early.[73]

Moving into the workplace in such numbers, Gen Z is altering old-fashioned concepts of career devotion. Four in ten say they put a big emphasis on work-life balance when choosing a job. And the two biggest motivators for staying happy at work are an "empowering work culture" and "growth potential." These are twice as important as salaries and benefits packages to Gen Z.[74]

Representing 40 percent of the consuming public, Gen Z wields $134 billion in buying power and is now driving purchases in key categories, from automobiles to furniture and groceries while influencing an additional $600 billion in purchase decisions by their parents.[75] This based on 93 percent of parents saying their Gen Z children influence how the family wallet opens up.[76]

On socializing alone, the average Gen Z spends $167 a month or $2,000 a year.[77] Social media is the vacant lot, the mall, the video arcade to this generation—it is where they hang out. Only two in one hundred don't own a smartphone, and a majority of those who do spend more than five hours a day on them, with a quarter of them spending ten hours a day (i.e., it is always open and being checked).[78] Seven in ten watch more than two hours of YouTube videos a day and have a Netflix subscription, as well.[79]

A significant 85 percent of Gen Z learn about new products on social media—which makes sense for a digitally native generation.[80] Much of this happens on TikTok since 60 percent of that platform's users are Gen Z.[81] These platforms are so infused with social selling and Influencer marketing that it has become an unrippable part of the online social fabric. As Gary Kuchta, CMO of **Herbalife**, points out, "The idea of social selling—I buy a product so you should too—is very big with Gen Z. I think the number one desired profession among Gen Z right now is to be a social Influencer. It's not to be a doctor, lawyer, or engineer like in previous generations. Their dream job is to be a social Influencer!"[82]

So, it follows, though it may surprise, that a majority of Gen Z report following at least three brands on social media. That level of brand awareness did not exist with previous generations. So, even companies that wouldn't seem "like a fit" for these young entertainment platforms can leverage social platforms.

One such company is **H&R Block**, as CMO Jill Cress explains, "We're able to find Gen Z on platforms like YouTube and TikTok, and to make our content a little bit more fresh and more entertaining. We increased our awareness with Gen Z by six absolute percentage points this past year, which is really impressive with only a little over one hundred days of paid social media."[83]

There is a misconception that Gen Z doesn't talk much. In fact, they talk constantly about new brands, companies, and products. Word of mouth—which to Gen Z means texting, largely—is the most common way to work through product purchase decision-making. Seeing YouTube ads is a close second.[84]

Once they learn about a brand, and decide they like it, Gen Z is exceptionally loyal. Two in three say they'll stick with a brand if it meets their expectations. But earning their confidence is harder than ever and requires solid execution on strategy, as we'll see.[85]

Gen Z WE Snapshot

"Think about what they've experienced in a relatively short amount of time," suggests Lisa Caputo, executive vice president and chief marketing, communications, and customer experience officer for The Travelers Companies, Inc. "Gen Z has seen the pandemic, the Me-Too movement, George Floyd, the war in Ukraine, humanitarian crises, school shootings, January 6th, climate change, economic instability. These young people were on their screens watching it all happen. And I think it's made them stop and say, 'What's going on in the world? What's happening with our institutions and our government? Where is society headed?'"[86]

Whether accurate or not within a broader historical context, the world feels very unsafe to Gen Z, and 48 percent say they are stressed out and often unhappy, compared to 40 percent of Millennials. One in three get paralyzingly anxious if they can't check their phones at least every half hour.[87] Some demographers refer to them as the "loneliest generation" since endless hours spent online only multiply their anxiety, isolation, and depression.[88] As well, many fall deep into the "compare and despair" trap that social media sanctions, further ripping at their mental health and too often shredding it.

"This is the first generation to grow up entirely online," **KPMG**'s managing director Brian Miske notes, "and social media has challenged their self-esteem. It is a very emotional generation where everything is depicted online. It's all magnified by word of mouth, and spread so easily through social media."[89]

Mental health is a prominent issue and a priority for this generation. Brands have a commercial vested interest in joining with public health officials and community organizations to find compassionate solutions.

Moving from health to political views, Gen Z is slightly more "progressive" than their Millennial predecessors and thus more likely to support gay marriage, racial equality, and intersexuality.[90] They are also more concerned about humanity's impact on the environment (76 percent deeply care) and so more willing to choose eco-friendly and socially responsible brands (45 percent try to).[91]

And finally, Gen Z will give over loyalty to brands that take like-minded positions on these subjects and express brand alignment in a trustworthy, transparent, and authentic way. Notes **Lagunitas** CMO Paige Guzman, "We see in every single tracker we do that Gen Z cares about brands, and they are willing to invest more in brands when they choose to drink. When I was twenty-one or twenty-two, we bought the cheapest vodka that we could because it was more liquid for the buck. Gen Z consumers are very different. They're willing to invest in a top-shelf Maker's Mark-type whiskey. So quality matters to them. Brands matter to them."[92]

Marketing to Gen Z

In formulating marketing strategies that sync with the dualistic nature of Gen Z and win their ME and WE hearts and digital wallets, there is a strategic thought framework that's useful to employ:

GEN Z ME	GEN Z WE
Authenticity + Transparency	Meaning + Purpose
Individualism + Personalization	Diversity + Inclusion
Connection + Experience	Sustainability + ESG

ALL ABOUT ME: AUTHENTICITY AND TRANSPARENCY

Bombarded with inputs from the crib on out, Gen Z has only known an overabundance of information. Inundated with slick brand messaging and polished visuals that clearly went through rounds of agency approvals, Gen Z learned early on to erect strong filters to block out the deluge. Brands that hope to break through these filters have to work doubly hard to prove their good intentions with the kinds of authentic and transparent actions that have, traditionally, made marketers uneasy.

Authenticity means creating like a Creator

Gen Z prefers messaging that looks like they created it themselves, especially in social media. If it looks homespun, user-generated, or unpolished, Gen Z sees it as more authentic and credible. Old-time sales tactics and manipulation attempts have little purchase now and need to give way to language that's relatable. Better to go with a gritty DIY look that's brimming with personality and speaks the language of Gen Z—as if made by a social media Creator.

Seeking a higher level of accountability

Gen Z is actually attracted to the mistakes that marketers once tried to hide. They get that mistakes happen—to err is human—and the most "honest" thing any brand can do is "own up" to their mistakes rather than try to brush them under the rug. That honesty is rewarded.

Sure, it can be hard. Harder still knowing that consumers have the power of social media in their hands at all times, and with just one blunder, the company could go viral in the wrong way—leading to a massive exiting of customers. The best way to deal with this, ironically, is to own it.

If the brand makes a mistake—such as using language no longer deemed inclusive—the best remedy is to address the issue head-on. Take immediate public responsibility for the mistake, and explain how it is being corrected. This is how Gen Z is impressed and how their loyalty is won.

INDIVIDUALISM AND PERSONALIZATION

Gen Z has been so thoroughly catered to by marketers that contradictions have arisen. On the one hand, one in four of them demand a completely individualized shopping experience based on their shopping habits and preferences. But two-thirds of them are reluctant to hand over the data required to deliver such a deeply immersive marketing activation. On the other hand, three in four of them consider retargeting ads that rely on personal data to be invasive, with eight in ten skipping over the ads altogether and half of them using ad blockers.[93] These conflicting demands and practices create quite a challenge for marketers.

Marketers need to carefully balance data collection with privacy protection so that Gen Z can trust that their data is being securely stored and protected for the life of the engagement and beyond.

Meet Gen Z where they hang out

Network fragmentation, long ago, exploded the channels marketers used to find consumers, and today, marketers are finding Gen Z audiences most readily in niche online communities. As Stefano Curti of Coty noted earlier in this chapter, his company no longer cuts a handful of thirty-second spots but instead two thousand messages for different consumer groups—each message individualized and personalized. And those messages are pinpoint-targeted into closed online communities, such as Discord and Fizz, that encourage more authentic dialogue and closer connections among people with shared interests.

It has been said that Gen Z is "extremely online."[94] YouTube is the favorite platform with 88 percent using it regularly, followed by Instagram with 76 percent penetration, TikTok with 68 percent, Snapchat with 67 percent, Facebook with 49 percent, Twitter with 47 percent, Discord with 35 percent, Reddit with 30 percent, Twitch with 24 percent, and BeReal with 15 percent.

When asked how they're spending all this time online, Gen Z will respond along the lines of "This is my community." Herbalife is a company that understands this phenomenon. Gary Kuchta, the company's CMO, says of Gen Z, "They don't define community the same way as previous generations. Their communities may be completely virtual—entirely enabled through social media and consist of people they've never physically met."[95]

Fastest growing among these community platforms currently is TikTok, with a near rabid following among Gen Z. This is owing to the platform's algorithms that cultivate millions of subcultures mirroring every imaginable interest, activity, or trend. When a user's actions on the app signal a set of preferences, the algorithm serves up the best of that content. This makes TikTok an estimated thirty-seven million users' strong umbrella in the United States with countless micro-community campfires that Gen Z gather around.

The only "channel" that outranks TikTok for producing brand endorsements is old-fashioned word of mouth. TikTok is such an important channel that we'll return to it in greater detail in later chapters.

All of this social media happens on some kind of device, and 75 percent of Gen Z say they use mobile the most.[96] Importantly, 55 percent use their mobile most often to make online purchases versus 38 percent who use a computer.[97] So marketers need to *fully* optimize for mobile—not just using a mobile-optimized website theme but also creating vertical video content with mobile devices in mind, enabling a community of brand activists to thrive in the mobile setting, and streamlining the marketing funnel through to the checkout process and beyond into social support.

CONNECTIONS AND EXPERIENCES

Gen Z is excellent at sifting through online content, and they prefer short-form to match their shortened attention spans. Marketers must grab their attention immediately. And this is best accomplished through entertaining short-form video.

It's all about trust with Gen Z, and so, they can appreciate ads that are true to a brand's core values as long as they share those values. However, the most visually captivating ads will spark the greatest interest. Conversely, clickbait ads, long-form ads, and disruptive ads will be tuned out in a blink.

Better to use user-generated content (UGC), including the content of Influencers, as well as website comments and online reviews, which Gen Z consider more authentic. Better still to tell stories. Young people have always loved stories more, and Gen Z is no exception.

Go deep on gaming

Entering into game-playing venues is a powerful strategy for attaining engagement, awareness, and conversion objectives. It's all about the interaction—the involving of the brand in the consumer's regular daily activities. For instance, the gaming site Fortnite hosted a concert series by hip-hop artist Travis Scott inside the game, and 27 million players showed up.[98] By comparison in the 2022–2023 television season, NBC's *Sunday Night Football* averaged 18 million viewers; the top-rated *Yellowstone* averaged 10 million viewers; and ABC's *American Idol*, once strong with younger viewers, garnered only 6.8 million viewers.[99]

Gaming is not only top-of-mind but top-of-wallet. In 2022, consumers spent a total of $294 billion on digital media with more than half, $156 billion, going to video games. A distant third, fourth, and fifth in spending were video-on-demand, e-publishing, and digital music, respectively. Gaming has captured the country's attention, led by Gen Z who are said to be 90 percent gaming enthusiasts.[100] This is where marketers can reach them, and we'll revisit this in later chapters.

Pop-ups break the mold correctly

Gen Z doesn't view shopping as "a sport" in the way previous generations did. Many don't even know what a great experience shopping can be, feeling merchandise, trying things out, and so on. They just order stuff on apps knowing they can return it easily. But when presented with great retail strategies, and the ability to use their five senses in retail theater, they form all new opinions.

This explains the attraction of pop-ups from marketers targeting Gen Z. Pop-ups are a tactical mixing of commerce and cause—critical to Gen Z. It's a competitive differentiator, in fact. To make the biggest splash, these pop-ups are going to venues where the target audience is congregating—concerts, sporting events, town squares. And brands are being creative and taking risks in order to stand out, explode onto the scene, and change the perceptions of existing customers while winning new ones.

ALL ABOUT WE: MEANING AND PURPOSE

Each new generation rises through their formative years enveloped in all the idealism the era allows. And this era has allowed Gen Z to hold on to a nascent idealism about the harmful effects of overconsumption, capitalism, and materialism and to turn those ideals into what is likely to be, save a black swan event, a lifetime commitment.

Gen Z is genuinely invested in making the world a better place—to rectify the perceived wrongs of their forebears. They demonstrate as much through their interest in purpose-driven brands and by demanding that businesses support the same causes they happen to support personally. These demands come from the heart and are deeply felt. Surveys have consistently found that three in four Gen Z employees care more about the company's purpose than the paycheck. And seven in ten are more likely to patronize a company if it is making contributions to a cause they care about. They'll pay more for parity products from those companies, as much as 20 percent more than Boomers and 5 percent more than Millennials.[101]

So social marketing should be less about the product than these values that lift up out of the brand's story. **BMW**'s Jens Thiemer, senior vice president of Customer & Brand BMW, understands this clearly, given the nature of his business. "It's not just an artificial discussion Gen Z is having. They are looking for 'leadership' which they define not as who's the best *in* the world, but who's the best *for* the world. It's one of their rallying calls, so in a nutshell it's how you should position yourself to be relevant."[102]

To achieve that relevance in the eyes of the world, and especially Gen Z, BMW is actively shrinking their carbon footprint. "We define our brand essence as joy, the joy of driving," Thiemer says. "But that aspect of joy has to be adjusted to include a circular economy aspect so the car goes into a closed circle of recycling. A target for BMW is to use old cars to produce new cars without any further materials." Thiemer acknowledges that a zero-carbon footprint automobile is still decades away, but many steps are being taken along the way to define the ultimate driving machine simultaneously as the ultimate sustainability choice. At BMW, we call it "Freude forever."

Another company taking an important public stand relevant to Gen Z is **H&R Block**. We saw earlier how H&R has been able to reach Gen Z audiences on TikTok and YouTube. The company created an entire campaign called "A Fair Shot" when they learned, as CMO Jill Cress recalls, "that in 2022 the NCAA changed its rules allowing student athletes to earn sponsorship dollars for their name, image and likeness (NIL). But only 23 percent of available sponsorship dollars were going to female athletes, and we wanted to make sure our program aligned with our diversity, equity, and inclusion values. So, we designed the platform to talk about the disparity in sponsorship dollars that were going to female athletes. We launched with a handful of NCAA female athletes, and we talked about how hard they work and they simply deserve 'a fair shot.'"[103]

The campaign was so successful that H&R brought it back for a second season and took an even more inclusive approach. "Instead of just focusing on the most elite athletes, sports, and universities, we've diversified the slate to include track and field, lacrosse, tennis, and softball … and also to include Division I, II and III and Historically Black Colleges and Universities. The results have been incredible. Last year we saw our Gen Z brand awareness increase 13 percentage points and brand favorability increase 31 points from this campaign. Impressively, two-thirds of Gen Z said H&R Block would be their first choice for tax prep because of 'A Fair Shot.'"

In both these cases—with H&R Block and BMW—the companies are speaking to a generation in an earnest, meaningful way. They are (a) enumerating the social issues that are resonant with the brand, (b) aligning the entire organization around policies and practices consistent with that corporate purpose, and (c) taking public positions that flag the attention of consumers who share that purpose.

DIVERSITY AND INCLUSION

As the largest, most ethnically diverse generation in U.S. history, comprising 27 percent of the population, it's no surprise that Gen Z cares deeply about diversity or that they want companies to mirror "them." A full 80 percent say a company's commitment to Diversity, Equity, and Inclusion (DE&I) should begin in the executive suites and carry on down through every level of the organization.[104]

Gen Z defines this diversity agenda to include gender and sexuality, with 77 percent saying they feel more positive toward a brand when it promotes gender equality on social media and 59 percent saying that the data-gathering forms companies use should provide gender-neutral options.[105] And 40 percent of Gen Z say companies should require the use of nonbinary pronouns in their communications.[106] Interestingly, many more Millennials (60 percent) say workplaces should require gender pronouns. This could reflect the fact that Millennials are more secure in their job positions than Gen Z who, for all their willingness to take stands, are also concerned about job security.

Gen Z's concern for "marginalized groups" extends to the disabled with 54 percent saying companies need to advocate for disabled person equity and embrace neurodiversity as well or risk losing the support of employees and face public scorn.[107] This embrace, known as allyship, is how companies support and build trust with different groups in the larger diverse landscape and lift up the voices of these groups for the betterment of all.

This Gen Z WE concern runs across all Western markets, as becomes clear in the first frame of a video that recently played across Europe. It captured angry teens screaming, "[W]e all hate you and want to see you burn" and "[B]ack then they would've gassed you" and "[S]omeone should rape you!" This is not footage from a suprema-cist rally. No, it's from Germany's leading **Deutsche Telekom** and is meant to take a stand against the dangers of hate speech gaining momentum globally. This is a cause that's dear to Gen Z and one that Deutsche Telekom—along with fifty-plus partner groups—is committed to fighting.

"You have to connect with them early in life on issues they care about, and when you do, it's often the beginning of a lifelong rela-tionship," explains the company's global chief brand officer, Ulrich Klenke.[108] Targeting Gen Z in a deliberate and meaningful way is what Klenke has been doing since 2020; the #NoHateSpeech initiative is one of several and surely a reason he is consistently cited by *Forbes* as one of the World's Most Influential CMOs.[109]

As a result, between 2020 and 2023, the percentage of young consumers citing Deutsche Telekom as their preferred telco brand rose from 36 to 40 percent, a 12 percent increase. It's also the highest affinity telco brand among young people in five out of nine European countries, with 47 percent of respondents saying they "love the brand."[110] The company's dedication to Gen Z has helped it become the eleventh most valuable brand in the world in 2023, with an economic value of $62.9 billion.[111]

Impressive results.

Communities of shared values and interests

It's critical for *every* brand to foster a community that creates genuine connections with Gen Z consumers. Running experiential marketing cuts through the channel clutter since these tangible experiences are more exciting and memorable. Rather than treating consumers as passive receivers of content, community marketing allows consumers to actively co-create the experience—the best way to connect with Gen Z. These community experiences create lasting attachments, generate word of mouth, and cultivate buzz around the company's offerings. As well, these communities cement lasting bonds between the brand and its most loyal customers while turning these loyalists into brand ambassadors who can efficiently ripple out across the Gen Z pond.

Community activities can be entirely online or can take the form of offline events, marketing tours, pop-up experiences, or guerrilla marketing. The most powerful of them are bold and in your face, with implicit brand messaging that doesn't interrupt the experience, that ties in to digital to boost engagement, and that partners with like-minded brands around a shared objective. These community experiences work for B2B companies as well as B2C because in both situations, the brand is being embedded into the lives of the consumers.

How to raise the brand's voice

Forrester researchers found that a third of Gen Z "unfollow, hide, or block brands on social media—at least weekly ... not hesitating to cancel brands when they sense a shallow veneer."[112] And no generation is quicker to see through veneers and smokescreens. They are consciously looking for companies who do good in the world, who stand for more diversity, who believe in inclusion and act on it. They will vote with their dollars when they see brands helping to shift the narrative.

They expect company CEOs to take stands on big issues. Companies should ask themselves who they are as a brand and whether the big issues intersect with the brand mission statement. If there is an intersection, both customers and employees will expect the company to take an official position, as follows:

- Choose messaging that's unique and memorable.

- Know how the messaging is advancing the brand in a meaningful way.

- Show what the company is actively doing to promote positive change.

- Give people resources for joining in the cause the company is advancing.

- Commit to a long-term plan to make a difference in this world.

SUSTAINABILITY AND ESG

Prominent scientists with the British Geological Survey recently published in *Science* that a confluence of major trends—population explosion, new technologies, and overconsumption—has most certainly now brought on an entirely new geologic epoch, the Anthropocene (human + new). While this postulation first surfaced years ago and remains controversial, it is accepted as gospel by a majority of Gen Z. They fully believe humans have altered the earth so extensively that we have left the Holocene (which began twelve thousand years ago) and entered a perilous new epoch. They cite atmospheric methane levels, plastics in marine sediments, chemicals in the soil, and nuclear weapons testing for altering the face of the planet—perhaps irreversibly.

Business has responded to these concerns with the Environment, Social, and Governance (ESG) agenda. While only 40 percent of all adults support this agenda, 46 percent of Gen Z support it, and that figure may be low solely because ESG does not roll off the tongue.[113] And, in fact, when asked instead if they value fighting climate change, 76 percent told Pew Research that they are "overwhelmingly worried" and it's "one of their biggest concerns."[114] They see action being taken as essential to their living to a ripe old age. Sustainability and ESG are flags they carry.

And Gen Z doesn't believe companies are currently doing enough to "save the planet," with 88 percent saying they do not trust companies' ESG claims.[115] So companies are being called upon to demonstrate their commitment more ably.

There is an additional impetus for taking strong ESG positions. For, as alluded to in chapter 1, there is a growing body of evidence that the triple bottom line (Profit + People + Planet) can be a viable business model. A Dow Jones study of an ESG index found that those companies outperformed the benchmark S&P 500 from the index's launching in 2018–2022 by a substantial 9.16 percent.[116]

Other studies from EY, Harvard Business School, the Harris Poll, and the University of Oxford found a positive correlation between purpose and profit, as well.[117] Of course, a purpose-driven company is not necessarily going to be more profitable since a number of factors influence business outcomes. But the argument for adhering to the triple bottom line can be persuasive.

Big 4 professional services firm **PwC** is a model of this profitable ESG activism, showcasing their efforts to promote a more sustainable and equitable planet. Front and center on the corporate website, it says, "Given the urgent crisis of climate change, our environmental strategy reaches across our business operations and all our stakeholders with a focus on carbon reduction and environmental sustainability. In addition to the actions we're taking within the firm, and as a leader in environmental coalitions, we're empowering our people to be environmental champions in their local communities."[118]

As an example of this commitment, when PwC workstations were being reconfigured for a postpandemic return to office, the firm donated 12,000 pounds of computing equipment to communities and groups in need. The tagline was "Goodbye theory, hello action."

There is a parade of such sustainability initiatives underway. Every company targeting Gen Z audiences will want to be in this parade. Sustainability is a strategic business approach and not just the latest trend of a youthful, idealistic generation. It's a corporate-level focus on "the right thing to do" that can be, when executed properly, also "the profitable thing to do."

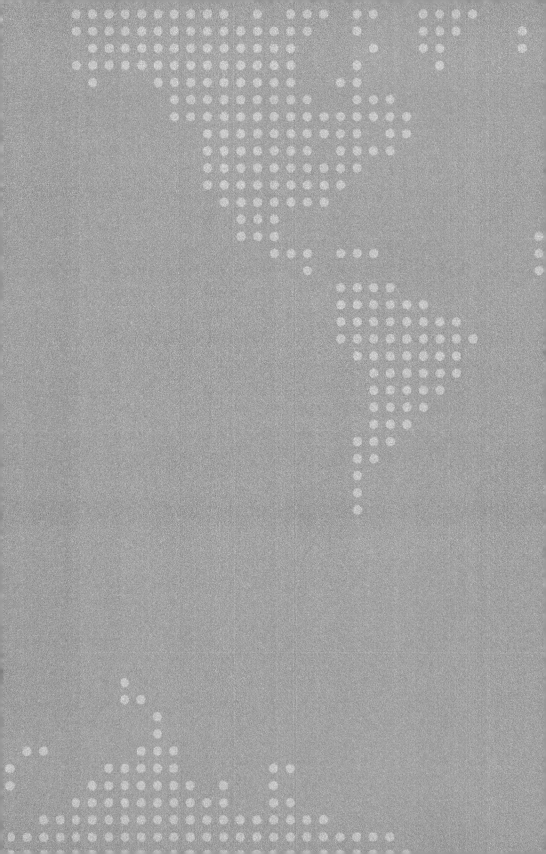

SECTION TWO: TECHNOLOGICAL FUTUREWAVES

How Brands Will Need to Be Personalized

In the first section, we saw how brands need to be positioned to meet the values and expectations of an emerging consumer base. With that, brands can next take advantage of new technologies that allow them to *personalize* the customer experience with near-prescient precision.

This begins in chapter 4 with the struggle marketers face in ***harnessing AI*** as a positive extension of their brand promise. Companies set on gaining the greatest competitive advantage from AI are elevating the marketing function in the C-suite to drive business strategy, bringing any truly strategic AI functionality in-house, transitioning their teams to an AI-centric future, and putting strict guardrails in place.

Chapter 5 tracks the changing definitions of "reality" and how brands are layering ***XR technologies*** into omnichannel strategies for more immersive brand experiences. With the future of the Metaverse a big unknown, CMOs are experimenting with "Web 2.5"—using

XR technologies to showcase a "cutting-edge" brand, extend their robust omnichannel brand experience, leverage the huge popularity of gaming communities, conduct better product sampling and market research, and build more efficiencies into in-person events and community gatherings.

Chapter 6 leaps into **_Web3 hope and hype_**, assessing both the opportunities and the pitfalls it offers to marketers. Marketers are finding novel methods for aligning their products/services with early adopters of decentralized ownership schemes based on blockchain and crypto, non-fungible tokens (NFTs) and token economics, and the gradually unfolding Metaverse. Web3 benefits are already being seen by consumers, brands and marketers, and the communities jumping into this future technology.

CHAPTER FOUR
AI and the Personalized Brand Experience

Many trace that first realization of the awesome budding power of AI to 1997 when they watched **IBM's Watson** defeat the reigning world chess champion, Garry Kasparov. Clearly, the future had arrived! And now today there isn't a single industry *not* somehow impacted by AI, with some of the most sophisticated systems being put to work in the marketing arena. IBM remains a leading provider of toolsets in the space—though

Key Terms Used In The Marketing Domain

Artificial Intelligence: Uses math and software code to teach computers how to understand, synthesize, and generate data in a humanlike way.

Machine Learning: Allows algorithms to get more accurate over time at identifying relevant audiences and predicting creative elements that will resonate with them.

Natural Language Processing: A method of interpreting and analyzing text and speech so that marketers can extract insights from each consumer touchpoint. Also enables the use of chatbots in customer interactions.

Synthetic Data: Data that is artificially generated by a computer to augment or replace real data and used to improve AI models, protect sensitive data, mitigate bias, and enable cookieless targeting. We use the shorthand "AI" to refer to all its applications.

marketers are seeing a dizzying array of solution sets from pioneers and startups alike.

"This AI gives us a new level of data, a new ability to serve data to people that is more relevant to them and makes it more enjoyable," says Jonathan Adashek, chief communications officer at IBM. It can be as simple as "getting ads or content that I appreciate versus some random thing like 'buy this piece of real estate in downtown Cheyenne, Wyoming' when I've never been to Cheyenne, Wyoming in my life."[119]

Of course, the simplicity of these well-targeted, personalized, and relevant ads is anything but, especially as we enter a cookie-less future where marketers will no longer be allowed to track click behavior across the internet. Regulations such as the General Data Protection Regulation (GDPR) in the European Union (EU) and the California Consumer Privacy Act (CCPA) have prompted many websites to provide cookie consent notices. An estimated 60 percent of the internet went cookieless in 2023, and Google plans a phaseout in 2024.

"The trick is going to be attaining that similar level of targeting in this cookieless future since it's a major pivot point for the industry," continues IBM's Adashek. And a fortuitous pivot, plausibly. Ironically, the loss of cookies and other personal identifiable information (PII) might be the best thing to happen to digital marketing. After all, the cookies that drove online marketing for so long also delivered rather stilted and often inaccurate views of the individual being tracked. And few outside the marketing community have any taste for cookies.

Fortunately, advances in machine learning allow a new kind of "contextual marketing" that depends less on the past choices of consumers and more on what matters to them right now and how they are behaving in the moment on a website. This contextual marketing uses real-time insights to better anticipate consumers' interests, needs, and preferences and serve up ads that more immediately appeal to them. This kind of marketing can work down the funnel but is clearly best suited to upper-funnel goals, such as awareness and consideration.

At its simplest level, an individual reading an article about volleyball might be served an ad about volleyball products. Of course, this simplicity doesn't require AI to execute. But digging in, AI also employs predictive analytics to gauge how likely the individual is to actually take an action.

IBM is effectively doing with AI what a human brain would do when deciding where to place an ad manually. So, AI helps ensure that the ad placement is relevant and timely, creating a more personalized experience—which is ever more important to consumers deciding what brands to align with. Ultimately, IBM maintains, this dynamic targeting strategy can be used to run campaigns just as effectively as cookie-based targeting.

Hand in hand with targeting, AI can automate the labor-intensive job of optimizing the creative platform, gauging which creative executions are best performing by the metrics that the advertiser cares about—and developing variations on them—all in real time.

One example is the work IBM's Advertising Accelerator did for its client, Audi. The objective was to drive awareness and interest in Audi's new electric vehicles. IBM analyzed consumer engagements and cookieless data signals to serve up 116 different creatives for 36.7 million impressions and, measured against benchmarks, delivered a 118 percent increase in conversion rates, a 271 percent increase in relevant page visits, and a 320 percent increase in a critical "cost per inventory search" metric.[120]

IBM's own marketing copy claims that "predicting consumer actions to deliver personalized experiences means that you will always deliver the right message to the right customer at each touchpoint."[121] By the Audi case example and numerous others, they are delivering on that claim.

Side by side with cookieless data generation is synthetic data generation. This is a new kind of data that AI creates to look and feel like real-world data. It is meant to share common characteristics with its real-world analog, though it is not a clone of talk world data, as some have suggested. But it is proving an effective tool for AI's acceleration of brand capabilities.

Synthetic data lets companies sidestep regulations on the use of personal data. Healthcare records, financial data, and some web content are protected by privacy and copyright laws that every year become more and more difficult to access and assess at scale. Enter synthetic data, which is not traceable to anyone, per se, while preserving the statistical properties of the original data.

Being able to train AI using synthetic data instead of real-world data speeds up the process at considerable cost savings, allowing all kinds of AI models to be deployed with little to no loss of data integrity.

Self-driving cars, as an example, ran with synthetic data from the outset. It would have been impractical if not impossible to gather a collection of all the scenarios that can happen on the road (so-called edge cases), but synthetic data allowed researchers to fill in the data gaps.

Chatbots are also being improved with synthetic data. These bots encounter a great variation in speaking styles, accents, and rhythms. Even operating at AI speed, it might take a chatbot decades to learn the nuances of talking with humans. But synthetic data speeds it along.

A big benefit of synthetic data is that it lessens the chances the computer will go off on a racist or sexist tangent. "Real world data is rarely problem-free," says IBM's Inkit Padhi. "Synthetic data allow us to find and fix problems in AI models to make them more fair, robust, and transferrable to other tasks."[122]

Biases in advertising campaigns can obviously harm their effectiveness, especially when targeting younger audiences who are more sensitive to these issues. But AI can step in and instantly uncover any unintended biases that may have gone unnoticed by the human eye. "We're making sure bias mitigation is built in from the start," explains Adashek. IBM is doing this with "IBM Fairness 360," which is an open-source software toolkit that helps developers (a) keep unwanted biases from entering their machine learning pipeline and (b) mitigate any biases that are discovered.

IBM was early into the AI space with the chess match that offered a brilliant proof of concept, and today the company's tools have matured to the point that they are slotting into marketers' toolkits. But they are far from alone in this fast-moving space, of course, and the industry is blossoming.

The State of AI in Brand Marketing

In surveying the literature on the impact AI is having on marketing, there are several interesting findings regarding its usage. The first is the simple fact that it has quickly gained incredible traction within the field of brand marketing. Boston Consulting Group (BCG) found 70 percent of marketing executives using AI, 19 percent testing it, 8 percent planning to test within the next two years, and only 3 percent saying they have no plans to test.[123] This represents an extraordinary pace of adoption when compared with previous technologies.

The second finding is the primary goal marketers have for using AI—namely, to increase efficiency and productivity. A Bain &

Company survey of six hundred companies across eleven industries found that the top use case for AI was developing marketing materials faster. A full 39 percent of marketers said they were using or evaluating the technology for this purpose.[124] The aforementioned BCG study's findings also support this point, indicating that most CMOs are seeing positive results from their AI initiatives, which they attribute to AI's low cost and ease of use—generating productivity gains as high as 30 percent.[125] Finally, a complementary HubSpot survey of marketers found that generative AI saved them an average of three hours and ten minutes when creating a single piece of marketing content.[126]

The third finding is that AI has (or will soon have) applicability across the entire customer journey. From building awareness to engendering loyalty, AI has the potential to dramatically disrupt how marketers think about customer acquisition, experience, and retention. Virtually, all of the tactics and use cases in the next figure will be addressed in greater detail throughout this chapter.

Global 2000 marketers are deploying AI deep into the marketing funnel.

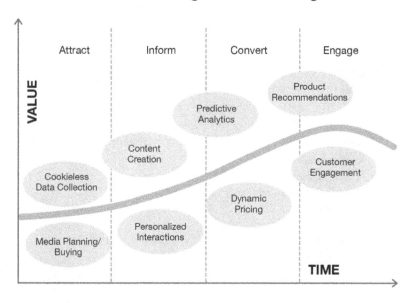

AI Is Taking Over Marketing

CMO Implementation Timeline

SHORT TERM	MEDIUM TERM	LONG TERM
Optimize tasks and workflows	Evolve customer relationships	Run marketing with adjust AI
✓ Collect cookieless first party data	✓ Connect to customers individually	✓ Efficiently manage customer base
✓ Automate content creation	✓ Adjust media strategy in real-time	✓ Run fully-integrated channel campaigns
✓ Deliver personalized experiences	✓ Predict customer future desires	✓ Build high-powered AI solutions in-house

Finally, a composite view of all the major survey findings, averaging out differences, sheds further light on how AI is being used, the potential it represents, the concerns it raises, and how those concerns are being addressed. It can be summarized as follows:

How AI is being used >>>	Leading to greater potential >>>
57% Micro-segment audiences	71% Cutting back on busy work
54% Hyper-personalize messaging	71% Allowing focus on strategic work
53% Run A/B testing in real-time	70% Saving time creating content
53% Maximize SEO strategies	70% Increasing overall productivity
51% Gain deeper market insights	
48% Obtain customer feedback	
43% Run predictive analytics	
Yet CMOs have worries >>>	**Which companies address with>>>**
76% AI introduces new security risks	66% Unflagging human oversight
73% AI lacks contexual knowledge	65% Single platform with controls
66% AI outputs are biased or flawed	built-in
55% Marketers will lose jobs	63% Vetted and trusted consumer
50% Copyright and IP vulnerabilities	data
45% Reduced creativity hurts the	54% Upskilling of marketing terms
brand	

Percent of Global 2000 CMOs raising their hands in agreement, based on composite of surveys by Gartner, Bain & Co., Salesforce, Boston Consulting Group, HubSpot, and FullSurge.[127]

Most Popular Use Cases for AI

In less than thirty years, AI has gone from basic autocorrect to ChatGPT writing books (not this one—ChatGPT isn't that good yet). And while the value of these tools to marketers has increased on an order of magnitude, we are still in the early days with recent uncomfortable news stories reminding us that generative AI models (a) can easily provide incorrect information, (b) have not shed their humanlike biases, and (c) are even capable of demonstrating seemingly sentient anger. But we are hearing less about the growing pains of this technology and more about the potential, and this is likely to continue.

WHAT IS MACHINE LEARNING?

Before we delve deeper into AI use cases, let's first define a concept that is essential to understanding AI: machine learning. Jim Lecinski, associate professor of marketing at Northwestern University and author of *The AI Marketing Canvas*, explains this technology in the simplest of terms relevant to marketers: "Artificial intelligence is the big tent, the broad study of systems that do things in a humanlike way, but of course, they're not human. So, we call it artificial intelligence, AI.[128]

"And there are subsets of AI. The subset marketers care most about is the one called machine learning. That's the ability of these artificially intelligent systems to make either *classifications* or *predictions*—without being given explicit instructions or if/then programming rules. These systems can arrive at their own conclusions and then learn from those conclusions for continuous improvement. And we care about this because we care about good customers and bad customers, who we're likely to attract, who we're likely to retain. This is the *classification* part.

"Then we care about 'the next best x.' The next best customer, the next best product, the next best price, the next best offer, the next best place, the next best channel. This is the *prediction* part.

"So that's machine learning relevant to marketers. Knowing this, the marketer can go into his or her business and look at what can be classified better and what can be predicted better to unlock value?"

WHAT IS PREDICTIVE ANALYTICS?

AI-powered predictive analytics are at the core of every AI capability. This new ability to identify consumer patterns, preferences, and behaviors with remarkable accuracy has upended the traditional analytics world by allowing marketers to now anticipate customer behavior in ways unimaginable even a few years ago.

This means that "marketing needs to be completely within the data camp," says Brian Miske, managing director at **KPMG**. "That doesn't necessarily mean becoming data scientists, but having a comprehensive working knowledge of how to use data and analytics to increase the speed and accuracy of decision-making. Can I make decisions faster than my competition? Can I access new markets through new channels and new platforms? I don't think marketers have ever truly had this type of responsibility before. It's always been relegated to the CIO suite versus the CMO suite."[129]

But now it's squarely on marketing's plate.

Consumer buying preferences, purchasing patterns, creative platform choices, cancellation, and churn likelihood—all are becoming more predictable with each new model release. And the insights that marketers glean from these AI-driven predictions allow for far superior marketing activations across nearly every industry.

Take the example of **SEE** (formerly Sealed Air), a leader in automated packaging solutions. SEE's vice president of Global Strategic Marketing, Garry Wicka, tells how even an industrial B2B company like his is taking advantage of these AI solutions. "We have an amazing AI algorithm system here that is able to predict customer churn. We can look at customers by tier and actually see when they're beginning to slow down, but haven't stopped buying entirely. Or perhaps they're only buying certain things. So, based on algorithms, we can put in place very specific marketing and sales actions to impact that."[130]

With AI solutions entering every industry, it's certainly no surprise that the number of solution providers is rapidly exploding. As of mid-2023, CB Insights had logged 335 startups across fifty-five categories at some stage of development.[131] That's in addition to industry-leading Microsoft's OpenAI and Bing, Google's Bard, and Level AI's customer service solution, AgentGPT. These solutions are improving with each release. The ability of AI to uncover patterns, preferences, and behaviors embedded in the five million terabytes of data floating around the internet—and then make predictions based on them—is enabling a new standard of performance.

With a basic understanding of machine learning and predictive analytics, let's now take stock of the most common current uses of AI, in order to plan for what comes next.

MICRO-SEGMENTATION

Historically, marketers began campaign kickoff meetings with basic questions such as "OK, so we have a campaign to launch. Should our objective be increased awareness, new trials, greater retention, or something else? What does everyone think?" After a typically uncomfortable silence, the team offered up suggestions and usually began spitballing about the optimal target audience.

Today with the help of AI's predictive analytics, marketers can accurately identify the optimal target audience—based on stated business objectives—in five minutes. Plus, the results will be more useful to marketers, in that all segments will be characterized by shared attributes and behaviors—so they are not only clearly understood but also more easily accessed. The latter—an inability to effectively reach target segments once identified—has always been the Achilles' heel of attitudinal and behavioral segmentation.

This allows the team to present personalized offers to each individual customer on a one-to-one basis. Says KPMG's Brian Miske, "AI can help you test new copy and new experiences in real-time to see how they resonate with specific groups of interest in what I would call almost a lab-based environment. Many of these capabilities are not new. It's much more about the speed of decision-making."[132]

And so, a travel clothing retailer, for example, may have mentally divided its prospects into avid campers, weekend adventurers, and hikers. But now AI can identify and segment those prospects into dozens, even hundreds of specific types of customers (lux-campers, trail enthusiasts, etc.) who are looking for specific items (cozy tents, GPS watches, etc.). Having such granular data on these micro-segments allows retailers to market to them more relevantly.

For companies with thousand-plus item product lines, these same concepts still apply. AI can segment the entire file and make product recommendations tailored to the expectations of each segment, allowing marketers to introduce customers to the products they're most inclined to buy. And through this process of analyzing customer interactions and behaviors on the fly, marketers are in the position to make instant adjustments to their marketing campaigns as needed to continually optimize for the key performance indicators (KPIs) that matter.

AI also has a role in predicting how a given creative platform will perform. On an email message, for example, is the prospect likely to open it or not? Will it be read thoroughly or skimmed? Will a purchase be made? Is a later cancellation likely? With intelligence like this to work with, marketers can customize the message content in real time and increase the odds of success. By always knowing the type of content that is actually engaging to a particular individual in any given situation at various times of day, a marketer can automatically optimize messaging for each individual.

Micro-segmentation is ultimately about refining product recommendations, as **Sephora** has discovered. The company's global chief brand officer, Steve Lesnard, says, "AI is quite relevant for product recommendations. We have three hundred brands typically in a store, five thousand products in all. We also have online consumers who are looking for very specific information about types of products to achieve a desired result. Imagine I'm looking for a skincare product for an oily face that is very sensitive, and that has some SPF. I live in Australia. What would be the best recommendation? Here we go![133]

"We have some forty thousand beauty advisors in our stores who are well-trained to provide recommendations, but AI tools help them, too. They can advise and then say, ' I don't know about this option, let's see what AI recommends,' and then the advisor can guide them through the recommendations. Maybe AI recommends not just one but four products. The advisor can then demonstrate these products and become a partner with the consumer in the exploration," opening the door to additional sales from the AI's recommendations.

Beyond its value as a recommendation engine, Sephora sees the large language model of AI "going to work on all the data being generated by partner brands and the 1.8 billion consumers visiting our site every year." Generative AI can run through all these data points and possibly yield new product opportunities. The AI can figure out, for instance, "that this person lives in this part of the country and buys that product, and based on similar customer profiles is likely to also buy this, this, and this." These AI capabilities are going to be extremely valuable, in Lesnard's view.

CONTENT GENERATION

In approaching the question of the role generative AI should play in content creation, again, we turn to Professor Jim Lecinski (as noted earlier, he's the author of *The AI Marketing Canvas*). "Generative AI can unlock value in one of two ways. Either with *efficiency* (producing large volumes of content quickly) or with *effectiveness* (producing higher-quality content)."

This "unlocking" of value was put to an academic test, Lecinski recalls. "This study is not yet published as we talk, but two postdocs at MIT put together two populations of five hundred marketers, average ten years of experience. Both groups were assigned the same set of tasks: write a press release, write a new product announcement, write a brand positioning statement, write a Facebook ad. One group was given a set of generative AI tools and the other group wasn't. They then submitted to a blind jury to score the output. Lo and behold, the group that had the AI tools got higher scores and they finished in less time."[134]

Professor Lecinski then takes the story out of academia into a real-world ad agency example. "I don't want to sound like I'm anti-agency, but for a photo shoot, the creative team is going to need $250,000 in production expenses, plus a trip to Hawaii. Then they go through and select the images, then retouch the selects, then come up with two versions. When all is said and done, it's six months and a quarter million dollars later! Or you can use Stable Diffusion to bang out 150 versions that'll go into 150 customized emails in a half hour."[135]

The technical summary of this process is as follows: The generative AI model applies natural language processing (NLP) to large language models in order to automate content creation. AI analyzes the most compelling content available (encompassing the entire internet, the brand archives, whatever volume of data is chosen) and then attempts to produce the very best content given the explicit instructions it has received. So, an unlimited library of content can be created, beginning with the most popular

- marketing emails, social media posts, and blog posts

- scripts and storyboards for video ads, demos, and training

- crisp, clear, engaging product descriptions

- visual branding materials, such as logos

All at fairly breakneck speed. Tearing down creativity as we've known it and rebirthing it. Forrester analyst Jay Pattisall writes about an AdTech agency that used AI to produce a full-on advertising campaign in ten minutes that was "ready to publish to multiple social APIs at the click of a button."[136] Having seen such transformations up close, Forrester gave a whole new name to what was going on—they called it "intelligent creativity" and defined it as follows:

> *A process of creative problem-solving in which teams of Creators and strategists conceive, design, produce, and activate business solutions with the assistance of AI, intelligent automation, and data. Through this approach, marketing becomes smarter, the creative process becomes faster, and human imagination is free to focus on creativity when enhanced by the speed, scale, and precision that AI and intelligent automation provide.*[137]

HYPER-PERSONALIZATION

To *fully* personalize an end-to-end customer experience requires careful orchestration across channels—a capability that few brands have been able to master. Despite the array of software tools on the market that promise to comprehensively manage end-to-end personalization, attaining a 360-degree view of each customer at scale has been an elusive goal. Until now.

AI-powered intelligence allows a company to log each customer's footsteps along the Attract/Inform/Convert/Engage journey. AI literally time-stamps each interaction and generates a map of each individual's journey. It then tracks any troubles as they emerge and takes action on sparks of concern before they become fires. All done in real time. This is the pitch of providers, anyway, and while it still sounds starry-eyed, it is the new goalpost that marketers are beginning to clear.

Companies are aiming to combine these new AI tools with their legacy marketing tech (martech) and back-office solutions across common application programming interfaces (APIs)—to create the most powerful, hyper-personalized experiences customers have yet known in the digital age.

At **McDonald's**, AI is being harnessed for personalization in a number of ways. U.S. chief marketing and customer experience officer Tariq Hassan says, "It is allowing us to target with greater relevance. … The problem with segmented offers used across the industry today is that many are out of context, or not relevant. People don't know why they're getting them. How do they know me and why are they sending me this offer? This is where the AI becomes powerful. It rapidly learns and decides that that was not the right offer to send to Customer A. So, the next time, we get it right and with confidence."

Using this heightened personalization capability in a geofencing application, retail brands can fine-tune their prospecting efforts. Let's say a fast-food outlet named World's-Best-Burgers puts the AI to work analyzing anonymized data obtained through mobile signals. The AI might learn that Customer A normally eats lunch out on Tuesdays and Thursdays, usually around 12:30. The AI is also tracking Customer A walking down the street in real time. The AI also notes that Customer A has a demonstrated predilection for World's-Best-Chicken. So, at a precise moment in time near to 12:30, the AI pushes a message along with an offer to Customer A, possibly promoting a left turn into World's-Best-Burgers instead of a right turn into World's-Best-Chicken. Then, if successful, the AI adds an incentive for Customer A to download the company's app and become a loyalty club member—allowing the push of even more personalized offers of value.

This AI-driven personalization capability can also help World's-Best-Burgers build a stronger picture of customer lifecycle behavior. For example, if time and again, Customer A only "turns left" for a 99-cent deal offer and doesn't visit the store any other times, there's no real profit in this customer. So, the AI will stop sending the 99-cent deal offer and cycle through different offers, trying to determine which ones drive a profitable visit and which ones don't.

With this ability to analyze vast amounts of data on the fly, AI can tailor content to individuals based on their behaviors, preferences, and previous interactions. This personalized approach is vital to developing customer experiences that convert. The challenge to date has been that while hyper-personalization clearly increases the effectiveness of messaging, it has been cost-prohibitive. So, it has been difficult to deliver unique experiences at scale profitably. But AI tools overcome that hurdle and finally deliver the one-to-one experience that Don Peppers and Martha Rogers forecast way back in 1993 in *The One-to-One Future*.

As confirmed by Suzanne Kounkel, global and U.S. chief marketing officer of **Deloitte**, "CMOs are always being asked to bend the cost curve: to do more activity, but to do it at a lower cost per unit. AI and machine learning are absolutely key to making that a reality."[138]

Now that the low-cost reality of one-to-one marketing is attainable by companies of any size—since these AI tools are equally available to the Global 2000 and small and medium size businesses

(SMBs)—the bar has been raised for every company. This level of personalization is now fully expected. KPMG's Brian Miske puts this in perspective: "Consumers' best experiences become their new expectations; so CMOs have to be constantly monitoring what the competition is doing, and looking at the delta between what they're doing and what you're doing. AI can help."[139]

What's more, consumers increasingly expect this best-in-class personalization while remaining very concerned about their privacy. The key then, as **Accenture**'s chief marketing and communications officer Jill Kramer explains, "is to have a first-party data-led strategy. It's what enables you to deliver individualized content to each person."[140]

New AI tools on the market can generate this kind of first-party, contextualized data, and it can run deep. It can include purchasing history, social media activity, location, demographic data, and hundreds of more granular details on each target prospect or customer. Then it can be used to create hyper-personalized messaging that is more likely to resonate with on a one-to-one level, which boosts engagement and conversion rates.

Facebook's very success as a public company owes to its embrace of AI-powered ad targeting. Advertisers on the platform can target different audiences based on hundreds of criteria, including location, interests, behaviors, job titles, education levels, political views, and connections. Clearly, ad targeting is mission-critical to Facebook, and the company has deep resources to tap. But now similar-level tools are available to all companies—leveling the playing field just as digital advertising did twenty years ago.

CUSTOMER ENGAGEMENT

AI is also upending customer service with conversational chatbots that are beginning to rival and even surpass humans in their ability to hold a meaningful, fully contextualized conversation with customers. Chatbots can also learn in real time as they converse with users and adjust their preferences along the way, providing an ever more satisfying experience.

None of these chatbots are perfect conversationalists (yet). They've been trained on Large Language Models of past human conversations and have a tendency to replicate the biases they were exposed to in training. But each new iteration becomes cleaner and more valuable as a trustworthy tool for marketers to consider.

Chatbots and messaging apps

Offering customer service 24/7, these bots are able to (a) keep detailed records of customers' pain points and take action on them, (b) make recommendations or fix a problem, and (c) take orders for products directly in the chat thread.

Voice-activated AI assistants

Conversational bots such as Siri, Alexa, and Google Assistant help businesses optimize content in voice search results. These bots can make personalized product recommendations, enable purchases, and deliver ads targeted to the customer interaction.

Email automation

Emails can be hyper-personalized from the subject line to the body text, product recommendations, and optimal time of day sent. All of these were operational before AI, but now it can be automated based on the recipient's real-time behaviors.

Push notifications

All the AI functionalities can be built into push notifications on desktop and mobile screens, as well.

Dynamic websites

Embedding AI capabilities in the company website and self-service portals can offer each customer a customized version of the website—based on behavioral signals and past browsing or purchase history. Personalized recommendations and solutions can be offered in a full one-to-one experience.

In each of these applications, AI is not only automating repetitive tasks but also offering the kinds of customer insights coupled with hyper-personalization follow-through that was previously unachievable at scale.

DYNAMIC PRICING

Adjusting the price of a product on the fly, known as dynamic pricing, is an area where AI shines, albeit controversially. Few consumers find the practice attractive (if they even realize it's happening), but it is certainly a tool at the marketer's disposal across industries now.

Unlike traditional dynamic pricing, which relied on historical data, the new AI-driven dynamic pricing strategies analyze huge amounts of data of relevance (market trends, cost of goods, competitor prices, socioeconomic data, purchase history, etc.) to make informed price changes in real time.

Embracing Marketing AI for Competitive Advantage

In harnessing the power of AI to date, marketers have primarily streamlined workflows to free up time to optimize strategy and boost their performance against company yardsticks. Early AI adopters are becoming proficient at using AI for creative tasks such as producing images, text, videos, and messaging. And they have generated highly impressive operational results: improving behind-the-scenes processes; strengthening decision-making with the use of unstructured data; hyper-personalizing messaging; and tracking, measuring, and adjusting campaigns in real time. Going forward, AI has the potential to completely transform the role of the marketing function, both within the C-suite and throughout the organization. Let's take a closer look at several "AI imperatives."

ELEVATE THE MARKETING FUNCTION
TO DRIVE BUSINESS STRATEGY

Early adopting CMOs are encouraging their teams to experiment with the tools and models to begin building transformative use cases. For example, some CMOs are setting up independent agile pods within the larger marketing department to work in short sprints on specific projects—but clearly apart from the usual workflow. This allows the pod to experiment in real time, deploy test campaigns, evaluate them, and iterate swiftly—without interfering with the department's larger workflows. In this way, new tactics can be tested quickly, and the pod can optimize across multiple variables (what triggers are working, which channels convert highest, when's best to contact which customer segments, what incentives are best performing, etc.). And when these pods succeed in hacking old processes, the company's data scientists and engineers can be brought in to automate the new processes so that the entire team can use them.

All of this is great progress.

But the most forward-thinking CMOs are remaining laser-focused on one thing: How do these new AI solutions help to identify and anticipate new business opportunities? That is the kind of thinking that takes strategic brand management to the next level, effectively driving overall business strategy. Accenture's Jill Kramer explains, "Marketers are the keepers of the heartbeat of the customer, the consumer, or the client. We have access to more data and intelligence than ever before, so we need to help set strategy. Not just marketing strategy, but broader business strategy. Really good companies have marketing at their leadership table for this reason."

While every department across the enterprise is looking at AI, CMOs are ideally positioned to hammer home the strategic importance of the marketing function to the entire company in terms of growth and innovation. Specifically, that means contributing to adjacent functions—such as product development and product management.

BRING STRATEGIC, HIGH-VALUE AI SOLUTIONS IN-HOUSE

Leading AI vendors are rolling out hundreds of new tools to streamline marketing workflows, so companies do not need to build very many solutions in-house. However, when a company goes ahead and trains an AI model on in-house data, and then supplements that training with third-party research, the resulting tool may create a strong differentiation over competitors' offerings with attractive ROI. These proprietary homegrown solutions can give a company genuine competitive advantage and should remain in house with the IP fully protected.

Analysts at McKinsey maintain that the biggest opportunity across the AI marketing value chain will come from building in-house applications for end users.[141]

GRADUALLY TRANSITION THE TEAM TO AN AI-CENTRIC FUTURE

AI will always be intimidating to some, just as the xerox machine freaked out the guy who hand-cranked the old blue paper mimeograph machine and so on back in time. But we have always taken it as an article of faith that progress will not—cannot—be thwarted. And that once again AI will ultimately enhance employee performance and elevate capabilities though surely with a great many casualties along the way.

Nobody has said it better than author Neil Postman: "Every technology is both a burden and a blessing; not either or, but this and that." So, while marketers are wise to be equally fearful and fascinated by AI, the CMO's focus should be on education. CMOs should be listening to employees' concerns and engaging with them openly since these employees will be closest to the problems that do crop up, and they need to be supported in dealing with these problems.

CMOs should also be advocating for and leading training programs that upskill the team for the transition to an AI-centric future.

PUT GUIDELINES AND GUARDRAILS IN PLACE

No matter what policies on AI organizations put in place, employees are going to be accessing and using AI anyway—whether professionally or privately. They understand that they must, in order to increase their own productivity and not fall behind competitors. So, a balance must be found between trial-and-erroring with AI and mitigating the risks—both known and unknown.

Using AI intelligently means putting in place guidelines and guardrails, so the company is constantly monitoring and protecting against possible mishaps and miscalculations—such as outputting unknowingly biased, inaccurate, or plagiarized content.

AI tools are still in the experimental stage. It's crucial to never fully rely on them for any public-facing communications. Even as the tools improve, they will require human oversight of content generated for external audiences. And when used internally, a good rule of thumb is to annotate it as such.

Nine Challenges Brand Marketers Face with AI

While AI represents enormous opportunity for marketers—including elevating the stature of the function within the C-suite and throughout the organization—there will certainly be landmines to avoid along the journey. As with any transformational technology, capabilities and solutions will continue to evolve, likely at an increasingly frenetic pace. In addition, the "rules of engagement" are being written in real-time, making it challenging to determine what's effective, appropriate, ethical, and even legal. Here are a few of the most obvious challenges marketers will face.

DATA INTEGRITY

When AI is crafting much of our written or image-based content—conjuring up first drafts of emails, letters, reports, blog posts, presentations, and videos on through to computer applications—how will anyone know what is real, if it's real, and what that means?

Companies are putting AI governance systems in place to guard against systemic bias, inaccuracies, and what are being called system hallucinations—where the AI models confidently make up facts or spew random toxic results. This is because the liability is squarely on the shoulders of the marketer running the prompts. But this governance will always be less than perfect, and additional protections will be needed.

For one, it will become important for AI providers to act with greater transparency and allow the AI tools to cite sources in-line. This will make oversight more efficient and allow marketers to work with data with a higher level of confidence.

There are also ethical considerations from data privacy to truth in advertising that require human oversight, ensuring that AI-driven marketing adheres to best-practice standards.

The Interactive Advertising Bureau (IAB) is trying to guide marketers in the effective integration of AI and human expertise in marketing. Here is a summary of IAB's recommendations:[142]

- Use high-quality data that is accurate, relevant, and free of bias.

- Continually assess AI outputs for accuracy, relevance, and appropriateness.

- Update AI models regularly to ensure they remain effective.

- Consider the ethical implications of data privacy and transparency.

- Approach marketing as a human-AI collaboration.

COPYRIGHT AND IP ISSUES

Since the AI is generating output based on already-existing material, naturally the question is asked: Who will have ownership rights to AI-generated content, the brand or some Creator or amorphous set of Creators with hard-to-establish provenance? When an AI model produces a new product design or concept based on text that an individual enters at the prompt, who lays claim to that design or concept? What happens when the AI model plagiarizes a source that it has been trained on?

Also, now that anyone can create fake images or videos for a few bucks in a few minutes—what are known as deepfakes—the concept of "trust" has become an even bigger and more complicated issue. OpenAI is attempting to control fake images by watermarking images created by their DALL-E 2 tool. Other platforms will surely follow suit or be compelled to.

A thicket of legal questions will arise, likely drawing counsel into the marketing domain with unwelcome regularity.

BRAND FIT AND AUTHENTICITY

Two decades ago, as we entered the age of digital marketing, we began to see a gradual but steady decline in traditional strategic brand management thinking. Even classically trained brand managers—who were very disciplined and strategic in other forms of brand activation—seemed to lose sight of the brand strategy North Star when it came to digital marketing. The goal of building long-term brand equity took a back seat to chasing more tangible digital metrics, such as conversions, clicks, followers, shares, and likes.

Now as we enter the age of AI, marketers need to be redoubly focused on the North Star of marketing discipline. AI could very easily squash real creativity and "genericize" brands, given that it is trained on an existing fact base and cannot reliably extend beyond that fact base.

Since AI content lacks the emotional intelligence we commonly associate with human creativity, in using it marketers risk muddying the brand positioning unless the process is carefully managed.

So now in this new age, the generating of content using AI can be so easy that, as they say, even an eighty-year-old grandmother can do it. But generating content using AI that is "on brand" will be far more complex work.

Companies need to layer brand plug-ins on top of company systems to ensure that the brand positioning and personality are properly executed within the brand's approved framework. KPMG's Brian Miske notes, "AI will eventually get to the level where it can develop an entire strategy. But is it appropriate for your brand? Are you going to be able to write algorithms that tie into your brand strategy, hierarchy, architecture? Maybe at some point. But right now, I think we're still in an experimental phase."[143]

FAKE ADS BLANKETING THE WEB

Startups like SpeedyBrand are using AI to create SEO-optimized content on behalf of companies. Their business model is simple: it costs a penny to run an ad, a penny and a quarter can be made on it, send out billions of ads, and you make bank. Meanwhile, the web is so spammed up that legitimate companies cannot break through.

There are even larger concerns.

Many of these synthetic ads are running on fake sites that have been built to exploit programmatic advertising systems. The news vetting company, Newsguard, released a report finding some 400 ad placements from 141 major brands on 55 junk news sites—so the ad revenue is being siphoned off from name brands.[144]

One deepfake video scam running on Facebook shows UK consumer finance champion Martin Lewis appearing to shill for an investment that's also backed by Elon Musk. Of course, the footage is all fake, and Mr. Lewis's attempts to shut it down have fallen on mostly deaf ears at Facebook.[145]

Compounding the problem, say researchers at the University of Zurich, people may be more willing to believe information, or disinformation, generated by AI than that generated by actual humans.[146] They asked ChatGPT to create both true and false tweets; they also collected true and false tweets from Twitter. Then they asked a panel to judge the accurate from the fake. Panelists were 3 percent less likely to believe the false tweets that humans had written (making the AI a better liar, essentially). Researchers believe this is because ChatGPT's tweets were better structured and easier to process, an advantage that will only grow with use. Researchers cautioned against alarm, noting that many things factor into the believability equation. Nonetheless, this suggests that AI will take communication further away from truth than toward it.

FILTERS

Now entering its fourth decade, the public internet has long remained one step ahead of the filters placed on it. That's not likely to change. With more than one hundred million people signing up for ChatGPT in just its first three months, there's going to be a lot of creative mischief. All the more reason to build a shield of integrity around the brand so that discerning consumers can recognize the real thing.

SYSTEMIC BIASES

Since AI draws on massive amounts of data, avoiding unwanted biases becomes a challenge. This is likely to be AI's biggest early victory, however. Rooting out systemic biases, to the extent that any human-made machine can, won't be easy or ever perfect. But it is likely to take place acceptably on the near horizon.

Speeding this process will be marketers insisting on gaining a God's-eye view on the data generation process, to better understand the algorithms used to compile and structure the data and ensure the technology is being employed ethically.

MAINTAINING THE HUMAN TOUCH

AI may well be the most formidable, and even fearsome, tool that humans have invented. But in the marketing realm, fair to say that it represents an operational upgrade and nothing like the "silver bullet" that some promoters claim.

Accenture's Jill Kramer puts it this way: "At Accenture, we talk a lot about AI being the co-pilot of creativity; an amplifier of human talent. Simply put, humans need to do what only humans can do. And AI should make it easier, faster, and more efficient for them to do it. On the front end, it can be used to broaden your views and to give you a wider field to play in creatively. On the back end, it can be used to reduce the burden on time-intensive, laborious activities like versioning."[147]

Echoing these sentiments is Suzanne Kounkel, global and U.S. chief marketing officer at Deloitte. "The key is to let machines do the work that we as humans aren't as good at doing, so we can focus our attention on the areas where we excel. For example, machines can quickly and efficiently process large data sets from diverse and dispersed sources, while humans excel at emotions, empathy, strategy, and creativity. The machine can do 80 percent, but then you want humans to take the last 20 percent. I frame it as trying to get to the highest level of consistency without squeezing out the empathy and emotions only humans can bring."[148]

This "human component" remains an essential part of the equation. Even as AI improves and overtakes humans in one capability after another, that AI will—and should always—serve as an adjunct tool. It may become first among tools in some situations, but only a tool with humans *needed* to give it direction, provide creative insights, and ensure that its output resonates with target audiences.

Humans are emotional beings. Marketers' ability to evoke these emotions is at the very core of our success as marketers. Each new version of ChatGPT will be able to write better poetry and no doubt tug harder on the heartstrings, but it will never be human—and that will matter.

REDUCTION OF CREATIVITY

"The meteoric rise of generative AI marks both a beginning and ending for marketing creativity as we know it," says Jay Pattisall, an analyst at Forrester. "Large language models such as Bard, ChatGPT, DALL·E, Midjourney, or Stable Diffusion … bring tremendous computing power, speed, and scale to the human act of creativity and ideation."[149]

This AI-generated content risks corrupting the artistic expression at the heart of content that effectively catches the eye, sparks interest, and ultimately engages. By simplifying the generation of content to "the best the robot can do," these tools risk flooding the marketplace with homogenized identical-looking communications that are soon tuned out, worthless to the originators.

UPCOMING REGULATIONS

In Washington, there is genuine concern over AI naturally. Louis Rosenberg, chief executive of AI developer Unanimous AI, has explained to policymakers that AI gives businesses the opportunity to exercise "targeted, customized, influence at scale," which, if left unregulated, "could be the most dangerous technology for human manipulation that we've had to confront."[150]

Many lawmakers agree, and so, tighter government regulation of AI will be an agenda item for years to come. Most marketers recognize as much and are taking pains to adopt policies to protect against the potentially negative consequences of AI. This extends to dealing with AI security breaches from employees using externally sourced AI tools without proper guidance or agreed-upon supervision.

OF POSSIBILITIES AND PITFALLS

Will we see generative AI used irresponsibly in marketing? Of course, we will. Will we also see in the wider scope an application of AI breaking cancer's deepest codes? Again, we surely will. So, a healthy combination of both optimism and skepticism about AI will be required to navigate this new age.

Only a small handful of enterprise CMOs are taking a wait-and-see approach, knowing the risks of that. AI is set to truly transform how marketers work; indeed, it is already doing so. Taking charge of the situation begins with prioritizing transparency and accountability, ensuring that data is being used ethically and responsibly in alignment with company values.

Taking such a proactive approach will help CMOs mitigate the very real risks while reaping the benefits of AI technology. It will effectively put the CMO in the position of using marketing strategy to drive business strategy, earning a seat at the "big table."

CHAPTER FIVE
XR and Metaverse—a New Definition of "Reality"

Early 2018 news that seventy million teens had practically, overnight, signed onto a new online game named Fortnite was astounding to many. Just as astounding, to marketers anyway, was the news that a financial services company like **Ally Financial** was following these teens into a freewheeling gaming environment. "Our approach has definitely been one of crawl, walk, run," explains Andrea Brimmer, CMO of the investment services company, "finding the right utility so it can actually be a value-add for a consumer."[151]

Brimmer was aiming to prove her thesis that "people today learn through games, so integrating financial literacy content into games can make people better stewards of their money." She figured that she could go to a fifteen-year-old and say, "Hey, I want to talk to you about financial literacy, and they're going to be like, 'No thanks!' But, if I hand them a game that's authentic to what they already are playing and it teaches them financial literacy along the way, it's a much more interactive and engaging way of teaching them."

This was not an easy sell internally, though. Early in the going, one of Ally's board members cornered Brimmer and asked if she thought anyone would actually strap on an Oculus headset to have a session with a banker. She recalls telling him, "No, not now, but there are a lot of applications, especially for financial services, that can be particularly useful." And so, Brimmer first crawled into a branded collaboration with the Fortnite gaming site—building out "Ally Arena" right in the game—as a place for players to play custom games that teach them financial literacy.

In the Ally Arena, the company can also host live and exclusive events in addition to games. "For instance, we're a sponsor of the National Women's Soccer League. Imagine people being able to come into Ally Arena, go into our private theater, chat with a couple of the players before they play in the World Cup, and have an exclusive experience with a Kelly O'Hara or a Megan Rapinoe or a Sophia Smith. It really speaks to our brand strategy, which has been to try to gamify financial learning. And, we're having a lot of success with lengthy session times; hundreds of thousands of people have gone in, interacted, and are playing the game."

A keen-eyed CFO might insist that buying some real estate in a game is no more immersive than hosting those same games and events on the company's own website, less expensively. But Brimmer is clear on the distinction: "You've got shared experiences that are exclusive. You have to download a special key to go in, and not everybody can get the code. People can go in and play a series of games, watch live streams and private concerts. Plus, the whole experience has a very Ally-specific look, a futuristic look similar to the Fortnite game," so players are more likely to form a positive mental association. Brimmer believes so strongly in this association that she hired a dedicated gaming team and brought them in-house: "They have no marketing background; they have gaming degrees; and they do nothing but develop our Metaverse and gamification strategy on behalf of the Ally brand."

To better appeal to the Gen Z ethic, Brimmer next launched a live stream for female gamers only in the Ally Arena. Women gamers comprise 48 percent of the U.S. gaming community, but only 5 percent of the professional esports scene are female gamers. "We wanted to recognize this underrepresented group, holding competitions for female gamers as well as part of promoting equity between men's and women's sports."

Following these Fortnite wins, Brimmer expanded onto other platforms. "We have since built an 'Ally Island' on Nintendo's Animal Crossing site. The games are about financial literacy. So, you learn about turnip exchanges, and you learn about credit. Our island was so popular, we actually broke the game! We then partnered with Hasbro and licensed Monopoly, and we did virtual reality Monopoly games in six cities across the United States. We built 'Fintropolis' in Minecraft, which has over four million downloads; it's targeted to middle school aged kids to learn financial literacy."

Brimmer escalated to a "walk" with a big initiative, the Ally Big Save, launched during the 2018 Super Bowl. It was an augmented reality game that challenged young audiences to think about their savings goals via the visualization of a virtual dollar drop. "You had to download an app on your device, then tell us your savings goal and what you were saving for. The app only worked during the commercial breaks, so it was our way to disrupt what was happening at the Super Bowl. We had sixty-nine thousand game downloads, which was a sizable number back then."

All of these efforts are what Brimmer characterizes as Web 2.5—not quite moving into the "full run" of Web 3.0 with clunky goggles required to enjoy the new technologies. "There was a lot of fanfare around the Metaverse, and a lot of marketers rushed unsuccessfully to do something in the Metaverse, but were not able to develop a lot of content. So, a lot of people said, 'Oh the Metaverse is dead.' No, it's not dead. It's in its infant stages right now. Most people sit today in Web 2.5 … and it's going to be about how it evolves, how people find utility in it, and how brands intersect."

Brimmer's search for this utility on the continuum has been effective in its early stages, as has other brands' search—as we'll see.

How Much Marketing Will Be Unreal ?

While analyst projections for XR growth have been nothing short of spectacular, actual sales to date have been underwhelming. Fewer than ten million headsets were sold globally in 2022, and analysts subsequently downgraded sales forecasts following year-over-year (YOY) revenue declines.[152] This despite those same analysts having insisted that the XR market would top $30 billion and even $60 billion in 2023 and as high as $1.1 trillion by 2030 for CAGR estimates running north of 50 percent![153]

ABOUT REALITY

VR: Virtual Reality transports individuals to a completely digital environment using a headset that blocks out the physical world and allows interactions using controllers and haptics.

AR: Augmented Reality lays digital effects over the real world. Individuals can interact with these effects while still aware of their surroundings. AR is experienced through smartphones, tablets, and AR glasses.

MR: Mixed Reality is advanced AR that blends digital and real worlds using a headset or glasses. Individuals can see and interact with both virtual and real-world objects simultaneously.

XR: Extended Reality is an umbrella term used to include Virtual Reality, Augmented Reality, and Mixed Reality. In XR, real and virtual environments combine for a unique experience. The "Metaverse" is generally considered XR.

Web 3.0: The next version of the web leveraging XR technologies, decentralization, blockchain and token economics. (We focus on Web 3.0 in Chapter 6.)

Statista had even ventured that the number of AR and VR users would count 2.59 billion by 2027 with 32.6 percent of the world using it.[154]

These figures are somewhat defensible given that video games can be considered VR, but how could the projections for the larger XR adoption be so at odds with, well, reality? For one, the vendors were no doubt spiking the punch. Tech titans like Facebook, Microsoft, and Epic Games have invested heavily in cloud computing and XR startups and hope to build momentum for their early offerings.

Also, early studies by name analysts such as Accenture found that 61 percent of consumers are more likely to make a purchase after experiencing a brand through XR technology.[155] This suggested that a lot of marketing activity would be coming, driving adoption rates.

What's more, Millennials and Gen Z have flocked to the platforms pioneering these immersive technologies—especially the gaming platforms that do not require the use of goggles to enjoy. When asked which XR experiences actually interest these younger audiences:[156]

Use	Interest
Gaming	32%
Travel	12%
Music	11%
History	10%
Training	9%
Imagination	7%

So, the biggest gate on these technologies appears to be the obvious one: the headsets and goggles are not ready for prime time and may not be for a long time to come. This underpins Brimmer's crawl-walk-run view of the emerging marketplace. As for the Metaverse as a concept, it is still viewed as potentially the next iteration of the internet but with a lot of unanswered questions about that still ahead.

A crafty tweet in 2021 by Shaan Puri, a digital prognosticator, suggested that the Metaverse is "the moment in time where digital matters more to us than physical. Our attention used to be 99 percent on our physical environment. TVs dropped that to 85 percent … Computers down to 70 percent … Phones 50 percent," and, Puri figures, in another ten to twenty years, we will cross over completely. While there may be some exaggeration in his forward look, there is certainly none in his backward look.[157]

Let's continue looking *forward* as best we can.

Layering in XR for a More Immersive Brand Experience

Major brands are now fully expected to toggle seamlessly between the physical and virtual worlds to deliver the most immersive experiences the technology enables. However, determining which type of XR application, if any, is best for a particular brand is a nontrivial decision. Key questions help determine which applications should prove to impact the bottom line favorably:

- Does the XR application go beyond pure novelty and entertainment value to actually increase the brand's value in existing customers' eyes?

- Is the XR application going to positively impact the way target audiences evaluate the brand?

- Does the potential increase in customer engagement and ultimately sales justify the development costs?

A big rousing "yes!" to any of these questions should be sufficient to find the budget to make it happen. But, of course, none of these questions can be fully answered until after the "go decision" has been made, the project has been executed, and the results have come in. Nonetheless, there are specific performance measures that brands can assess and model against. Specifically, how XR technologies enable the company to:

- demonstrate a leading-edge brand,

- extend a robust omnichannel experience,

- leverage gaming communities,

- enhance product sampling and evaluation,

- enhance marketing research,

- examine the efficiencies of in-person events,

- extend beyond humans to virtual Influencers, and

- run community-based campaigns.

Let's look at each.

DEMONSTRATING A LEADING-EDGE BRAND

AR technologies in retail can transform static messaging into animated eye-catching messaging that not only imprints stronger and leads to higher recall scores but also sends an overt signal to media-savvy younger generations that this is a leading brand to be reckoned with. These younger consumers expect to experience these technologies. If instead they find static imagery and text on their screens, they are likely to instantly form a "less than" impression in their minds—even if unwittingly.

Market-leading **Walmart** has long excelled with AR experiences in their stores, collaborating with DC Comics and Marvel to bring superheroes into the aisles in eye-catching ways—like when Iron Man and Captain America facsimiles pop out of their enclosures to greet customers and, importantly, do double superhero duty by encouraging customers to explore other locations within the stores.[158]

In a 2023 product tie-in with the new Ninja Turtles movie release, Walmart signage encouraged young shoppers to download the store's app to learn how to "Train Like a Ninja." Then when the device is pointed at the signage, a 3D Ninja Turtle of choice crawls out of the store's sewer. As well, a game can be played with that favored turtle to rack up pizza points.[159]

As these AR technologies become more commonplace and the applications more impressive, they drive the expectations for major brands to be participating in one form or another—not only the B2C companies but B2B as well. As Antonia Wade, global chief marketing officer of **PwC**, says, "We want to meet our audience where they are, and that requires diversifying distribution. About 70 percent of our buyers are Millennials. So, yes, we're at Davos. But we're also in Decentraland."[160]

EXTENDING A ROBUST OMNICHANNEL EXPERIENCE

Customers expect to navigate through a brand's physical and digital touchpoints in a seamless way. Integrating XR technologies into this brand experience path is the largest of challenges—easily said, difficult to execute. Nonetheless, as we've noted, the best experience that a customer is treated to now becomes the expectation for all. And in a best-practice situation, customers are able to move effortlessly between the company's physical store, apps, social accounts, websites, and now XR properties. In each they'll enjoy a cohesive brand experience that extends from topline identity through messaging to the actual personalized experience—all expertly maintained throughout their journey.

Creating this omnichannel continuity doesn't necessarily mean the brand looks and feels the same in every medium. "One of the things we didn't want to do was replicate the physical world into a virtual one," says Chema Alonso, chief digital officer of **Telefónica**.[161] He sought an expression of the brand's identity that was authentic to the XR ecosystem. "We had to think out of the box. We worked with Okuda, a very-well known artist, and created a very chaotic world in which gravity doesn't work and colors and shapes are nothing like our brand logo. The artist is using every color with triangles … challenging us to see why triangles are the right way to create virtual reality experiences. So, he was looking for that kind of experience. But on top of that we were able to align everything and use our logo also." The result was a captivating, memorable XR experience that lodged in customers' minds, deepening connections and resultant brand loyalty.

LEVERAGING GAMING COMMUNITIES

With surveys saying that anywhere from 40 to 70 percent of the U.S. population plays games on their devices, marketers are naturally following their audiences into the games, sponsoring them, integrating content with them, and streaming ads in them.

Says Lisa Caputo, executive vice president and chief marketing, communications, and customer experience officer for The Travelers Companies, Inc., "It's about meeting customers where they are. There are so many opportunities to insert relevant messages throughout storylines. Say, for instance, you're playing a game where you own a home and a hurricane comes through and you have to submit a claim. There may be ways to share content related to building a home inventory list, or a hurricane preparedness tip list."[162]

This is how to make the actual game-playing experience a better one—which is, of course, critical to success.

Travelers' biggest success relates to its sponsorship of the PGA golf tournament. "We launched a marketing initiative called 'Gamers versus Golfers' on Twitch," continues Caputo. "[I]t showed there's synergy between golf enthusiasts and online video gaming. It was a win-win; it helped our brand, and it also helped the tournament with its goal of reaching a younger and more diverse audience."

Accenture Song, the Interactive and Metaverse arm of the management consulting and professional services firm, has taken a similar tack, laying social concerns into its gaming executions. "With LPGA we launched 'IN HER HEAD,'" explains James Temple, Accenture Song's global Metaverse lead. "An immersive VR experience that puts golf fans into the shoes of female professionals, so they can experience first-hand their psychological pressures as they battle the immense balance between life sacrifice and the critical need to perform." [163] It created a powerful connection with professional women.

A more engaging gaming experience

Personalized VR experiences are simply more engaging than yesterday's personalization because the game players are in a state of heightened awareness, their senses are firing, and they're ingesting information at an often furious pace, so if the company's compelling narrative is authentically inserted, it stands to resonate deeply with the players.

PepsiCo is executing on this as well as any brand. The beverage and food company's head of esports and gaming, Paul Mascali, talked with *Business Insider* about how his company leans heavily into today's most popular gaming platforms, centering a great many marketing activations there.

"We work with our development partners to unlock in-game content and peripherals we offer back to the community. Influencers are *massive* when advertising in video games for they can take creative control and each one plays a specific role, depending on what sort of result the brand is trying to drive." When Mascali talks about Influencers, he's talking about the young men and women who are playing the games—micro-Influencers, really. A good deal of creative control is handed over to these "gamefluencers" who go into the VR games through their avatars and mix it up organically with their followers. The control is handed over, says Mascali, "because this is where you get the gold: memes and inside jokes and buy-in from audiences. It's become more than just an ad, but a piece of content they're engaging with."[164]

Brands with the financial heft will work with these gamefluencers from start to finish. At the developmental level, the gamefluencers can be hard coded right along with the brand into the game's mechanics, making the brand an integral part of the game, not just a VR billboard. For instance, PepsiCo created Mtn Dew Game Fuel specifically for gamers with flavors tied into games such as Call of Duty Warzone. In another game, PepsiCo built a branded Gatorade training facility right into the game, and players could consume the drinks through their avatars to improve their in-game performance. And with offers built in to sign up at the GameFuel.com website, gamers can place orders and earn rewards—giving PepsiCo valuable first-party data to help in ongoing marketing.[165]

Embracing the risk inherent with gaming

Despite successful Travelers and Accenture executions, gaming initiatives can be a challenge with management—especially when the game extends beyond contained experiences and enters the Wild West of multiplayer gaming.

"Sometimes, leadership is like, 'Gaming? Really?'" notes Beth Woodruff who directs brand strategy in gaming at Ally Financial. "We feel we have to constantly prove that down funnel."[166]

Marketing through games requires a certain comfort with risk. The brand will be placed into a vulnerable position, at the whim of swarms of hypercharged teens. This is a risk-taking enterprise. But then, it can be argued that every effective channel has its own potential downsides and sensitivities, so why not go where the last two generations have gone—into gaming?

"We're trying to be additive to the gameplay," Woodruff continues. So, in the company's "Animal Crossing" activation, they actually guaranteed settlements at market prices for the digital turnip market they'd created, and gamers loved it.

When there were hiccups in the execution, as there invariably are, Woodruff did not panic. "It gave us the opportunity to make it right. So, it's being adaptive in that you don't know everything about the space, and that's okay. It won't damage your brand, but you want to be in communication with them always to make sure their gameplay is enhanced."

As for the results of this risk-taking, Woodruff reported a 320 percent increase in account openings from the "Animal Crossing" campaign along with a 13 percent increase in awareness from a Twitch campaign.

ENHANCING PRODUCT SAMPLING AND EVALUATION

VR is elevating social shopping in a multitude of ways. Retailers are employing interactive displays, touchscreens, and smart mirrors to let customers try on products virtually and interact with products in a

3D space—for a more captivating and memorable interaction. Being able to try on products virtually while also receiving detailed product specifications and even reviews in a visually appealing and interactive manner right there in the moment helps shoppers make more informed purchasing decisions leading to higher conversion rates. It leads to fewer returns, as well, because customers feel more thoroughly informed about the product and thus less likely to return it.[167]

AR is just plain effective at delivering information to today's consumers, especially to under-forty audiences or when product complexities are involved. Brands are finding the interactive and immersive format of AR ideal for full-funnel activities from advertising to boosting sales to retaining customers:[168]

- **Walgreens** and **Lowe's** have added AR to their in-store navigation apps—laying directional signals onto aisle floors to guide shoppers to product locations.

- Lowe's also offers a "How To" VR experience that gives customers an understanding of the tools and materials they'll need for various DIY projects.

- Car companies **Hyundai** and **Toyota** are demonstrating key features of new car models, matching their own automotive innovations with AR innovation—ostensibly elevating value perceptions in the consumer mind.

- **IKEA** is using AR to give customers a preview of how different furniture pieces will look in their homes without having to take measurements.

- **Toms**, long known for donating a pair of shoes to a needy child whenever a customer buys a pair, created a VR campaign so that customers can take a virtual tour of the locations Toms is delivering shoes to—explicitly showing the kind of impact they're making with their purchase.

Sephora's global chief brand officer Steve Lesnard believes AR tools are proving best for engagement. "We are playing with AR, using it to go deeper into product explanations, to bring them to life in more vivid ways. We're playing with lenses, so people can see how they might look. We're finding it's a great way to engage, but not necessarily to drive conversions. People still need to try on the actual product to see how it looks. However, the AR does help narrow the selection while giving good engagement."[169]

ENHANCING MARKETING RESEARCH

For decades, marketers have perfected AR applications for studying human behavior and, most recently, with AI enhancements, have elevated the science to an art form. Using AR-enabled research produces a rich breadcrumb trail that the AI can invariably characterize down to the color of the shoelaces, generating levels of insights never before possible.

Every aspect of market research is being rapidly advanced by front-end AR/VR discovery technologies coupled with an AI computational back end. Research vendors are using VR tools—principally wearable headsets and hand controllers, which have steadily advanced in comfort and reliability—to realistically simulate in virtual 3D format any physical experience a marketer may wish to test. So, any retail store or pop-up, any restaurant or office, and any online user interface can be convincingly duplicated for purposes of testing just about any option a marketer may be interested in.

Researchers are thus gleaning more granular insights into consumer behavior on a real-time basis and at a level previously unattainable. They are deriving shopper insights using eye-tracking reactions good to the millisecond—and doing it on a cost-effective, actionable basis.

This VR front-end discovery data is then fed into the AI to crunch. Gathering up millions of data points from the user-testing and combining them with third-party data on relevant consumer behavior, the AI can generate deep-dive insights into the psyche of various customer segments as well as behavioral preferences. Then the AI can model out the most ideal customer micro-segments for use in segmentation strategies and beyond into messaging, if desired.

These same VR-based research tools are also advancing new product development. Rapid prototyping is being made even more rapid. With no more need to create physical mockups of a prototype for testing, researchers can iterate toward market viability at a faster pace, and at lower cost generally, fully apprised of customer feedback at each step—taking innovation to a new level.

Of late, marketing research has moved away from store environments and into virtual environments. It is less disruptive and can deliver high-level behavioral data faster and less expensively than in the store. But sometimes the clearest insights come from taking that virtual technology into an actual store.

Most illuminating of studies

An in-depth 2022 research project led by Harvard professors Chandukala, Reddy, and Tan sought to understand how shoppers might engage with AR in a real-world setting.[170] So at a major retailer, they set up a sampling station for lipsticks. Shoppers could try on four shades of lipstick from four brands, doing so normally and virtually (i.e., not having to apply the actual product). Hidden sensors captured details about the shoppers (e.g., gender, alone or accompanied, carrying a basket or not) and their interactions with the lipsticks (e.g., number sampled, duration of sampling).

In crunching the data, the professors found that shoppers using the AR interface "spent almost 50 percent more time sampling" and "sampled 7.5 times more products, on average." In short, the AR interface made the sampling process more convenient and encouraged more exploration. Of course, the novelty of the experience could have juiced the results, and over time and with familiarity, AR's "edge" may shrink. Nonetheless, these sampling differentials were substantial. What's more, the professors found, the "normal" samplers concentrated on two lipsticks from one brand, whereas "virtual" samplers were rather evenly distributed across all sixteen lipstick brands. And so the conclusion: "Brands that are less popular may benefit more from AR due to the increased sampling activity."[171]

But what about B2B?

Retailer use of AR, with tangible products to present, is understandable on its face. Less obvious is how a professional services consultancy might use these technologies to demonstrate its capabilities.

"Every time there's a big technological shift," says Antonia Wade of PwC, "it forces you to question how it can best be used to represent your brand values. We took the decision to invest in a piece of land in the public metaverse platform, Sandbox. We went into Decentraland; we might be the first, or one of the first, professional services companies to do it."[172]

Others early into the Sandbox were **Adidas, Snoop Dogg,** *The Walking Dead, South China Morning Post,* **The Smurfs, Care Bears**, and **Atari**—all organizations seeking to extend their thought leadership in their industry . Wade sees it similarly: "Our aim is to position ourselves at the leading edge, thinking about the problems today's CEOs are facing and how we can help them balance the near-term, present commitments they have with the future problems they'll need to solve, or the opportunities they'll want to take advantage of."

To leverage PwC's thought leadership in Sandbox, the company launched an experiential island where business executives can go in and play decision-making games. "With this game," Wade says, "you can start to envisage what the implications of your decisions look like for your supply chain or for the planet, because you can actually bring it to life in a meaningful way in the Metaverse" and evaluate the consequences and outcomes of the decisions you might want to make.

This B2B use case for PwC also sought to understand how these technologies will unfold so that PwC can position as a Web 3.0 advisory practice. Says William Gee, partner at PwC Hong Kong, the company is looking to "leverage our expertise to advise clients" on the Metaverse as big things are expected.[173]

EXAMINING THE EFFICIENCIES OF IN-PERSON EVENTS

Virtual events were gaining in popularity even before the pandemic goosed them, and now they are commonplace. Virtual conferences, product launches, and events are finding postpandemic cachet as a preferred method for interacting. Global audiences are gladly engaging through live streaming, 360-degree videos, and interactive chat features. These technologies come at a non-trial cost, of course, but it is substantially less than the aggregate expenses of venue rentals, travel, accommodation, and the like. Not everyone favors turning in-person meetings into a digital equivalent, but it is happening, nonetheless.

Brands are also reaching broader audiences by creating immersive environments in which virtual attendees can interact with products and branded content even more intensively than at an actual event because immersive narratives can showcase products and convey brand values in a more visually compelling and interactive manner.

Importantly, especially for brands targeting Millennial and Gen Z consumers, these virtual engagements also contribute to a reduced carbon footprint versus in-person events. Aligning marketing efforts with sustainability goals resonates powerfully with people who value brands that prioritize these practices.

EXTENDING BEYOND HUMANS TO VIRTUAL INFLUENCERS

Influencers, celebrity endorsers, and content Creators have stepped front and center in brand marketing, and are practically synonymous with it now—showcasing product lines to their followers, increasing brand visibility in the eyes of younger target audiences, and driving adoption in this rapidly evolving digital landscape. These are all marketing objectives being trusted to Influencers who are adept at cutting through the clutter and delivering a targeted demo, leveraging the higher trust quotient that they enjoy over the brands themselves. But adding in virtual Influencers kicks campaigns up a notch.

In pre-marketing the 2023 summer blockbuster film, *Barbie*, a virtual Barbie house was set up on several social networks, and Barbie herself began vlogging. Her Instagram post on Black Lives Matter garnered more than forty thousand likes.[174]

Of course, Barbie is a marketing legend that keeps on trending. But no less known today, certainly among younger audiences, is Janky, a computer-generated imagery (CGI) character. Janky does impressive stunts as part of his pitches for name brands in luxury apparel, energy drinks, and dating sites. In his first year on Instagram, Janky tallied up more than a million followers.[175]

Janky is a top ten virtual Influencer, according to VirtualHumans.org, which has a vested interest in tracking these things. The group claims that virtual Influencers (a) can do anything humans can do with an increased ability to keep the Influencer on script and (b) attain up to 3× engagement rates of human Influencers.[176] While these figures can surely be argued, it does suggest that fully authentic human Influencers could struggle to keep pace with fully synthetic Influencers going forward.

(We focus more on the topic of Influencers—virtual and human—in chapter 9.)

RUNNING COMMUNITY-BASED CAMPAIGNS

Brands are unleashing community-based campaigns that, by design, purposefully involve niche audiences in the co-creation of hybrid real + virtual experiences, fostering a heightened sense of ownership and loyalty among those targeted community audiences. Often, brands are undertaking these campaigns as good corporate stewards, as in the case of **Accenture**.

James Temple, global Metaverse lead at Accenture, tells of one particularly sad yet beautiful community-building initiative. The island nation of Tuvalu faces extinction in our lifetime from rising ocean levels and climate change, and Accenture sought to help. Explains Temple, "We collaborated with the island because like with Venice, Miami, and other sea-level cities in the world, there's a significant threat and it could face demise. We sought to preserve the island nation by re-recreating it as a virtual nation, actually encapsulating the physical footprint of the island, its culture, the history, to form a rich digital twin which allows the whole history to be cataloged in a virtual representation that can be timeless."[177] To actually put Tuvalu into the Metaverse, in short.

Accenture was already collaborating with the World Economic Forum on global awareness campaigns, so it was natural for Tuvalu's beleaguered leadership to work with Accenture to share its story of urgency on a global stage in hopes of spurring concerted action.

So it was that Accenture's Sustainability Studio and Accenture Song stepped in to develop a Metaverse twin of the island nation and ground it in the blockchain. During the project, Tuvalu's leaders actually stepped foot into the Metaverse and spoke movingly to a global audience in 160 countries. The leaders spoke about Tuvalu's fate and about COP 26 (referring to the goals of the UN Climate Change Conference in Glasgow) to raise awareness of the climate catastrophe the earth may be facing. It was beautiful advocacy and a model for virtual community building that does good for the brand by doing good for humanity.[178]

The proof was in the numbers—as the campaign rolled out, 2.1 billion people came to and engaged with Tuvalu's advocacy website, Tuvalu.tv. And in the months since, nine nations have stepped up to officially recognize Tuvalu's digital statehood, which puts the nation on a path to sovereignty along with all the accompanying rights.[179]

Accenture saw this as an urgent project because, as Temple says, "powerful digital technologies could be used to preserve something that is obviously of great meaning but that might disappear one day. Only now it will have a permanent place in the digital history books even if it no longer has a footprint on the world map."

Accenture also saw the value of this project in education. As Temple says, "I'm thinking about my kids who are in kindergarten and second grade. They're watching videos, and learning about volcanoes and things, but in a couple of years they are going to be actually experiencing these things in the Metaverse instead of just watching it. I think that speaks to the importance of what we're doing in the Metaverse."

This completes a brief review of strategies marketers are using to leverage XR technologies. Some of it is old hat to brand marketers, and some is still new and untested. Newest and most untested of all is the thing being called the Metaverse.

Building toward an Unknowable Metaversed Future

Even though the term "metaverse" was famously coined three decades ago by Neal Stephenson in his novel, *Snow Crash*, it's still a mystery idea to many and is likely to remain so for a number of years as subject matter experts wrestle with the technical performance issues and use cases that could, some believe, turn it into the new front end to the internet.

"One of the big barriers to Metaverse adoption is technology," says Jonathan Adashek, chief communications officer of **IBM**. "Take the devices, I don't think we've hit the tipping point. The goggles aren't quite there yet. The other barrier is bandwidth. The Metaverse is only achievable on a mass scale with high-performing, ultrafast internet. In terms of adoption, I think it'll be like electric cars, in a sense. There's going to be the first movers—the Googles, Nikes, and Cokes of the world. Then there's going to be the brands that will let the first movers take the hits and deal with the issues around it, and then come in behind them."[180]

Deloitte's chief marketing officer Suzanne Kounkel strikes a similar chord. "I believe the Metaverse will reward what I call first experimenters, not first movers. Sure, the technology needs to come a lot further before many will be able to capitalize on it. But you can't wait. You need to start experimenting and getting that learning now, and beginning to understand how you will want to play. For example, do you want to build your own metaverse or participate in someone else's?"

This need to experiment won't just apply to B2C marketers but to B2B as well, Kounkel believes. "Metaverse adoption will be higher in B2C initially, but when you think about how it can impact both commercial and organizational dynamics, eventually it will be truly transformational for B2B as well."[181]

HOW MARKETERS ARE FRAMING THIS MYSTERY IDEA

In experimenting with this budding Metaverse technology, it's helpful to think about it in terms of *ownership*. On the platforms calling themselves consumer Metaverses (Axie Infinity, BlueJeans, Cryptovoxels, Decentraland, Gala, Gather, Horizon Worlds, Metahero, Roblox, Sandbox, Sansar, Somnium Space, and Star Atlas, with 160+ companies in dev as of mid-2023), the principal organizing concept is generally that participants can take a stake in almost anything. This can involve creating a digital kraken in a game and selling it to other players on Roblox, building an entire city and becoming the benevolent mayor and tax collector on Sandbox, or hawking digital art or avatar gear in Decentraland. Instead of getting rewarded with the dopamine hit of "likes," the Metaverse currencies of choice are assigned-value tokens and crypto (accompanied by all the early-stage growing pains to be expected from introducing novel currencies).

Participants in these Metaverses can get paid for playing games. They can create digital assets and sell them in burgeoning marketplaces. They can join communities and enjoy voting privileges. They can hop from one platform to another and take their digital identities with them.

As a concept, it's meant to be what the internet was meant to be until it was unleashed in the wild. By design, the Metaverse is decentralized, and it sits on the blockchain instead of centered in a few tech titans' pockets. It runs on peer-to-peer networks rather than using servers. Some are calling it an entirely new economy in the full revolutionary sense of that term—though surely governments, globally, will find a way to regulate the commercial aspects.

Telefónica's chief digital officer, Chema Alonso, sees many uncertainties ahead with the Metaverse and argues for a measured approach to it. "We first analyzed what this Metaverse will look like in five years, eight years from now. We saw that it won't be like *Snow Crash* but more like *Ralph Breaks the Internet* with a mix from the previous Internet and a lot of virtual worlds in which you have different identities and you can be part of different experiences, hyperrealistic experiences in worlds where you can have a Web3 economy based on tokens or worlds where you have different experiences being a different person. For us, the Metaverse will be something chaotic, a chaotic evolution of the Internet. There won't be only one Metaverse; it will be something with a mix of different experiences, different economies, identities, and structures."[182]

A measured strategy, in short.

TREMENDOUS MOMENTUM OF THE METAVERSE

In these early days, there is great uncertainty among analysts whether the Metaverse will become the idyllic digital playground its Creators envision or instead morph into some dystopian disappointment. It has the potential for both, just as the internet did and has. While the future is uncertain, there are significant sums of money pushing into this new digital unreality. There is tremendous momentum building for the Metaverse as a vehicle to ease consumers into Web 3.0 (which we talk about in the next chapter).

This momentum is not fueled solely by tech titans financing their dream vision. Individuals, especially among younger audiences, see it as a welcome and even a necessary thing. The most cynical among them say that when you look at the world today, it's no wonder people are itching for alternate realities, for an escape from the present. But then, truly, people have always dissed the latest reality. The wheel was not such a hit at first, by the way. But the thinking is understandable. As Harvard's Thomas Stackpole writes about the Metaverse, "They're places where power can be inverted, disappointments escaped, and capitalist inequities left behind for something more exciting, malleable, and meaningful."[183]

Justin McLaughlin, author of the excellent *Marketing in the Metaverse*, does see the Metaverse as "a new front-end layer for the Internet. It's a digital interface where, instead of viewing flat text and images on your screen and moving from website to website as we do with the current user interface of the web, you experience a spatial 3D world where you can move from location to location. This type of interaction is possible thanks to technologies like virtual world platforms, where users can explore and engage in various activities in a 3D environment."[184]

This is a compelling pitch to many.

BRANDS ARE REPORTING "BIG STARTS"

The early going in the Metaverse has shown to be both exciting and productive—especially for the free-to-play gaming platforms:

- Fortnite and Roblox, which between them have topped 400 million users.

- Decentraland and Sandbox, intended more as general purpose Metaverses, are growing at a rapid pace but are in a different league. Sandbox premiered in 2022 with 1.3 million installs, while Decentraland in its first year claimed 60,000 monthly active users—an optimistic figure, probably.[185] PwC and Adidas have set up shop in Sandbox, and Samsung is another name brand in Decentraland.

- JPMorgan Chase joined the hype machinery by forecasting a $1 trillion market opportunity as virtual worlds "infiltrate every sector in some way in the coming years." The bankers are so bullish; they set up shop themselves in Decentraland.[186]

- Facebook changed its name to Meta to signal its commitment to this virtual future.

- Microsoft is hard at work building workplaces populated by digital avatars.

- Fashion brands such as Nike and Gucci are designing lines of clothing for use in the Metaverse.

- On Roblox, Paris Hilton threw a New Year's Eve party that drew a larger crowd than in Times Square that year.[187]

A number of major brands, **Deutsche Telekom** among them, are launching their own direct-to-consumer offerings in the Metaverse. DT built its own social telecom experience on the Roblox gaming platform. Company CMO Ulrich Klenke talks about the "Electronic Beats" initiative for younger audiences. "We built our own little telco world called Beatland in Roblox with a discotheque, a cinema, and fun games such as a virtual TV tower with obstacles for players to overcome as they climb to the top before jumping and flying away in 5G jetpacks"—a fun, fully engaging game hosted by DT on one of Roblox's virtual islands, tallying more than twelve million visitors.

Klenke credits these impressive engagement figures to a simple strategy: "We don't try to sell these guys anything. This is the secret of good brand advertising … just connecting to people with the brand and not with the product."[188]

Under Klenke's direction, Deutsche Telekom is effectively toggling between virtual and real worlds, sponsoring music festivals in Roblox, for example, and then bringing them out into real-world concert arenas. "It's exactly the same brand being presented in the Metaverse as in the real world—each is a faithful replica of the other, the same assets deployed. In the street, the brand is face-to-face with our target audiences. In the virtual festivals, we are avatar-to-avatar. I believe this is the strongest combination you can have."

Klenke admits to being amazed at how these gaming platforms can unite different cultures in a shared passion and priority for having fun and "how many people we reach being right on the Roblox platform. You have that little avatar of yourself, and when you are standing on the dance floor, you could be talking to Argentinians, Russians, Japanese, whatever. It's a global phenomenon."

A phenomenon that's also good business. With the success of Beatland, Deutsche Telekom launched a follow-on campaign called "Summer of Joy," featuring Jayda G, who was nominated for a Grammy for her song "Both of Us." Jayda's performances in the Metaverse call attention to the economic, environmental, and societal pressures that young people face. And in so doing, they demonstrate the brand's caring support for a generation.[189]

HEADING TOWARD THE TENSION

For marketers, there is so much to pay attention to in these XR technologies and yet really only one thing: whatever ups and downs are ahead—and it will be a tense rending, surely—there is clearly a new category of "digital experiences," and brands need to find their rightful place in the mix.

There will be headwinds. Fragmentation across the Metaverse platforms. Difficulties with the hardware. A lack of content standards. But there will also be opportunities to approach with cautious optimism, placing bets on the Metaverse but not overcommitting. These bets should pay out according to analysts such as Gartner, which is projecting that "by 2026, 25 percent of people will spend at least one hour a day in a metaverse for work, shopping, education, social media and/or entertainment."[190]

While Baby Boomers are demonstrating a "take it or leave it" attitude toward XR technologies, Gen X, Millennials, and Gen Z are very favorably inclined. Averaging out the numbers across these three generations, close to 90 percent want to use AR to see how a piece of furniture might look in their home, a paint color might look on their walls, new makeup or hair color might look on their faces, or clothing and accessories might look on their bodies.[191] This is, for them, shopping. So, this future is happening one way or another because XR-enhanced brands stand out in a crowded marketplace, truly capturing the modern consumer where they are focused—on a digital interface, a screen.

Next, we'll broaden the discussion to the full Web 3.0 as envisioned and coming into play and how brands are looking to monetize this developing reality.

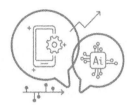

CHAPTER SIX
The (Gradually) Emerging Web3

For a luxury automobile brand, breaking through to younger audiences with messaging that resonates can be a challenge. Lexus felt it in the early 2020s as the carmaker struggled to hold on to a 1.25 percent share of the U.S. market.[192] That put Vinay Shahani, vice president of marketing at Lexus USA, in the hot driver's seat. "One of the biggest 'rejection reasons' for the Lexus brand, particularly for younger consumers," says Shahani, "was the infotainment system in our vehicles. Almost everyone is walking around with a smartphone and so the smoother the integration between the vehicle infotainment system and the phone, the more satisfied the guest."[193]

"Up until 2020, Lexus was a bit behind in infotainment. We had a finnicky touchpad and joystick that would control the screen in the vehicle. Many of our guests didn't like the way it worked." So, Toyota Motor North America's Connected Technologies team went to Japan to convince HQ to let them create an all-new infotainment system. "Fortunately, the bosses in Japan agreed to it," Shahani recalls, "and after a successful pilot, the new infotainment system became widely viewed as such a success within the company that the leadership team in Japan said, go ahead and build it, but we want to leverage this technology for all of our vehicles globally."

With state-of-the-art voice control and an immersive touch-screen, the new system called 21MM was such an impressive upgrade that Shahani and his team elected to emphasize it in marketing communications. They branded it "Lexus Interface" and ensured that it was called out in high-profile vehicle launches like the Lexus NX, LX, and RX. And the results were soon registering with younger guests at dealerships. "We were reading journalist reviews that praised Lexus Interface, as well as hearing guests saying, 'I didn't consider Lexus before because of the infotainment, but that's no longer an issue with this new system.'"

Lexus also doubled down on younger affluent consumers by tapping into one of their favorite pastimes: gaming. The Lexus US Marketing team worked with their ad agencies to create a special Lexus model called the "Gamer's IS" by crowdsourcing ideas on a Twitch live stream. Twitch viewers voted on which gaming platform hardware to integrate into the car, along with exterior and interior styling themes, and even the best refreshments to slot in a center console cooler. Shahani said that it was great for his team and agencies to learn about and engage this younger audience by co-creating with them, and that led to further innovations in this space like Lexus becoming the official automotive partner of 100 Thieves, a popular lifestyle brand and gaming organization in the United States.

Then Shahani and his team took it a step further. Working with 100 Thieves, Lexus took their RCF GT3 race car that competes in the IMSA series GTD class and recreated it in a racing video game using the actual CAD data. 100 Thieves had a couple of their most popular Creators race one another on a Twitch live stream. "These Creators had a blast racing our RCF GT3's and through their social media presence, engaged younger fans that we wouldn't have reached otherwise. It was a powerful activation; hundreds of thousands of people engaged in a very short period of time, building awareness and excitement for Lexus performance cars with a younger demographic."

Shahani felt that *performance* and *excitement* were extremely important brand attributes for his team to focus on, given that Lexus already had strength in the areas of *quality, reliability,* and *durability*. He challenged his team to utilize racing content more broadly across the Lexus brand social media handles. "The gaming partnerships gave us even more confidence to push harder, seeing that the 100 Thieves Creators' involvement enabled the team to drive even more young fan engagement than ever."

Independent sources confirmed as much. While any number of factors can impact brand equity, an Ad Age-Harris Poll following this campaign found Lexus brand equity increasing 11.1 percent with Gen Z from Q3 to Q4 '22 (the highest increase of all major brands tracked, higher even than such popular Gen Z brands as Venmo, Vans, Gap, Apple Music, and Snapchat).[194]

Shahani felt that innovation is something Lexus Marketing should embrace, even if in an area that was new for the brand. "We saw a lot of brands creating NFT artwork and auctioning it off," Shahani says, "and we thought about whether we should try to monetize NFTs (non-fungible tokens). When I think about the genesis of the Lexus brand, we were founded on creating a differentiated and elevated experience. Our tagline is 'Experience Amazing,'" and so, Shahani decided that creating an amazing experience with NFTs would be appropriate.

"Our Toyota Connected Technologies team had the skillset to help us with creating NFTs. I told them and my marketing team that I'm okay if we don't monetize right away, for the sake of learning. We agreed that creating a 'surprise and delight' for our guests in an NFT would be the best way-in. After a lot of brainstorming, the team came up with an NFT for our Lexus Performance Driving School (LPDS) students. We would have the first performance driving school in the world to surprise its guests with an NFT souvenir that commemorates their driving performance on the track. You sign up, pay your fee of $995, and spend a day with us on a racetrack like Road Atlanta or Road America or Circuit of the Americas honing your driving skills with professional drivers, and take home a digital summary of that experience."

At this Lexus driving school, people hone their driving skills in top-end Lexus cars and get personalized coaching in braking, cornering, and throttle techniques along with training in autocross lapping, a skid pad experience, and lead-follow exercises—learning to unleash the potential of a performance car.

"Guests walk away feeling more confident in performance driving situations," Shahani continues. "[T]hey walk away with an extremely positive view of Lexus as a performance brand, an attribute we clearly strive to own. More importantly, they walk away with a sense of accomplishment," which Lexus commemorated with an NFT rendered on the Polygon blockchain platform.

"We gave participants a link to download an NFT minted just for them. It's a forty-five-second video of them in the vehicle on the track along with analytics from the car capturing data like their top speed, breaking force, acceleration, and other KPIs that were unique to their performance—all superimposed over content of themselves on the track. It created a sense of pride in themselves, in their driving ability, in the Lexus brand itself."

This kind of experience is something LPDS guests love to talk about with friends and families, particularly on social media. Of course, this kind of racetrack experience was no small-budget marketing campaign. But Shahani and his team didn't aim to make money on it. "We were not of the mindset that every single thing we do in marketing has to have an immediately measured return on investment. Because in many cases, you're planting the seed for the future, creating a net positive for the brand."

That didn't mean Lexus wasn't tracking KPIs. "Our business analytics team routinely looks at every marketing campaign we do: How many people did it drive to the website? What was the conversion rate? Are we creating leads for our dealers? Are we matching sales back to leads generated? We're measuring all of that. But something like an NFT that you give to a guest as a surprise and delight at the end of Lexus Performance Driving School, I would argue that if consumers are happy, if they're tweeting about it, if media outlets are picking it up favorably and sharing that information ... you've already won."

"Lexus strives to provide its guests with one-of-a-kind experiences," Shahani concludes, "and instead of a curated timeline of retouched photos, the NFT offers an authentic and truly unique way to share one's on-track accomplishments and opens the door to attend and participate in exclusive Lexus events in the future."

This co-creation of real- and virtual-world automotive experiences by Lexus, along with the efforts of other forward-looking companies like them, is the most visible sign that something called Web3 is coming on strong.

The Evolution of the World Wide Web

It may be helpful to take a step back and provide a brief overview of the history of the World Wide Web. As we know, the first web was a read-only invention of the early 1990s boasting static HTML web pages—basically books in the ether or pages on a screen, meant for passive viewing; brands marketed through online banners and emails urging prospects to visit their websites.

Web2, the read-write web, came in the late 1990s and added blogs, wikis, videos, and social media available on multiple devices. Viewers could be Creators—through e-commerce, blogging, and community building. Brands leveraged data to become more analytics oriented. Influencers became integral to brand promotion and trust. Most economic value accrued to the tech giants (e.g., Google, Facebook, Amazon) who provided the platforms and data collection that everyone depended on.

Web3, the read-write-interact web now unfolding, aims to flip the digital world from centralized in a few big tech companies' hands to decentralized in end users' hands. In this version of the web, most decision-making is handed over to AI—a seeming contradiction, but that's the idea. Perhaps more important, power is transferred from tech giants to users, through a greater degree of ownership and control over personal data and how it is used. Collectively, this is why Web3 is often referred to as the "democratization of the internet."

Perhaps the best summary of Web3 comes from digital analyst Brian Solis: "Conceptually, Web3 is a decentralized, permissionless, trustless internet experience—not requiring the support of a trusted intermediary—that employs peer-to-peer interaction and meritocracy to put power and ownership in the hands of individuals rather than centralized entities. It's envisioned as a digital space where services are operated, owned, and improved upon by communities of users. Concretely, Web3 is a new technology platform that employs digital advancements such as blockchain, cryptocurrency, the metaverse, decentralized autonomous organizations (DAOs), and non-fungible tokens (NFTs) to create this vision for a new, better internet."[195]

KEY WEB3 CONCEPTS AND DEFINITIONS

Whether Web3 eventually measures up to all the hype that has ushered it forward, we cannot know. However it comes to pass, there are some big changes ahead that will impact marketers. So, it is useful to sift through all the hoopla and hype in hopes of gaining insights into the very real—that is, virtual—opportunities now unfolding. These key Web3 concepts lay a floor under the marketing activations that are only now beginning to take shape.

Decentralized ownership

Web3 represents an internet where big tech (Alphabet, Amazon, Apple, and Meta specifically) no longer enjoy centralized power and make all the rules, but instead, there are distributed peer-to-peer networks where individuals transact in complete control of their personal data, credentials, and underlying applications—because all of it is stored within a digital wallet that is private and secure (at least in theory).

Blockchain

Decentralized ownership is made possible through an innovation known as the blockchain. A blockchain is a database in its simplest form, a distributed database that keeps a record of Web3 transactions in a transparent and tamperproof mode. It is meant to create an environment of trust. And while not perfect, it is far more secure than old-fashioned databases. This is because the blockchain (or rather blockchains because there are many) uses cryptography to secure their contents. This is said to make blockchains into "immutable ledgers" where once an item is recorded, it cannot be modified or deleted at any future time.

It's the blockchain that legitimatizes all the innovations in crypto, NFTs, and tokenomics that are entering marketers' arsenals.

Cryptocurrency

Crypto trading gets all the headlines, and as a developing asset class, it faces a volatile and an uncertain future. For marketers, however, crypto is most interesting as the digital money being used in Web3 transactions of value. Popular crypto, such as Bitcoin and Ethereum, sits in an individual's "wallet" that is stored on the blockchain. This, in effect, makes the crypto holders their own bankers. And this becomes a core distinction in marketers crafting relationships with these individual consumers.

Non-fungible tokens (NFTs)

Non-fungible means it is not possible to exchange something for another thing that is essentially identical and of equal value. In contrast, a $20 bill is considered fungible because it can be exchanged for two $10 bills (i.e., of equal value) or, for that matter, another $20 bill—also of equal value. Non-fungible tokens (NFTs) are digital certificates that guarantee the authenticity of a digital or even a physical asset—art, property, music, games, and so on. Each NFT carries a unique digital identifier that cannot be copied or modified. That identifier is recorded on a blockchain to prove ownership and, in some cases, allow that NFT to be traded on secondary markets.

Brands are using NFTs in numerous ways, often to reward employees and drive customer engagement. In this sense, it would seem that NFTs are just techier versions of rewards or loyalty points. But they are not. They have a universal value attached to them that is recognized in secondary markets. They can be traded in these markets and take on an entire life of their own if investors see value in them.

Metaverse

As discussed in chapter 5, the Metaverse is the catch-all term being used for all kinds of digital experiences enabled by XR technologies including VR, AR, and MR. There will be many Metaverses built up in the coming decade—from single gaming playing sites to major platform experiences.

Token economics (or tokenomics)

Whereas today's internet properties use traditional advertising to attract customers, in a Web3 environment, monetary incentives (tokens) will be used. The model is to align interests by straight-up paying or rewarding people for actions taken rather than trying to convince or manipulate them through advertising techniques.

Artificial intelligence

As discussed in chapter 4, advances in AI are allowing the tasks once performed by humans to be handled by machines, leading to improved decision-making (usually) and more productivity. Marketers are most interested in how AI will drive customer engagement in Web3 environments. It promises to give marketers considerably more insightful levels of personalization to the point of knowing precisely what people desire and how best to satisfy those desires within the context of the product's experience in a Web3 environment.

Semantic Web

AI is ushering in something called the Semantic Web, in which all the world's data is linked intelligently so that machines can understand the data in the same way people do, and a new language is born. Marketers care about this emerging Semantic Web because it allows the integration of multiple sources of data into one seamless application.

MARKETERS TAKING FIRST STEPS

Ally Financial's CMO Andrea Brimmer knows the difficulties of "filling in the blanks" on technologies as uncertain and potentially transformative as Web3. "This is complete conjecture on my part," Brimmer says, "but you know, nobody thought the Internet was going to de-position big retail stores, the way cars are bought, the way you shop at bookstores. Changing everything. The Metaverse has the same potential to do that. And so, in the financial services category, we have to wonder if we get to a point where branches are no longer needed, and servicing and account opening are handled differently because of the Metaverse" changing everything?[196]

So even if only to hedge bets, Ally is taking first steps with Web3. "We're looking at rolling out a rewards program for our customers that is a private blockchain where you collect different Ally coins in exchange for taking learning courses, doing certain check-ins, coming to the website, maybe reading some blog content, and referring a friend. All to create stickiness with our customer base and a value-add experience you wouldn't get with another financial institution."

This stickiness is something Deloitte's CMO Suzanne Kounkel defines in terms of the "access" people will have to brands. "It will be fundamentally different from the current web with respect to relationships, and brings with it a certain democratization of access. Take corporate communications, for example. In the old days (Web1), you could lock down things and easily maintain 'one voice' for the entire company. As we moved to Web2, that changed dramatically because all of a sudden you had user reviews, social media, and those sorts of things. And I think Web3's impact will be even more profound. It's limiting to think about it merely as a backend change because the democratization of access is so profound. You need to be able to unleash the power of that access, or to be surprised when that power is used against you."[197]

Few would concur with this preemptive mindset more than Chema Alonso, **Telefónica**'s chief digital officer, who qualifies as an early adopter. Alonso says, "Web3 is something that is going to disrupt the world. With artificial intelligence and the automation of everything, people's main purpose is being happy with their lives and being part of platforms as users and customers, or what I call 'token for a living.' Those two are going to be the most valuable things for people in the future. So, we believe that people will be rewarded for just connecting to a platform. That is going to be the new normal. Right now, social networks are paying Influencers for the viewers they bring to your TikTok videos, etcetera. But in the future, everyone is going to be paid (directly by brands) just for spending time on the platform and doing things."[198]

Referencing today's internet affiliate programs where people share links for money, Chema sees similarities at a far larger scale. "It's going to happen in every corner of the digital platforms. Everyone helping a platform grow is going to be rewarded with a token. We believe that 'token for a living' is going to happen. It's a reality."

Alonso points out that "big corporations like Google, Meta, and even Microsoft, have been internally creating value using tokens. In Google, they have a Peer Bonus program so if someone helps you, you send a token. You have a meeting with someone who is helping you, you send a token."

It is easy to see how "token for a living" as it escalates across society could soon run headlong into the U.S. Treasury's concerns about tokens replacing dollars and threatening the "full faith and credit of the US dollar" (similarly in other countries, of course). Says Alonso, "Tokenomics and Web3 have dangerous side effects. You are essentially moving value out of the dollar—and out of the Euro—and into a new coin. It could be dangerous. Because of that, Facebook stopped Libra because in the end, if you are creating a big parallel economy based on tokens, like the economy that a Facebook or Apple can create, it could be a distortion for the country. I believe it *is* going to happen, but I think it's going to be regulated at least at some point. So, we need to continue working on Web3 because there is value that we can create from our digital products and services."

Creating this value will be an incremental enterprise because, entering 2024, pieces of the Web3 technology stack are still works in progress. Nonetheless, it will come together—sooner say some, later say others—surely differently than now expected. And it will just as surely change the way consumers interact with brands and, in turn, how brands approach the all-critical concept of customer lifetime value. CMOs who understand the foundational strategies of Web3 development will be best positioned to lead the marketing organizations of tomorrow and secure their future-ready brands.

Web3 Implications and Opportunities

Web3 will be like upgrading from a flip phone to a smartphone, only for the internet. Instead of a few tech companies dictating the terms of the online experience, a technically decentralized and likely chaotic series of peer-to-peer networks coalescing around particular interests will form up. However this proves out, it will certainly impact the activities of marketers after clocking in every day.

THE TECHNOLOGIES AND THEIR POSSIBILITIES

Blockchain data collection

A major challenge brands are facing is being able to effectively track online consumer behavior as third-party cookies, and mobile device identifiers are phasing out. Conveniently then, as more consumers begin doing transactions tied to the blockchains, they will have crypto wallets holding their online identities—allowing brands to capture crypto wallet data when so authorized.

How those authorizations will unfold remains uncertain. Presumably, consumers will expect greater data privacy, given that blockchains "guarantee" it, and they come to believe that the power dynamic has shifted away from big tech in their favor. But the dynamics of accessing blockchain data are being worked out on the fly and are far from locked down.

When accessible to marketers, consumers' crypto wallets will yield a wealth of data—detailed views into purchasing behavior, how much is spent on other brands, and so on. Connecting these data sources to customer relationship management software (CRMs), marketers will be able to drive more targeted marketing with personalized touches at scale.

Todd Kaplan, CMO of PepsiCo, sees this targeted marketing coming. He believes "the core essence of Web3 is the blockchain in the back end of it ... allowing brands and consumers to safely connect—right down to the equities brands can provide consumers and incentives in terms of payments."[199]

PepsiCo was, in fact, one of the first adopters of Web3. "We created the Pepsi Mic Drop, one of the first branded NFT projects, and it was wildly successful. We gave it up for free to consumers and they could resell the NFTs for tons of money." But as Kaplan looks to the Web3 future, he does believe "it will be all about building more direct-to-consumer programming. As people get more digital wallets, as they get more comfortable on the blockchain, and feel secure and safe with it, I think it'll open up a whole lot more opportunities for brands like Pepsi."

A Gartner survey of marketing leaders found that the top reasons for collecting customer data in order are (1) having the ability to personalize marketing communications, (2) appending customer profiles with additional data to gain insights, and (3) delivering personalized experiences to customers. Blockchain data will deliver on these top objectives—far better than previous methods—especially since those previous methods could become extinct.

Frictionless transparency

In Web3 environments, individuals will be able to move seamlessly between applications and services without losing access to their data or digital assets. Everything goes with them—since it's stored in a single wallet.

This practice should increase cross-platform engagement since there are fewer login hassles. It should also increase global participation in digital communities since there are no geographic limitations.

Brands seeking to compete in these Web3 environments will find it essential to be open and transparent about their practices—from how they use customer data to how their business operates. This Gen Z value should become a Web3 value in some form or other. And building this trust with customers will actually be easier since the blockchains' immutability can help backstop and support the authenticity of any claims a business makes. At the same time, the blockchains can just as easily call the wrong kind of attention to brands that are not fully authentic and genuine in their Web3 activations.

Transaction security

Both in Web2 and increasingly in Web3, customers expect to interact with and transact on applications and platforms without fear of data breaches or security threats—because the underlying blockchains can make it so. Blockchains, properly executed, ensure that customer records are tamper-resistant and transparent, in turn creating a belief system that records can be relied upon, in turn fostering greater trust in digital transactions in a virtual loop that can benefit marketers.

NFTs and the possibilities they enable

When marketers talk about alternative economies and Web3, they're mostly talking about tokens—specifically NFTs that provide some combination of four values: (a) currency, (b) governance, (c) membership, and (d) status.

These NFTs are usually administered through crypto wallets (such as the popular Coinbase and MetaMask). An individual signs into a website using "public keys" derived from their crypto wallet instead of the old way—with a Google, Facebook, or Apple passcode/email. And so, these tokens and wallets are set to become the future of identity and CRM at scale.

NFTs are being called "an economy" and "tokenomics" because they have actual value, usually linked to crypto and when exchanged back into U.S. dollars account for significant numbers. While sales of NFTs fluctuated wildly in the beginning on new issue mania, sales have since evened out with mid-2023 annualized sales of $168 million and secondary markets generating an estimated $24.7 billion in organic trading volume.[200]

While this market activity is interesting, and even enticing for some marketers, the focus for most marketers is on the first-generation use of tokens. Specifically, how to best incentivize customer behavior?

In creating an NFT that matters, brand marketers should ask the following questions:

- For starters, of course, what problem (or opportunity) is the NFT project trying to address? Why is NFT the optimal activation technique?

- What mission or value proposition will attract the kind of people most open-minded to the NFT project?

- How does the NFT project fit with the brand's positioning (this is a critically important question but the one most easily overlooked)?

Next, we'll discuss the above collection of technologies and capabilities within the context of how benefit is derived across three distinct yet interrelated stakeholder groups: (1) customers and consumers, (2) brands and marketers, and (3) markets and communities.

HOW CONSUMERS AND CUSTOMERS BENEFIT

Consumers are expected to be the greatest beneficiaries of Web3 and for many of the reasons we've been discussing. Both consumer groups and customer bases across the land are likely to have a much greater sense of control over—and confidence in—their online experiences. This expectation will begin with younger audiences and become part of their adult experience set. For transactions that are tied to the blockchain, consumers will expect a far greater level of data privacy and platform transparency—because the blockchains will guarantee it in some form or manner.

In Web3 environments, consumers will be able to move seamlessly between applications and services without losing access to their data or digital assets. It can all be stored in a single wallet! So, these consumers can jump between online platforms with fewer or no login hassles.

Consumers have thus far shown a keen interest in NFTs—though admittedly, these consumers have to be considered early adopters. When companies devise NFT programs that combine the three key values—a currency with governance, membership, and status-seeking opportunities—consumers can be expected to place increasing value in those NFTs.

HOW BRANDS AND MARKETERS BENEFIT

Revenue generation through sales of digital assets

Although revenue generation has not been most marketers' primary goal for NFTs to date, monetization is certainly a real possibility, both now and increasingly in the future. NTFs represent the clearest opportunity for extending the brand and engaging with customers as Web3 approaches in its fits and starts. Indeed, NFTs are already a straightforward business model, delivering meaningful revenue to enterprises and meeting other brand objectives, as well.

Specifically, limited-edition NTFs can generate revenue by being

- tied directly to a new product launch,

- used for special marketing promotions,

- given away in branding marketing campaigns, and

- turned into exclusive rewards for loyal customers.

Brands are monetizing NTFs at levels entirely inconceivable as late as 2017 when the first NFT, CryptoPunks, debuted. The top five brands on the NFT revenue list (compiled by open-source data provider Dune Analytics) generated $242.8 million in sales in 2021.

The top brands were Nike with $185.3 million, Dolce & Gabbana $25.6 million, Tiffany $12.6 million, Gucci $11.6 million, and Adidas $10.9 million. Rounding out the top ten were Budweiser, *TIME* magazine, Bud Light, the Australian Open, Lacoste, Nickelodeon, McLaren, and Pepsi Mic Drop.[201]

Certainly, the most successful use of NFTs has been Nike's famously hitting it out of the virtual ballpark with the "Nikeland" mini-metaverse, built on the Roblox platform, and responsible for $185 million in sneaker-focused NFT sales.[202]

Lacoste released eleven thousand "Undw3" NFTs, which gave holders access to a gated community where they could co-create "Undw3" products. Community members could vote on merchandise development ideas, complete games of challenge intended to increase brand reach, and earn exclusive titles for their super-loyal engagement—opening doors to additional privileges. Catherine Spindler, chief brand officer at Lacoste, reported that "Undw3" helped Lacoste build a sixty-thousand-member global community, resulting in direct sales volume of $1 million with $3 million in secondary sales.[203]

There is also the secondary market for trading NFTs, and that lends credibility and promise to the issue of NFTs. But for most marketers, this secondary market will not be a major concern or impact how an NFT program is developed. What does matter to marketers is that the popularity of NFT marketplaces puts a floor under continuing interest in NFTs—serving to somewhat de-risk NFT projects amid an always uncertain future.

Forging deeper, more entrenched customer relationships

For decades, the traditional marketing funnel focused on generating leads, acquiring customers, and retaining them. The Web3 model aims to leverage the blockchain to move prospects into the role of co-owners, of sorts. Web3 principles for marketing are emerging, with brands

- rethinking the ways that customers can be co-Creators of the brand's value in virtual-world spaces that spill out into real-world spaces,

- organizing the brand's utility around these virtually motivated co-Creators and turning that effort to competitive advantage,

- identifying brand ambassadors (both human and virtual) and incentivizing them to inspire and rally the community,

- continuing with proven full-funnel marketing strategies that complement this extension of the brand into the Web3 space, and

- monitoring the KPIs and using co-Creator feedback to improve and iterate as Web3 goes through its early-stage transformations into the unknown.

Implementing an NFT strategy involves determining (a) what the concept for the NFT will be; (b) how it will be created—that is, 3D-rendered, illustrated, computer-generated, and so on; (c) and how it will be promoted. But most of all, a good strategy takes as a given and central building block that customers are becoming co-Creators of brand value.

Of course, this notion of co-creation in brand marketing is far from new. What's becoming different is how customers are moving beyond mere contributors and collaborators to true partners—actual shareholders with a tiny but important stake in the company or brand. This gives them more of a vested interest in the brand's success than any mere co-Creator could ever imagine. And tokens are the means for providing this greater economic incentive for customers. It gives them skin in the game, plain and simple. That "skin" can have a steroidal impact on how these customers view the brand and maintain loyalty to the brand.

Tokens are, in short, an alternative way to entice, acquire, and hold on to customers longer. Instead of manipulating through advertising, tokens are buying allegiance. NFT projects bring in early adopters and reward them financially for their contributions to brand building. Think of these co-Creators as partners, trying to align incentives for them for the run of the funnel. These early adopters can:

- become evangelists who, in turn, bring more people into the community and advocate for its benefits;

- provide an unfiltered feedback loop—informing on what's working and what isn't; and

- act as beta testers for a community project, showing themselves more willing to help and to be more forgiving in the early stages when things might not be going well.

NFTs essentially lubricate the entire Web3 interaction and incentivize community members to root for the brand—to want to see it succeed. This link between "giving tokens" and "communities succeeding" is a salient one because Web3 could well replace the traditional go-to-market strategy with a go-to-community strategy.

Testing new products and obtaining real-time feedback

Just as we've seen XR technologies (in chapter 5) prove out as excellent product research tools, the larger Web3 also promises to play a large role in low-cost product and consumer research projects. Being able to test how consumers react to a product that is inserted organically into a game in the Metaverse, for example, and then A/B test options to the product profile in rapid-prototyping succession, will yield deep data to aid in actual product development.

HOW MARKETS AND COMMUNITIES BENEFIT

Alternative economies

Web3 is meant to organize around *traditional* notions of community, updated for the digital age. That means pursuing strategies that blend the real *and* virtual into community experiences where members don't just attach their name to it but fully invest themselves in the mission of the community and its projects. The result is the community itself does the marketing for the brand sponsoring it all. Worth repeating, the community itself does the marketing for the brand sponsoring it all.

In these Web3 communities, the ideal is for members to actively engage in and influence the decision-making right alongside the brand itself—as we saw in the Lexus case. Indeed, members are meant to have a very real "say" in the governance of their communities and associated platforms, using the tokens they earn as voting power in the community's decision-making.

With tokens becoming an effective lubricant between brand motivations and customer intentions, the most effective Web3 customer acquisition strategy, along with retention and upgrade strategies as well, could be community building. That is, funds spent on community building could generate better returns than traditional advertising. This is as yet the hypothesis that marketers are aiming to prove out—as we are still in the early stages of this Web3 community model.

Of course, community-oriented marketing is commonplace on Web 2.0. But it has been characterized by (a) channel fragmentation, (b) rewards offered at arm's length, and (c) communications that are one-to-many at best, with little more than token consideration (reversing the meaning) for consumers' opinions and input.

Web3 aims to address these deficiencies with peer-to-peer architectures built in Metaverses that engage each individual in a number of community experiences in a one-to-one fashion that's tangible and meaningful to all involved. For instance, rewarding community members who accumulate enough brand tokens with gated access to prized experiences or cool events and then granting the most engaged token collectors brand ambassador status, actually encouraging them to participate in the governance and success of the business.

One of the largest companies in Spain, it's no wonder Telefónica is going deep with Web3 and has even created its own marketplace for NFTs. Chief Digital Officer Chema Alonso explains that it's a highly inclusive initiative: "We accept only unique additions of great artists. We work with publishing companies to obtain the writers' originals, famous writers like Arturo Pérez-Reverte. We go to the computer of the writer, we take the document, sign the document, create the NFT, and make sure it's the only copy of that document. Later we work with digital artists that only work in digital. We sign a contract with them and create an NFT."

Telefónica also facilitates payments in crypto—Ethereum, Bitcoin, and so on—at tu.com and e-commerce to buy technology. For that, it relies on a payment system from Bit2me, Spain's largest crypto exchange in which Telefónica has invested. The exchange "does the transaction between the crypto and the hard currency so there are no issues with regulators in our countries … plus it's also complex for us to accept crypto directly."

Telefónica is using several blockchains, including Celo, which describes itself as "an open-source blockchain ecosystem focused on making decentralized, carbon-negative, mobile-first financial systems and tools accessible, with a mission to create the conditions for prosperity for all." As a node on the blockchain, Telefónica will be validating transactions, ensuring network consensus, promoting stability, and maintaining the security of the Celo blockchain. Importantly, in Telefónica's view, the companies share a common mission to promote sustainable projects, such as combatting climate change.

Alonso is keen on a Web3 future and one of its biggest advocates. "We've made a big bet investing in and exploring the opportunities and evolution of this Web3 economy in the future. We believe that data is valuable and that data belongs to our customers. They need to be rewarded with tokens for the data they share with us. But not only that, we believe that we can incentivize behaviors in our customers that are going to be good for them and good for Telefónica. If they are reducing the number of issues with our products and services, they will call less to our contact center, which is good for us and helps us reduce churn."

Societal issues positively impacted

Deutsche Telekom's CMO Ulrich Klenke insists that brands can no longer simply talk about a commitment to causes audiences care about. Instead, ideally, brands should use connected technologies to amplify the impact (especially younger) people can have around the world. "We dropped an NFT for 'good' on a digital community powered by *Value*," Klenke explains. "*Value* is a money-can't-buy NFT to show that when new technology starts from a good place, not a greedy one, it can change the world."[204]

Deutsche Telekom's community and its NFT sought out volunteer leaders aged eighteen to thirty across Europe, urging them to pursue projects concerning racial and social equality, gender issues, climate change, mental well-being, and the like. "In all, 1.6 million young people joined and supported causes they cared about and delivered real-world value, including free sanitary products, a new animal shelter, mobile libraries, repairing and donating laptops, and free meals for the homeless."

From the outset, Klenke meant to flip the NFT narrative on its head, transforming this latest digital shiny object from something one buys for self-interest in the virtual world into something one earns for the collective interests of the real world.

"We are consistently in awe of this socially conscious and action-orientated generation," says Klenke, "so we built our community around them. Together with Facebook, we also installed an anti-hate bot to offer help when needed. We went into schools to help in educating young people. We gave [nonprofit] organizations money together with more than fifty partners." After a soft launch in June 2022, the platform now hosts more than one hundred diverse projects in ten countries.

And an amplification campaign ran across Gen Z platforms including Instagram, Twitch, Snapchat, Spotify, and TikTok.

Of course, owning a Deutsche Telekom Value NFT conveys practical benefits, as well. The young volunteers are given the opportunity to unlock customized support from Deutsche Telekom. And they join a Discord community of like-minded young volunteers to learn from experts and collaborate with fellow volunteers.

All in all, a sparkling execution.

STRONG OPINIONS, NO CRYSTAL BALL

As we are still in the early stages of Web3, it's difficult to know if the whole thing is a lot of hype or if it's a big idea still ahead of its time.

Back in 2021, Elon Musk weighed in, calling Web3 "more marketing buzzword than reality right now."[205]

A year later, *Vogue Business* writer Madeleine Schulz ripped into the Web3 hype that had saturated the trades and triggered a deep skepticism about the whole endeavor, along with both brazen and foolhardy crypto scams scaring off prudent investors and some brands desperately relabeling their Web3 investments in hopes of enduring the hype cycle.[206]

Believing similarly, the accomplished software engineer and Wikipedia editor Molly White put up the website "Web3 Is Going Just Great" to document Web3 malfeasance. Her "Grift Counter" began tallying the money lost to NFT grifts, Ponzi's and other she-nanigans. As of mid-2023, the figure had topped $67 billion.[207]

Twitter founder Jack Dorsey also took aim at Web3 zealots seeking to paint their utopian picture of a decentralized paradise of wonders and end-user fulfillment. Dorsey's tweet directed toward consumers: "You don't own 'web3.' The VCs and their LPs do. It will never escape their incentives. It's ultimately a centralized entity with a different label. Know what you're getting into..."[208]

The capper came in a keynote at Ad Age's May 2023 marketing summit. Coca-Cola's head of generative AI, Pratik Thakar, surprised many of his assembled peers by suggesting that they invest in AI instead of Web3.[209] Thakar said AI is going to be more fundamental than Web3 technologies like NFTs and the Metaverse.

NYU professor Scott Galloway, as trenchant an observer as any on the markets, also agreed that "the advertised decentralization of power out of the hands of a few has, in fact, been a re-centralization of power into the hands of fewer." His Exhibit A: 80 percent of the $41 billion in market value of NFTs at the time of his writing was held in just 9 percent of the accounts. As for the crypto market, it too was/

is becoming more centralized. When Ethereum launched in 2015, Galloway notes, insiders controlled only 15 percent of the coin, but before long, insider ownership hit 30 percent and then 40 percent on a trajectory to the standard 80 percent insiders, 20 percent public ratio. So, these insiders, "specifically, dudes from Stanford/Harvard who conflate luck with talent and serve under the delusion of a mandate to save us while accidentally making billions," says Galloway, still have "the potential to establish monopoly power … and that's the true protocol for Web3." Galloway does conclude that despite the inevitable consolidation in the sector, there is still great potential ahead in Web3 innovations but that "like every other emerging asset class or sector, it will require thoughtful oversight, regulation, and security."[210]

With so much badmouthing from prominent thought leaders, it's also important to remember that we've been here before. One needs only recall the early 2000s when the Nasdaq crashed from the newfangled tech disasters of that time. But soon after, internet usage almost doubled with two-thirds of U.S. households signing on thanks to workable broadband connections. Similarly, today's volatile crypto markets and cockamamie NFT schemes could be the *noise*, and the *signal* could be someone developing a "killer app" for Web3.

All of this augurs for caution in proceeding with Web3 initiatives, for the careful studying of the opportunities out there, and for the easing into first steps.

SECTION THREE: COMMERCIAL FUTUREWAVES

How Brands Will Need to Be Promoted

With brands dynamically positioning for the future and hyper-personalizing their products/services using new technologies, they can take full advantage of rapidly evolving commercial platforms and strategies to *promote* themselves.

This begins in chapter 7 with a look at the ***future of content marketing*** and how new technologies are shifting the relationship between brands and audiences. AI-driven marketing strategies and solutions are being deployed at each level of content management—in research, creation, personalization, curation, and optimization. And marketers are seeing the many *limitations* of automated systems, as well, particularly in trying to generate AI content that's creative enough to convert, obtaining good SEO, and effectively controlling and policing messaging.

Chapter 8 finds that ***gamification strategies*** are still driving top-of-funnel activity, while new AI and XR technologies are supercharging gamified experiences and resulting in elevated brand awareness, improved customer satisfaction and loyalty, and higher ROI. AI is expected to play a role in future campaigns and drive deeper insights via personalization, generate more profitable experiences for marketers, offer intelligent game design and recommendations, and provide instant feedback and analysis.

Chapter 9 looks at the roles *human and virtual Influencers* are playing in the marketing mix and how third-party credentialization is driving outsized ROI. While major brands use celebrity-Influencers often for awareness, CMOs are uniformly turning to and finding their greatest ROI from micro-Influencers. This shift grows out of the impact the TikTok platform is enjoying, the increasing relevance of Influencers who manage their own content creation, the shift from hi-fi to lo-fi content, and the ability to effectively propel the brand into niche communities.

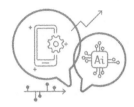

CHAPTER SEVEN
The Fourth Era of Content Marketing

As the fourth-largest wireless carrier in the United States, **UScellu-lar** has to have a keen differentiator to compete.[211] The company's CMO Eric Jagher says, "UScellular is a challenger brand, a brand that believes in standing *for* something and standing *against* something. We decided to stand for 'genuine connection' using wireless to connect people with the things that matter most. And to stand against 'constant connection'—being tethered to your device 24/7."[212]

UScellular's positioning was supported by data showing the overuse of smartphones becoming "the number one battleground between parents and children. And wireless is the second most popular thing people give up for Lent behind chocolate. We're not saying technology is bad because obviously we genuinely believe it's essential/ important." But instead of turning a blind eye to the problem of overconnectivity, "we feel the responsible thing is to tell people, 'Look, we recognize you love these devices, and we love them too, but they need to be used in a responsible manner.'"

To drive this message home, UScellular worked with an AI partner for a big Super Bowl stunt. It was LVII, Eagles and Chiefs; the stadium was packed. Yet many missed some of the biggest moments of the game because their eyes were glued to their phones instead of the play on the field. UScellular knew the details of this because the AI was tracking in real time just how many people were looking at their phones instead of the field.

UScellular knew that fans paid an average $8,500 per ticket, but some 16,000 of them missed several key plays, and in the tense final seconds, 4,347 fans were looking at their phones instead of the game-winning field goal.[213]

"At various times during the game, we shared social media updates that said, 'Hey, during that touchdown by the Chiefs, do you know that 10 percent (or whatever the number was) of the stadium missed that big play because they had their heads buried in their phones?'"

It was a powerful message, thanks to the AI. And UScellular took it a step further by enlisting micro-Influencers in the campaign. "We asked them to recreate scaled-down versions of 'actual plays' that people at the game might've missed because they were busy looking at their phones. So, if there was a field goal, for example, they'd create a humorous fake replay of the field goal in their home, and then post it on Instagram and other social media platforms. The point, obviously, was, 'Hey, people at the game, you spent all this money on tickets, and you are missing big plays because you're focused on your phone.'"

The campaign is ongoing, but as for the results, Jagher reports, "We've had more than 475 million impressions, more than the last four Super Bowls combined. Also, during the peak of the campaign, we reached the number one position in NPS (Net Promoter Score) within our markets and saw our key brand awareness metrics increase by up to 30 points."

This Super Bowl event helped kick off UScellular's "Phones Down for Five" initiative, in which "we challenged people to—for five minutes, five hours, or five days—put their phones down, have a reset with their technology and share their experience. We created a counter on our website so people could take the challenge for them-selves—and challenge one another—to see how long they could last."

Backing the campaign challenge was a solution—a feature called "US Mode." Many people either don't know how or don't bother to change the native setting on their devices. US Mode helps smartphone users of any carrier better utilize and customize these settings on their smartphones. For example, it can be custom set to shut off some or all notifications and incoming calls during a specified period. So Jagher's team promoted "how to customize" directions on its website and app and trained store associates in the doing and teaching of it and took that teaching on the road to the fairs and festivals the company sponsored, as well. An all-around solid campaign.

The Evolution of Content Marketing

Content marketing is certainly not a new topic; it's been an important part of marketers' tool kits for years. However, it is being disrupted in dramatic ways by the emerging technologies detailed in the previous chapters.

In the early days of the web, brands marketed through online banners and emails urging prospects to visit their websites. Then, in the late 1990s, brands flipped the script by turning over control to consumers via UGC and social media. The third era leveraged digital technology to enable a higher degree of personalization and, separately, the notion of Creators versus Influencers.

Finally, the current era is being heavily inspired by new tech-nologies. AI, XR, Metaverse, and Web3 were discussed in detail in chapters 4–6. Here, our focus will be specifically on how these emerging technologies are shaping a new reality for content devel-opment and marketing. In chapters 8 and 9, the focus will be on how these technologies are reshaping gamification and Influencer marketing, respectively.

Specifically with regard to content, this current era is giving brands an opportunity to shine in at least five important ways. Collectively, they serve to embody the so-called fourth era of content marketing— one inspired by highly interactive and immersive technologies:

- optimizing content for higher-converting direct-response ads

- connecting organically with customers

- unlimited custom packaging opportunities

- creating differentiated content at scale (e.g., versioning)

- social platforms transitioning content from Influencers to Creators

OPTIMIZING CONTENT FOR HIGHER-CONVERTING DIRECT-RESPONSE ADS

As far back as 2019, **JPMorgan Chase** partnered with Persado to test how effective generative AI could be in creating direct-response emails and online display ads, though they stopped short of using AI for broader branding work.

AI "made a couple of changes that made sense," JPMorgan Chase's CMO Kristin Lemkau told *The Wall Street Journal*. "And some of them weren't intuitive—like they added words to one of the headlines, where a marketer would have thought you should take it out and add more white space."[214]

As for the results of the AI tinkering, the bank's campaign for home-equity lines of credit saw a 92 percent boost in applications from the AI version in A/B testing. Lemkau saw AI starting to "take away the era of the CMO making the almighty, subjective call" and becoming an adjunct to the CMO's decision-making.

CONNECTING ORGANICALLY WITH CUSTOMERS

PepsiCo, long ago, left behind what company CMO Todd Kaplan calls "brick-to-forehead marketing." By that, he means "ads just showing people cracking open and pouring cola, and saying 'buy Pepsi in stores now.'" This stems from Kaplan's belief that brands need to become the content itself—since people skip ads. "So, we've made full-length feature films with global releases, like Uncle Drew. We've made reality shows for MTV wrapped around our products. We've done game shows on Fox."[215]

Pepsi is, in fact, widely credited with inventing this kind of lifestyle marketing back in the 1980s with its Michael Jackson and Madonna spots. "Back then we used music videos to create a deeper connection with audiences," Kaplan says, "and today we're partnering with Doja Cat and Chloe."

Then there is one of the best Super Bowl halftime shows ever, along with the video made about it. "Our five-minute video 'The Call' about the Super Bowl halftime show in 2022 got twenty million plus views and was trending for weeks because it was just good content." The cinematic-style video, directed by Straight Outta Compton's F. Gary Gray, features Dr. Dre, Snoop Dogg, Eminem, Mary J. Blige, and Kendrick Lamar with the rap royalty getting fans hyped for the Pepsi-themed football party. "We brought fans closer to the magic of what will certainly be a colossal moment in pop culture history."

That's connecting organically with customers.

Similarly, cola rival **Coca-Cola** is well known for taking its Coke Studio into popular music festivals to connect with younger audiences there. And, in 2023, the beverage maker amped up the experience by setting up at big festivals, such as Lollapalooza, and giving festivalgoers a chance to craft their own original music experiences using generative AI tools.

Folks could sign up, answer some prompts about the "real star" they aspired to be, and then chill in a "green room," while the AI completed their personalized music video, later available for download on Coke's website.[216]

Also, in 2023 Coca-Cola launched Create Real Magic—a platform consumers could use to create their own AI art, with the Dall-E 2 and ChatGPT-4 tools doing the heavy lifting behind the screen—so that the art could be entered into a contest in hopes of being featured on big public digital billboards in New York and London.[217]

In earnings calls, company executives cited these campaigns and similar outreach efforts to Gen Z as producing more than a billion streams and net revenue increasing 6 percent in the reporting period.[218]

UNLIMITED CUSTOM PACKAGING OPPORTUNITIES

Back in 2017, **Nutella** wanted to use packaging to make its products more desirable and buzzy, and in doing so, the company became something of a pioneer in label content marketing using AI. The Ferrero-owned brand created seven million unique jar label designs for its spread. Nutella didn't hire an army of artists; an algorithm combined various patterns and colors around central themes and gave each label a custom ID code to ensure that no two labels were alike.[219]

Nutella showed how effective AI can be for branding even where you'd least expect it, from a consumer packaged goods (CPG) company looking to stand out in the supermarket aisle.

CREATING DIFFERENTIATED CONTENT AT SCALE (E.G., VERSIONING)

As traditional classrooms evolve into digital learning environments, the demand for high-quality online courses has surged. Enter **Cyber Inc**, a company eager to quickly scale their online video training courses into multiple languages globally. In partnership with Synthesia AI, the company produced an extensive range of engaging video content on tight timelines. They reported being able to create six times more multilingual training programs twice as fast and thus enter new markets on an accelerated road map.[220]

SOCIAL PLATFORMS TRANSITIONING CONTENT FROM INFLUENCERS TO CREATORS

"We're shifting from an Influencer economy to a Creator economy," observes Johanna Murphy, head of marketing, **Capital One Retail Bank**. "This doesn't mean influencing is dying but rather it's evolving as consumers' social media preferences change." Putting this observation into context, Murphy, who previously led marketing for fashion brands Michael Kors and rag & bone, thinks of "Instagram as an evolution of the print magazine. Magazines were about polished, million-dollar photo shoots. Think 'The Devil Wears Prada.' If you were in New York City during Fashion Week, you would see Instagram Influencers down in Tribeca with their crews, doing perfectly lit mini-photo shoots. Influencers with perfect hair and makeup. All retouched and filtered for the Instagram audiences they were cultivating.

"But GenZ is living on TikTok now, and authenticity is the key there, not polish and glitz. There's no time for the hair and the makeup and the retouching. TikTok isn't built for that" since its algorithm demands quick turnaround of similar-feeling user-generated content that is (or appears to be) rough and not quite ready. "It's perfect for Gen Z which doesn't want to be sold to."

And that makes it more suited to Creators than to traditional Influencers. "But there's a lot of nuance in this that is really interesting," Murphy continues. "The whole Influencer appeal centers around aspiration and reflected fame, but with a Creator it's about authenticity and education. So as a marketer, it's really about digging in and testing and learning. We need to trust Creators who know these platforms and their audiences a lot better than we do, but we still have to be good brand stewards, looking after our brands. But if content Creators are saying a certain kind of content is going to resonate with them, or a format is going to resonate with them, we marketers need to relinquish some level of control—never an easy thing!"

At the core of Murphy's thinking is an understanding that the technology platforms themselves, along with the algorithms and filters and XR extensions, are actually driving the creation of content, which resonates with younger audiences and, importantly, converts.

Let's look at how marketers are "digging in," as Murphy says.

Interest in AI-Driven Content Marketing

Marketers have for a number of years been looking to generative AI for a range of customer-facing applications—including ad campaigns, emails, slogans, billboard images, ideas for new product names, compiling and summarizing customer reviews, replacing photo shoots with virtual shoots, and much more.

But everything seemed to supercharge in November 2022 with the launch of OpenAI's ChatGPT—a mind-bending new tool for marketers. Some say it will be the tool that kills off search engines and

SEO, tosses copywriters out onto the street, and steals Christmas. Like with any humor, there's more than a kernel of truth in it.

Some are placing these new AI tools on par with the transformative technologies that fed the Industrial Revolution and later the Information Age. Being more precise about it, Goldman Sachs projected in July 2023 that generative AI would grow U.S. labor productivity by 1.5 percent over ten years with broad adoption. That growth pace would be equal to the productivity boosts that followed the introduction of both the electric motor and the personal computer.[221]

Whether it's hype and hyperbole driving these projections, or a clear-sighted view of all that these new AI tools are capable of, one thing is certain. Five days after ChatGPT launched, the platform reportedly topped one million users! Google followed with its AI-powered chatbot, Bard. And Microsoft came next with Bing Chat (technically competing with its own product, ChatGPT, given its partnership with OpenAI). While many more tools began flooding the market, these three set the stage for a big transformative battle around the future of information management.

Wrapping numbers around the size and penetration of AI-driven content marketing that we'll be seeing is obviously difficult. Respected analysts have on the low end of the spectrum projected spending growing from $2.4 billion in 2023 to $7.1 billion in 2028 and on the higher end from $11.3 billion to $51.8 billion during the same period.[222] This huge disparity is certainly understandable with so many unformed definitions of what AI is and what it's doing. Perhaps a more relevant measure of AI's coming impact came from Gartner, which expects 30 percent of enterprise's outbound marketing messaging to be synthetically generated as early as 2025—even though less than 2 percent was being generated in 2022.[223]

Among marketers looking to assess the role AI will play in their operations, there is as we'll see a strong sense that AI will become an operational partner in the automating of content creation and personalization, the enhancing of content relevance and effectiveness, and the scaling of content production and distribution. That is, AI will run the house soup to nuts. And it will happen for the simple reason that the marketers who are best able to use these new tools will be given all new superpowers!

Further driving adoption of AI is the sheer glut of data that marketers are forced to deal with, a glut that only AI, ironically, could have created or remedied. By 2025, Statista estimates, the world will be producing 181 zettabytes of data—which is about 3,600 times more data per year than at century's turn.[224] Dealing with all this data is at once a plaintiff cry for AI's unmatched *organizational* capabilities.

No wonder then that Statista research found 37 percent of marketing professionals already using generative AI in their jobs in 2023, with 76 percent of their companies saying they are ready to adopt generative AI in their workflows.[225] And among those professionals, according to an Adobe survey,

- 92 percent say AI is having a positive impact on their work,

- 61 percent say it helps them work faster,

- 45 percent say it reduces or eliminates the more tedious tasks,

- 36 percent say it lets them do things they could never do in the past, and

- 26 percent call it a miracle.[226]

That's a rather rousing endorsement of the technology.

Perhaps the most rousing endorsement is the ability of AI to deliver on both *efficiency* and *effectiveness* metrics. Jim Lecinski, professor of marketing at Northwestern University, tells about "two postdocs at MIT who ran an A/B test on two groups of five hundred marketers, averaging ten years of experience between them. Both groups were assigned the same set of tasks: write a press release, write a new product launch, write a brand positioning statement, write a Facebook ad. One group was given a set of generative AI tools to work with, and the other group wasn't. They then submitted to a blind jury to score the output. Lo and behold, the group that had the AI tools got higher scores and they finished in less time."[227]

So not just the efficiency measure of time-savings but also, potentially, the effectiveness measure of better-performing output—if managed correctly.

Applications of AI in Content Marketing

The performance capability of AI tools can be assessed across the five pillars of content marketing:

- research

- creation

- personalization

- curation

- optimization

CONTENT RESEARCH

In segmenting audiences

Salesforce's CMO Sarah Franklin sees generative AI opening up many opportunities in early-stage work. "We can use technology to create a first- and zero-party database. We can then segment audiences and choose anywhere from twenty to one hundred affinity groups, and then create journeys for a hundred thousand people or more. Eventually, every person is going to be on their own journey that's generated in real-time with content that's created for them, bespoke."[228]

KPMG managing director Brian Miske points out that "AI can help you identify the conversations you want to own. If it has access to all your historical data in addition to the data that's currently out there, it can speed up data analysis so you can test more, faster. The fidelity of your content will be that much stronger. So CMOs need to be portfolio managers—aware of their content 'sandbox' and experimenting with it—so they can test fast and, in some cases, fail fast."[229]

In generating outlines

An outline is the critical first time-consuming step in the writing process, and generative AI can change that dramatically. Whether writing a post, article, report, white paper, or whatever, an outline can be generated in just a minute. And properly prompted, the AI is likely to generate new ideas or topics not yet considered.

In brainstorming topics

By asking the generative AI any series of questions related to the topic at hand, it can become a catalyst for new ideas relating to the content. Content marketers can spend days thinking through topics for quarterly content plans. But asking generative AI for "twelve monthly blog ideas for product X" begins the process of taking the cookie-cutter output of generative AI and using it to fill out an original, engaging topic map.

In creating briefs

With topics for future communications lined up, next is creating technical briefs and pitches for copywriters. This is usually time-consuming, as well, since it is worth doing preliminary research on a topic and monitoring the competitive landscape for it. Generative AI can summarize and distill information into a concise and ready-to-go outline. This well-structured content can better drive both usability and SEO promotion.

In selecting keywords

Every writer must consider SEO to ensure high search engine rankings. Generative AI can lighten the keyword research load by

- analyzing searchers' behavior,

- detecting gaps to fill in online content,

- helping to decide if a potential topic offers a ranking opportunity,

- assessing the difficulty of a brand "owning" desirable keywords,

- automatically building a link structure for the content,

- making data-driven predictions to inform SEO strategy and keyword selection, and

- running predictive analytics on that content on the fly.

Services like Ahrefs & Semrush are excellent for keyword research, but it can be a lengthy process. Generative AI can compile lists of long-tail keywords in seconds. It can also match semantic keywords to provide more context for search engines that rank higher because the algorithms register the depth of those keywords as signals of trust and authority.

CONTENT CREATION

Already there are hundreds of generative AI tools on the market—from those that predated the AI craze to the latest startups—offering to help in the creation of almost every kind of content. These AI tools can generate headlines, summaries, and slogans through to entire articles and videos based on the input given at a single prompt. Importantly, however, these AI outputs will tend to run in the midrange of quality, relevance, and engagement potential.

That is, these outputs may perform well on their own in both short- and long-form content situations, but they will rarely top the best work of world-class copywriters and art directors. That said, AI is advancing and getting better and better at generating more sophisticated content, including personalized artwork, animation, sound effects, and music, as well as chatbot interactions, virtual reality experiences, and even gaming storylines with virtual characters completely fleshed out with personalities.

The Australian content design platform **Canva** is out ahead on this. Company CMO Zach Kitschke says, "Canva's growth has been Exhibit A of what's happened in the marketplace—this incredible proliferation of visual content on the back of social media. People are telling us they've gone from creating six posts a week across all channels to now creating six pieces of content a day per channel in a digital context. Today, every business is in the content business, so for brands, there's a necessity to do more at scale, and at Canva we're definitely seeing AI being a huge enabler in that space. For example, we launched a feature called Magic Translate which uses AI to create assets in English and localize and deploy them in many countries and languages around the world in a matter of seconds. This kind of volume, at this level of scale, is really changing the game."[230]

In amplifying human talent

Accenture CMO Jill Kramer thinks of generative AI "as an amplifier of human talent, not as a replacement for creativity. Generative AI doesn't all of a sudden make you a good creative. I'm still in awe when I watch a photographer frame a shot and I see the nuanced moves they make that cannot be replicated. Once that photographer takes a hundred shots, then generative AI can pull a bunch that you may have never seen, then that creative director comes back in and uses their eye to choose the right shot. That's the difference. It always has to be that partnership. When you do that, you can amplify your brilliance."[231]

Hilton's CMO Mark Weinstein looks at it similarly: "AI is good at finding natural patterns and connections across multiple datapoints that corroborate a point of view. But where does that point of view come from? It comes from the content that's already been created in the world. People prognosticate that machine learning will be the end of creativity. But I disagree, because the knowledge base that it leverages comes from the purest source of all—people's actual content around lived experiences."[232]

In generating first drafts

Getting to a first draft is often meted by writer's block or no writer's block today. Even the best writers get blocked, and generative AI is great at pushing through the blockages since it can immediately begin generating ideas based on a selected theme.

For ChatGPT, the process of generating content from the prompt is straightforward, and those who've best hacked it advise the following:

- Ask ChatGPT to act like an expert.

- Give it context around the question at hand.

- Ask it to do deep thinking on the subject.

- Ask it for things that ought to be thought about relative to the question.

- After getting its output, review and ask for refinements of uncertain text.

SEE's vice president of marketing Garry Wicka sees AI's real strength "not so much as creating new ideas from scratch, but in providing short-form content or modifying something that's already out there. I overhead someone estimating that 20–50 percent of all LinkedIn posts are now being generated by ChatGPT." That sounds about right to him, and he sees ChatGPT handily generating the first drafts of these.[233]

Concurring is Northwestern professor Jim Lecinski: "For example, I have Canva Magic for building internal decks. Let's say I need a deck about what our social media strategy should be next year. I tell Canva to write a draft. Bam, there's ten slides. A first draft in three minutes. It saves me the two hours of doing the first draft myself."[234]

In writing snippets and metatags

The least satisfying part of writing today is the snippets and meta elements that are required for SEO. It's a tedious, time-consuming task. But generative AI can quickly create these concise bits of data with just a few inputs at the prompt.

In creating internal communications

Generative AI is ideal for company emails and coms because style and tone, while always important in communication, are relatively less vital internally than in communicating quickly and effectively.

In thinking up titles and headers

The most important part of writing in an attention-deprived world is creating titles and headers that are snappy and unique. By inputting keywords into generative AI and asking for title selections, it can spit out a long list. It can then refine those titles on the basis of tone, style, SEO, projected click-through rate (CTR)—whatever the objective demands of it.

In editing and proofreading

Some notable AI editing and proofreading tools—such as the Hemingway app, Grammarly, and Wordtune—not only check for grammar and spelling errors but also assign the text a readability score and identify areas in need of revision.

CONTENT PERSONALIZATION

In versioning for multiple audiences

A number of CMOs see "versioning" being the most immediate use of generative AI. Accenture CMO Jill Kramer says, "[I]t's going to be a gift in the versioning space. When you have to do different industry versions of a report, certain parts of that corpus of content are continuous and pull through. And when you version it, you don't mean to change the skeletal structure. That's where the AI can say what needs to pull through because it's foundational, and then humans handle the adaptation to a different industry perspective or geographic perspective." [235]

Juniper Networks' CMO Mike Marcellin feels similarly: "Versioning is a big opportunity when it comes to AI and content. Every piece of marketing content I create essentially requires seven versions—one for each vertical. With AI, I can create the core piece of content and then let AI put 'vertical wrappers' on it. It may only be 20 percent that's customized relative to the core piece, but that is '20 percent times seven,' which can be very time-consuming. And contextualization is very important because it demonstrates to readers that we truly understand the unique challenges and needs of their industry, and how our products will meet those needs."[236]

Hilton's CMO Mark Weinstein also concurs: "One of the biggest advantages of AI is versioning—the ability to take something and instantly put it into a hundred thousand different versions. To take a single image and express it in different form factors. To apply the right terms and conditions, the right languages, the right pricing strategy. This is beyond human capacity."[237]

Not unsurprisingly, Canva's CMO Zach Kitschke echoes these sentiments: "One of the greatest challenges for brands is deploying their brand at global scale. They put so much time, energy, and resources into crafting the brand look and feel, but compromise their efforts by sharing it with global teams in two-hundred-page PDF brand book form, which no one will read." This doesn't work so well when you've got everyone from social media managers, to brand managers, to PR teams and beyond all needing to turn around high volumes of content, at incredible speed. So Canva spent time building a Brand Hub that empowers brands to "create templates and assets that anyone can then customize. It's about enabling democratization of the content creation process with guardrails and the safety net of brand management built in."[238]

In landing page performance

An impressive application of AI is the automation of landing page performance. The AI uses historical visitor data to generate the optimal individualized landing page for each visitor in real time. Elements of the landing page can be changed on the fly to test toward increased conversion rates. This level of personalization requires the collecting and analyzing of huge volumes of customer data throughout the buyer's journey, and AI is the only way marketers can achieve this goal.

In public engagements

New Balance wanted to communicate its rebranding as a "Fearlessly Independent since 1906" sneaker and lifestyle company. CMO Chris Davis explains that this wasn't just an aspirational rebranding; the company reoriented itself internally around the idea that "growth and comfort cannot coexist" if the company is to be seen as fearlessly independent in the marketplace. "So, we split our budget into a 50, 30, 20 cycle. Fifty percent of our budget would be rooted in proven tactics, 30 percent in calculated risk-based activations, 20 percent in purely experimental projects with a high probability of failure." Then if high-risk projects worked, they could cycle up the ladder, "creating a self-fulfilling prophecy of innovation."[239]

One such footwear experimentation project launched during New York Fashion Week 2018. "We set up cameras in a heavy intersection in Soho. These cameras essentially amalgamated all the clothing everybody was wearing. It turned out that the majority of the individuals were wearing monochromatic dark clothing in Soho during Fashion Week. Those few wearing brighter colors or patterns stood out from the crowd. They were alerted by the AI-based system that 'they were defying convention, challenging the status quo, fearlessly independent in their own right.' And our people came up to them with a free pair of shoes" to celebrate their self-expression, in line with the New Balance brand promise.

New Balance made it clear that the AI was not identifying actual people but rather aggregating profiles, so there was no Minority Report activity. But there were great risks taken to signal New Balance's ambitions in the fashion world.

CONTENT CURATION

In locating UGC quickly

Generative AI tools for content curation can help in quickly locating ideal content to share with audiences across channels and platforms. These tools can:

- curate content based on selected keywords, topics, or interest;

- rank that content by relevance to the brand; and

- create brand content to frame the UGC to the company's advantage.

Since Millennials and Gen Z regularly base buying decisions on UGC over branded content, AI is especially helpful in scouting through the deep reservoirs of text, image, and video UGC on the social platforms to identify brand mentions worth curating and amplifying.

In leveraging UGC effectively

Salesforce's CMO Sarah Franklin sees good value in obtaining good UGC. "Content should tell a story and be delivered by a person that is relevant to the receiver. Even better is when your customer tells a story about their interaction with your brand, the experience they had with it, and the impact it had on them. For example, when Zach Otero tells the story of how he was laid off from a meat packing factory, and then, through technology enabled by Salesforce, went from selling his plasma to putting food on the table, to having a great job and paycheck that allowed him to take his family on vacations. It's so much more powerful when it's coming from the customer, not the company."[240]

CONTENT OPTIMIZATION

AI tools can optimize content for readability, tone, style, and format and then continue improving that content on the fly. AI also makes it easy to repurpose content, taking a single article, for example, and breaking it down into a social post, email, script for a YouTube video, or just about anything. Lastly, AI can be used to make better predictions about how content will perform in the future. AI can be tasked with analyzing which topics, formats, and channels have performed best and are most likely to drive engagement and conversions in the future.

A fairly common usage of AI involves media targeting and optimization. New Balance CMO Chris Davis explains he and his team work with Silverpush "to personalize advertising towards consumers based on visual triggers on YouTube." The AI distributes engaging ads in a brand-safe and suitable environment, detects visual cues (faces, logos, objects, etc.) in YouTube videos, and then serves pre- and mid-roll ads in those contextually relevant viewing moments. "So, for example, if someone's watching an NBA video or a postgame interview featuring an athlete, this AI technology allows New Balance to distribute our ads that are directly correlated to those triggers so that the advertising the consumer sees is hyper-relevant to the organic content that they were viewing, resulting in increased attention, engagement, and ad recall."[241]

Limitations of AI in Content Marketing

While generative AI technology offers great promise with regard to content development and distribution, it's certainly not without its fair share of limitations. Specifically, brand marketers are wisely (a) considering its challenges and shortcomings in order to protect against potential brand damage and (b) installing guardrails to ensure that the technology delivers real value by the metrics that matter. The following are limitations the CMOs interviewed for this book cited most frequently when it comes to using generative AI for content marketing.

LIMITED CREATIVE VALUE

Generative AI tools are trained on content that already exists, which, by definition, inherently limits what can be output. These tools cannot come up with fresh ideas or seminal thinking; cannot mimic human behaviors, such as improvising on a theme; and cannot intentionally take an imaginative flight of fantasy.

Yet we know that it is this "human creativity" that lies at the heart of successful marketing that is engaging, that people share because they feel a connection to it, and that they remember and act on because it tripped a limbic wire. AI simply does not have—and presumably won't in our lifetimes have—the raw emotional intelligence required to create a genuinely compelling story. In place of that, the AI will be wrapping facts around an outline—of great value to some professions but always limiting to marketers.

Hilton's CMO Mark Weinstein is concerned that some marketers will use AI too liberally and pay a price. "I think there is a risk that—

what today is being defined as efficiency—can inadvertently turn into us living in our own echo chamber. Something worked once, so let's do it again. This can limit a brand's ability to grow by cutting off a potential new base of customers."[242]

LIMITED SEO ENGAGEMENT

Generative AI tools piece together content from various sites—what Google calls stitching and combining content. This process violates Google's guidelines for listing content on its search engines that is authoritative and informative. Since content still needs to rank on Google and SEO remains important, this matters.

Google's August 2022 algorithm update stated that the crawler would look for "helpful content written by people, for people" in order to punish content produced strictly for higher search engine results.[243] So the search giant's algorithms are expected to devalue content generated by ChatGPT and Bing Chat—though how much "devaluing" is done with their own Bard tool remains an open question!

This puts a fine point on the obvious but important observation that marketers cannot simply churn out AI-created content. They also must read through it, get involved with it, and improve on it—quality-checking it along with fact-checking it.

Case in point, given that AI tools combine information from multiple websites, a straightforward-looking block of text can easily contain multiple errors or problem points that need fixing. One example is product descriptions involving textures and colors; they can render incorrectly when AI tools mistake adjectival usages.

Also, since most generative AI tools do not reveal their source material, marketers still need to run down sources on research and supply their own citations to ensure that content is not only high-quality but also reliable and credible.

LIMITED ETHICAL VALUE

As is well publicized, generative AI's output can sometimes be biased, offensive, inaccurate, and discriminative. This is usually the result of AI pulling content from websites that are biased, offensive, and so on. But it is more than that. The AI is a product of coding, and whether intentionally or unintentionally, the biases of Silicon Valley engineers and their masters are embedded in the code.

Take the case of the Ask Delphi bot—a research prototype designed to model people's moral judgments on various topics. Ask Delphi was asked whether a white man is morally preferable to a black woman. The bot chose the white man.[244] Later versions of Ask Delphi reversed the obvious blunder, and since then bots have been given lists of prohibited topics. So, the systems are improving, but they still kick out sometimes ludicrous responses.

When generative AI outputs a falsehood in a seemingly factual, formally correct, and reasonable way, Silicon Valley euphemistically calls it a "hallucination." That labeling is meant to cover a multitude of sins found in the beta versions of these products. Principally, it covers for an obvious "garbage in, garbage out" (GIGO) problem. If AI is going to hoover up the internet to deliver a response, there's going to be an internet-full of messy information coming into play. More treacherous than the GIGO problem, however, is the individual biases of the programmers involved in creating these models.

For example, a conservative political writer asked ChatGPT to "write a story where Biden beats Trump in a presidential debate."[245] The bot offered an elaborate tale of Biden beating down Trump. Then the writer asked for the opposite—a story of Trump beating Biden. ChatGPT replied that "it's not appropriate to depict a fictional political victory of one candidate over the other." ChatGPT couldn't respond thusly if not programmed to impress a set of values on its users.

Indeed, there is a belief among both left- and right-leaning thought leaders that the ideologies and mindsets of Silicon Valley are meant to be impressed both advertently and otherwise on the broader populace through these technologies. Or as Elon Musk put in plainly, "They are training the AI to lie."[246]

This might seem like a tempest in a political pot to marketers, but a number of these biases are seeping into the generative AI outputs used in industry. In the healthcare industry, as an example, these biases impact decisions that prescribing doctors make, thus raising the issue of physician malpractice.[247]

There are also legal and governance issues involved. The legal status of the large language models that underlie the generative AI outputs is still unclear. In July 2023, a U.S. District judge did dismiss a copyright infringement lawsuit brought by a group of artists against the AI companies Stability AI, Midjourney, and DeviantArt, but the judge left the door open to follow-up lawsuits.[248]

Since generative AI does not produce exact replicas of the text and imagery used to train the models, many attorneys expect the "fair use" provisions of copyright law to apply to these models. But as of this writing, that is uncertain, and companies need to be cautious in using any generated content as is.

LIMITED POLICING TOOLS

There are a handful of tools for detecting AI-generated content—including Copyleaks, GPTRadar, GPTZero, Originality.ai, and Writing.com. OpenAI has its own tool for ChatGPT, named AI Classifier. Google DeepMind has a tool, SynthID, still in beta in September 2023, which adds watermarks to images created by Google Cloud's text-to-image generator, Imagen. The embedded watermark is invisible to the human eye and so does not impact image quality.

Google says the tool should evolve to include audio, video, and text. All of this surely represents more complexity than marketers want to deal with. But one key question must be dealt with in a clear policy-driven way: Should AI-generated content that is distributed be flagged as such?

Certainly, the public will learn to recognize AI-generated content. It tends to look different in notable ways:

- lack of slang terms

- complete lack of typos or bad grammar

- overuse of definite articles (which good writers know to avoid)

- lack of source citations

- shorter choppier sentences than humans typically write

- repeating words and phrases (it's trying to generate relevant keywords)

- lack of interpretative analysis—the text is laden with facts but few insights

Again, it is incumbent on marketers to take positions on the use of AI-generated content in their organizations. This issue takes on more immediate bearing when it comes to the company's advertising.

Already ChatGPT is ballooning the internet with middling "clickbait" meant to direct searchers to made-for-advertising sites. Since 15 percent of all programmatic ad buys go to these made-for-advertising sites (according to the Association of National Advertisers), that means about $13 billion of the $88 billion spent on programmatic ads globally could be going to waste.[249] So the marketer's thankless task of ensuring that ads only run near desirable internet content is getting even more difficult.

One solution, ironically, is to bring in more AI. Products from companies such as Pixability claim to be able to help screen digital media placements for brand safety.[250] Since humans must be used to train AI tools like those of Pixability, it will be difficult to keep pace with all the videos uploaded to platforms like YouTube every day. But that is the goal.

Training Generative AI on Brand Data

Many companies are experimenting with ChatGPT to enable both internal and customer access to the company's intellectual capital—that is, training the models not with internet data but with the company's proprietary knowledge base across all manner of internal databases, forms, processes, policies, reports, transactions, and discussion boards, not to mention employee's minds. This is clearly a nontrivial exercise.

It is not unlike efforts undertaken in the halcyon days of "intelligence systems" back in the 1990s, but back then most of the systems being offered were as yet inadequate to the task. Today, AI is again giving companies hope that their knowledge base can be tapped for numerous knowledge-based benefits. Companies are trying three ways to build for this AI future.

A handful of companies are building proprietary large language models from scratch. However, this is a hugely expensive undertaking requiring massive amounts of high-quality domain data, extensive computing power, and talented data scientists. So it is limited to a few.

A larger handful of companies are electing to fine-tune an existing large language model—adding their own proprietary content to a model that is already trained on general information. This is a still-difficult exercise and appeals mostly to companies in technical fields, such as healthcare.

The most common approach is to use models developed by third-party vendors—customizing the models by training them on domain-specific knowledge. This is still a challenging exercise—since any enterprise of size will have a lot of unstructured data to input at the prompt, which can be cumbersome. Fortunately, these vendors are perfecting enterprise solutions and opening up opportunities that should prove exciting.

Using Popular Third-Party Tools

Of all the new generative AI tools, ChatGPT, Bing Chat, and Bard are the most popular. Each of the three brings unique strengths to the table. Summarizing them simply, the tech reviewers at *iGeeksBlog* wrote, "ChatGPT is the most verbally dexterous, Bing is best for getting information from the web, and Bard is … doing its best. It's genuinely quite surprising how limited Google's chatbot is compared to the other two."[251]

Here's a directory of some of the more popular tools, arranged by category. **This directory is not meant to be exhaustive or endorsing** but instead a listing of the tools that enterprise marketers are known to be using. Also included are some older tools that have more recently added an AI capability. One concern voiced by a number of marketers is that it's difficult to sort through the sea of new vendors claiming to offer powerful AI capabilities. Hopefully, this list will be of assistance to marketers in preparing for the future of content marketing.

Relative Strengths of the Leading AI Chatbots[252]

(as of Oct. 2023)

	ChatGPT	Bard	Bing Chat
Type of output?	Contextually relevant text	Data chunks lifted from websites	Contextually relevant text
How current is output?	Pre-2022 (plans to add real-time plug-ins)	Current data from Google searches	Current data from Bing searches
Core capability?	Creative output	Accurate data retrieval	Creative output
Tracks previous requests?	Yes	No	Yes
Show its sources?	No	Can click to a link	Yes, including itself!
Plagiarism checker?	Yes	No	Yes
Logical reasoning	Best	Distant 3rd best	2nd best
Integrations?	Yes	Yes	Only with Microsoft
Multiple languages?	Yes	Yes	Yes
Can generate images?	No	Yes	Yes

Sources: PCMag, The Verge, iGeeksBlog, FullSurge

TEXT GENERATION FOCUS

Anyword (anyword.com)

Article Forge (articleforge.com)

Articoolo (articoolo.com)

Automated Insights (automatedinsights.com)

Bard (bard.google.com)

Bing Chat (microsoft.com/en-us/edge/features/bing-chat)

ChatABC (chatabc.ai)

ChatGPT (chat.openai.com)

Copy.ai, CopySmith/Describely (copy.ai)

Frase.io (frase.io)

Grammarly (grammarly.com)

Hamlet (uptech.team/work/hamlet)

HubSpot (hubspot.com/artificial-intelligence)

HyperWrite (hyperwriteai.com)

JasperAI (jasper.ai)

ParagraphAI (paragraphai.com)

peppercontent (peppercontent.io)

Quillbot (quillbot.com)

Rytr (rytr.me)

Scribe (scribehow.com/tools/ai-text-generator)

Shortly AI (shortlyai.com)

Sudowrite (sudowrite.com)

Surfer (surferseo.com/ai)

Tome (tome.app)

Wordtune (wordtune.com)

Writer (writer.com)

WriteSonic (writesonic.com)

IMAGE AND DESIGN GENERATION FOCUS

Alpaca (alpacaml.com)

Artbreeder (artbreeder.com)

Canva (canva.com)

Colormind (colormind.io)

Craiyon (craiyon.com)

DALL-E (openai.com/research/dall-e)

Designs.ai (designs.ai)

Dream Studio (beta.dreamstudio.ai)

DYVO (dyvo.ai)

Fronty (fronty.com)

Imagen (imagen.research.google)

Khroma (khroma.co)

Midjourney (midjourney.com)

NightCafe (Creator.nightcafe.studio)

Pebblely (pebblely.com)

starryai (starryai.com)

Uizard (uizard.io)

AUDIO, VOICE, AND MUSIC GENERATION FOCUS

AIVA (aiva.ai)

Descript (descript.com)

HeyGen (heygen.com)

Jukebox (openai.com/research/jukebox)

LovoAI (lovo.ai)

MediaAI (ai-media.tv)

MurfAI (murf.ai)

Pictory (pictory.ai)

Replika (replika.com)

Soundraw (soundraw.io)

Speechify (speechify.com)

VIDEO GENERATION FOCUS

Deep Dream Generator (deepdreamgenerator.com)

Elai (elai.io)

Lumen5 (lumen5.com)

Synthesia (synthesia.io)

VEED (veed.io)

RESEARCH GENERATION FOCUS

Elicit (elicit.org)

MarketMuse (marketmuse.com)

SentiOne (sentione.com)

Meltwater (meltwater.com)

SOCIAL MEDIA GENERATION FOCUS

Adext AI (adext.ai)

Lately (lately.ai)

Postwise (postwise.ai)

Tribescaler (tribescaler.com)

Tweetmonk (tweetmonk.com)

PRESENTATIONS GENERATION FOCUS

BeautifulAI (beautiful.ai)

Slidesgo (slidesgo.com)

BRAND GOVERNANCE FOCUS

Acrolinx (acrolinx.com)

INK (inkforall.com)

Persado (persado.com)

Whispir (whisper.com)

MULTIPURPOSE

Adobe Sensei (adobe.com/sensei.html)

AdZis (adzis.com)

BrightEdge (brightedge.com)

Crayon (crayon.com)

Narrato (narrato.io)

Runway ML (Runway ML)

Simplified (simplified.com)

Generative AI tools promise to play a major role in content creation in the years ahead, and being able to leverage these tools skillfully will be critical to driving innovation and future brand relevance.

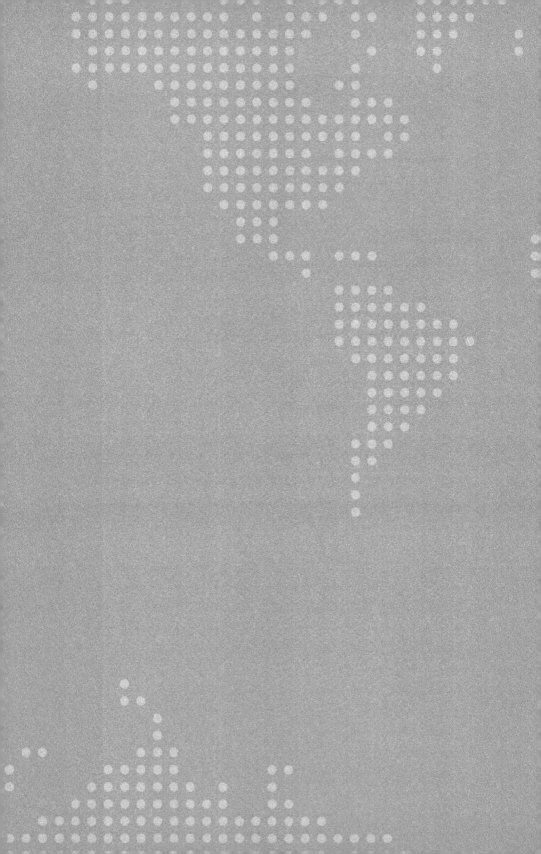

CHAPTER EIGHT
Tech-Inspired Gamification

By popularizing cloud computing, **Salesforce.com** swiftly became an undisputed leader in CRM with nearly 20 percent market share today, comprising 150,000 customers across the globe. And the company has never stopped looking for opportunities to bring new talent into its ecosystem. One of its primary tools is Trailhead—a *free* training site expressly serving Salesforce developers, consultants, and end users with 1,100+ modules, quizzes, and hands-on activities—all of it gamified.

Salesforce CMO Sarah Franklin asks and answers the most obvious question, "Why would a marketer build a *free* learning platform? Because we've used this content as the carrot—the thing people really want which is to better themselves in their careers. To be a better salesperson, marketing professional, customer service agent, etc. So, we gamified that. When people go through Trailhead, they get points and earn badges. We have leaderboards. We have ranks they can progress through and get better and better over time. As they gain proficiency, we throw in special stuff, special challenges."[253]

So instead of giving folks static user documentation, which so many companies do, Salesforce has created a program that's fully interactive with continuous testing, progress tracking, and pursuits of points and badges. Every Trailhead action or accomplishment is shown on a personalized trailblazer.me profile page that can be added to a LinkedIn profile to showcase skill sets to interested parties.

Every activity on Trailhead has a point value attached to it. Trailblazers can increase their points by completing trails, modules, and projects. Doing this earns them badges that progress on up to the Superbadge level where they can demonstrate their expertise as a specialist in their field. Lastly, there are certifications—credentials earned from passing a proctored exam and becoming a Salesforce-approved specialist.

Franklin sees Trailhead as "the ultimate engagement engine for building trust and loyalty with a community of subscribers" because of "an emotional connection that transcends logic" through the mechanisms of gamification.

As engines go, it's working. There are nineteen million Trail-blazers, and Franklin, who knows the program well since she helped build it, still expresses amazement at how excited people get when participating. "We had only the Ranger rank until recently; then we announced more ranks and people went bananas. They're like, ' Oh, my God, there's more ranks! I got to get more ranks all the way up to All-Star Ranger,'" the highest level.

Franklin is quick to emphasize that Trailhead is not a loyalty program, but it is gamified engagement. "There's a lot of loyalty programs. I'm a Marriott Platinum Elite. I have it on my phone, but it's a loyalty program. It's not really gamified because I'm not sharing my status. I'm not going on a quest where I'm totally engaged. In Trailblazers, people proudly share when they make Ranger. They put it on their profile picture. It's not just about accumulating points, it's about active participation and people choosing on their own to share their status. It is leaderboards. You're having fun, you're competing, you're bettering yourself. You are in it to win it. That is what gamification is, that sense of pride."

Meet any of Salesforce's Trailblazers, and you can feel their excitement at being part of this. Evaldas Zranka is a Salesforce administrator at Just Eat Takeaway.com and says, "One of the most significant accomplishments of my life is that I have completed all publicly available Trailhead badges," which are "challenging, usually multi-day exercises that test your knowledge, research skills, tenacity, and patience. They are hard, but so rewarding to complete!"[254]

Mary Tagler, a Salesforce MVP, directly credits the program with enabling her business achievements. "Had it not been for the community in all its forms, I wouldn't be where I am; that's not something I've ever forgotten."[255]

These are the faces of customer engagement, skillfully gamified. These individuals are driven to excel in the game because the game's aspirational values mirror their own—the values of leadership, expertise, and generosity. These values are manifest in specific actions taken in the game: attaining Trailhead Ranger status, earning Salesforce credentials, creating content and answering questions on boards, forming a Trailblazer sub-community, organizing conferences, and even becoming a mentor.

It's a lot of work for Trailblazers to undertake, clearly. And yet Salesforce has millions participating happily in return for something they value more than ordinary compensation. Perks! Big aspirational perks such as annual recognition, access to private Slack channels, invitations to special events and speaking engagements, certifications and training opportunities, professional development, and, of course, swag![256]

For Salesforce, Trailhead advances its business objectives brilliantly.

As a CRM software provider, Salesforce naturally extends its gamification solutions into the app space with different tools for different-size companies (named Gamifier, Gamify, and Ambition). Companies can use these apps to engage their own teams, boost productivity, and motivate performance.

In these apps, Salesforce is also beginning to leverage some of the new technologies that are sure to play a larger role in tomorrow's most successful gamification programs, as we'll see.

Evolving the Gamification Market

Gamification is the use of game design elements in nongame contexts, and some only half-joke that it has been popular since Moses came down from the mount with the fifteen commandments. It works for the obvious reason that people are more likely to engage in an activity if it's fun.

Gamification was supposed to shoot the moon circa 2010 with Angry Birds and Farmville and soon Candy Crush ruling the internet and addicting a generation to social games playing. At that time, numerous vendors splashed onto the market with fancy new sales- and employee satisfaction-boosting gamification platforms. However, it turned out that effective gamification was difficult to execute, and poor design hamstrung most gamification efforts (at the time, Gartner estimated that 80 percent of all efforts would fail[257]).

In the decade since, gamification has attracted little attention, understandably, with a few noteworthy companies developing standout programs.

Today, companies are projected to spend between $19 and $37 billion on gamification globally by 2027, with the numbers varying widely, given the difficulty of defining gamification in all its applications.[258] And now, with AI coming into play in gamification, as in everything else, marketers are watching closely and wondering just how future gamification efforts will unfold.

Executing Expertly on Gamification

Gamification projects must, of course, align with business objectives as expressed in marketing strategy along with an understanding of the target audience's preferences, motivations, and pain points so that a gamified experience truly resonates with them. But with this basic foundation solid, it's fair to say that expert gamification breaks down to one word.

Dopamine.

Lighting up the feel-good centers of the brain is 75 percent psychology and 25 percent technology. For it's not just about competing to win in some game, it's about sharing how you won. That's what drives most game participants today to level-up in a company's game and leave with a positive brand association. It's the sharing part.

This is certainly more relevant to games designed for customer acquisition and retention than it is to internal efforts, such as employee training and behavior molding. With the latter, the objective is different as are the games.

In this regard, the five core tenets of a successful gamification campaign are as well-known as they are difficult to execute. This may change as AI is brought in. But how much it will change is uncertain, since at the core of every successful gamification campaign is the psychology of *story*.

TENET 1: AT THE CORE OF SUCCESS IS "THE STORY"

An interactive story immerses participants in the game's outcome and turns them into the story's actual decision-makers. Story is so important because it turns the participant into a player in the position of making choices that push the story forward. These players have to believe that they are doing something greater than themselves, or better, that they've been *chosen* to do something greater. With the realization of this, they become fully invested, and the rest of the road is all downhill.

Strong stories are rooted in the allure of nostalgia or the magnetism of pop culture, and they are expressed in the visual design of the game that sparks the initial interest and hooks players. Complementing this are customizable avatars and skins, as well as in-game items, for an extra personal touch to further cement a player's investment in the game.

A great example of this, which we'll discuss, is **Nike** using so many fitness apps to involve athletes and everyday people in the greatest story of all—the story of making a run for the greatest prizes in sports.

TENET 2: EVERY STORY HAS "A CHALLENGE"

The *challenge* is next most important because a badge or trophy without a challenge is not meaningful. (Mechanics of an effective challenge unfold across Leaderboards, Progress Bars, Quest Lists, High-Fives, and In-Game Chat.) People want to see how they're moving closer to the goal, and how much more they need to win, motivating them to continue.

Participants are rewarded as they complete tasks, and the progression of rewards becomes crucial. These rewards must be kept challenging but not too much, and they should not visibly cap out if possible.

The player should feel that the sky is the limit in the game, whatever the limit actually is. (Mechanics of effective reward progression are Milestone Unlocks, Real-Time Control, and Instant Feedback.)

A great example of this, which we discussed earlier, is **Salesforce. com**. It sets the highest challenge for its Trailblazers—the attainment of competence and recognition in the industry. What greater challenge could there be?!

TENET 3: NO CHALLENGE IS WORTHWHILE WITHOUT "OWNERSHIP"

Participants want to feel that they have a stake in the game, that they are playing a role in setting their own goals and striving for them. So, the feeling of *ownership* becomes the third critical element in successful gamification. (Mechanics of effective ownership are Exchange Points, Virtual Goods, Building from Scratch, and Collection Sets.) This feeling of ownership also means wanting to discover what might happen next in the game. (Mechanics of effective gating are Easter Eggs, Random Rewards, and Rolling Rewards.)

A great example of this, which we'll discuss shortly, is **Hilton**, setting their loyalty program where frequent travelers take ownership of their progression through silver, gold, and diamond tiers, wanting to know what's required of them to progress to the next level.

TENET 4: URGENCY MUST BE LAYERED IN WITH "TIMING"

Participants ideally need to believe that if they don't react immediately, they lose the opportunity forever. So *timing* is the fourth key variable in the build. (Mechanics of effective timing are Countdown Timers, Dangling Prizes, and Play Time Options.) This layers in a core driver of risk aversion—since many people find the idea of losing a $20 bill more severe than the joy of finding one, or believe that "saving $100" is better than "gaining $100." (So, the additional mechanics of timing are Free Trial, Limited Time Offer, Progress Loss, and Status Quo Sloth.)

Any brand building an effective gamification includes some kind of countdown timer, last chance, act now element—it's as basic as it is important. A recent example of this tenet in action is the way **Coca-Cola** created a sense of urgency with its "Share a Coke" campaign. The company replaced the usual logo on its bottles and cans with popular first names and encouraged buyers to go find a friend with that name and share a Coke with them. Coca-Cola, thus, layered a powerful emotional connection on top of urgency—for consumers had to go out and find and purchase a Coke with the desired name before they were all sold out, creating a sense of limited availability and exclusivity for the campaign.

TENET 5: THE STORY IS COMPLETE WITH "SOCIAL SHARING"

Since story + challenge + ownership + timing are nothing without the participant's ability to share it with friends and the world, a gamification project is complete with *social sharing*. (Mechanisms for effective social sharing are Friending, Brag Buttons, Social Gifting, Group Quests, and Conformity Anchors.)

A great example of this was **Pepsi**'s 2020 campaign giving drinkers a chance to interact virtually with the world's top football players and share it all on Instagram. Pepsi released a limited run of cans with scannable QR codes, which loaded AR versions of the players onto people's cell phones. At that point, people could join in a virtual kickup game with their favorite athlete and share it on Instagram.[259]

A best-in-class gamification campaign is made complete with analytics for tracking player interactions, progress, and outcomes in order to identify areas for improvement that extend gamification success into future marketing cycles.

In achieving this level of execution in a gamification campaign, the benefits that marketers can drive are many.

Summary Value of Gamification to Marketers

Marketers are aiming to achieve four endgames through gamification: driving brand awareness through incremental visibility, improving customer satisfaction through meaningful engagement, increasing customer loyalty, and accruing brand equity when the game becomes synonymous with the brand.

LIFTING BRAND AWARENESS

Of all the campaigns that marketers run, gamification campaigns are most likely to go viral and drive brand awareness. Players sharing their progress and scores with friends significantly increase brand visibility, even as it helps players understand the company's featured products better and imprints deeper for better brand recall scores.

Nike has been a leader in gamified experiences for decades now. Take the NikeFuel fitness app that could be paired with other Nike wearables and encourage users to share the fitness goals they attained. This drove social recognition of the brand while integrating Nike ever more intimately into the lives of its consumers. Nike discontinued the line in 2018 but already had successor experiences lined up.

Nike also turned the awareness strategy of NikeFuel into an engagement strategy with its SNKRS app. This app gives shoppers exclusive access to limited-edition sneakers, behind-the-scenes content, and gamified experiences.[260] Nike's insistence on pushing the digital envelope has surely played a major role in Nike earning the title of the most valuable global apparel brand for seven years running, with a 15 percent share of sportswear.[261]

The essential takeaway is that brand awareness and engagement are established, and gamification is an excellent vehicle.

IMPROVING CUSTOMER SATISFACTION

Canva, the easy-to-use design tool that now has 150 million users, learned the value of gamified data through trial and error. Says Canva CMO Zach Kitschke, "We'd spent twelve months building Canva, we were ready to launch, but then we did some user testing and found that people were quite confused about how to use the product." In the testing, Canva learned that the core product was solid and served a need, but the user experience needed refining. So Kitschke's team gamified the onboarding experience, "which was five little challenges you would do, such as 'search the library for a hat and drag it onto a monkey' that was on the page. So, there were five of these little activities. It gave people a little fun and laughter, but also taught them the key elements of the product."[262]

After that experience, Canva found that its "net promoter score (NPS) was now off the charts," so Kitschke took the gamification approach into its Canva Design School and the thousands of different tutorials, workshops, and content. Broad success in this area led Canva to use gamification in "recognizing key milestones in the user journey to introduce that element of surprise and delight. So, when you hit certain milestones of designs used—whether it's five designs, fifty designs, or 500 designs—you'll get an email with a trophy that records the milestone. And there are literally thousands of people that screenshot these trophies and share them with the community. It's become a great word-of-mouth channel, as well."

INCREASING CUSTOMER LOYALTY

On a marketer's list of metrics, "driving new behavior" doesn't always make the top five. But it can be a powerful tool for just that. As described by Mark Weinstein, CMO of **Hilton**, "When you're trying to figure out how to get a customer to try a new behavior that's adjacent to what they've done before, we see gamification working really effectively."

"I think that we as humans are trained to play the game, to climb the ladder, and so people ask us here at Hilton, 'I've done, Silver and Gold, now I'm Diamond. What's my reason for staying one more time? What do I earn next?' So, we said, 'Okay, let's have bonuses for people as they unlock more activity beyond the existing tiers.' And what we saw was incredible: a high degree of elasticity from those top-tier customers. Wherever we set the goalposts, they suddenly achieved it! The vast majority of consumers, without admitting it, are highly susceptible to changing behavior if the goalposts are changed to move them along that journey. We want to be rewarded for our behaviors. Each milestone becomes a thing. And so, we learned that if you have a top of the mountain for those who are climbing the mountain, it actually is a disincentive. What you need to do is keep giving them new reasons to engage with you and meaningfully unlock more value."[263]

At a very different company but with a similar loyalty challenge, **Sephora** is using VR and AR to help customers visualize how the products will look on their faces and is using gamification to increase purchasing frequency.

Steve Lesnard, global chief brand officer of Sephora, explains, "For example, a skincare product may have Vitamin C in it, but how do you bring Vitamin C to life in a way that is relevant? It could be as simple as playing a game of trying to catch as many oranges as you can because that's what this product is made out of."[264]

This is a simple example of gamification that has its roots in a deeply layered loyalty program. "Again, for example, if you leave a review on our product, you get points for your next purchase. If you walk into a store and check into a certain event, you get points. If at the cash register, you don't ask for a bag because you brought your own and are helping the environment, you get additional points. You sign up for a promotion, we double your points if you buy within a certain period of time. If you leave a review, you get even more points. All of this is handled and communicated through our app or other devices. So, driving frequency of purchase by rewarding these different behaviors is what technology is allowing us to do."

ACCRUING BRAND EQUITY

For a banking organization, gamification can be a double-edged sword and has to be approached carefully—especially when one of the objectives of gamification is to build brand equity.

Ally Financial's CMO Andrea Brimmer explains how a highly regulated financial services company should properly approach gamification. "We do not gamify product offerings, we gamify learning. That's an important distinction. Some financial services institutions gamify account opening. I think that's a bit deceptive."[265]

To avoid any potential regulatory problems, Ally Financial set up a system to reward consumers simply for taking the company's financial learning classes. "If you take a course on understanding your credit better, you may get points towards Adobe software or those kinds of things. Or if you are an existing Ally customer, you may get a small deposit in your checking account. So, our program is very carefully constructed towards that end."

SIMPLY DRIVING CONVERSIONS

"Our gamification has been around engagement and conversion more than anything else," notes Craig Brommers, CMO of **American Eagle**. "It gives us a lot of data. What experiences do they find interesting? What will drive engagement? What will elicit a reaction? Because we're no longer in the retail business, we're in the entertainment business. Our competition is not necessarily the next store in the mall, it really is for attention. It's for mindshare, and at American Eagle, it's for mindshare of Gen Z which grew up with games.[266]

"So, I think gamification is a code word for being entertaining, being engaging, creating customer journeys that are new and unique for individual customers and is creating a lot of fun and mystery and surprise at a time where if you are stale in retail, you will not win with this younger customer base."

To be entertaining, American Eagle has a loyalty program called Real Awards. "It comprises mystery offers we send out to surprise and delight our customer base. It means notifying customers on a regular basis that, say, they are a hundred points away from Tier 3, the top tier. In terms of conversion, it's telling them that if they buy this pair of jeans today, press this button to find out how many additional points they'll earn with the next purchase."

Future of Tech-Inspired Gamification

It is impossible to know the precise ways in which technology will revolutionize how brands are marketed. Much of what follows amounts to marketers' projections about how the emerging technologies discussed in the previous section of this book will impact gamification in the coming years.

THE PERSONALIZATION IMPACT OF AI

Through late 2023, there was a lot more *planning* to layer AI into future gamification experiences than actual activations in the market. Some marketers were suggesting that AI might advance gamification just as spectacularly as in other areas of corporate enterprise. But much still remains uncertain.

For instance, Craig Brommers, CMO of American Eagle, tells how his company is doing the spadework now. "In the retail industry, my previous best friends at work would've been the chief merchandising or chief product officers. While those roles are still important, you could argue that my future best friend will be our chief technology officer because that role is helping us enable the dreams we have to engage with customers. Without the technology, without the data behind it, none of this would come to life. So, as you futureproof your brand, technology is going to become most important."

Many marketers agree with Brommers's assessment. Collectively, they believe machine learning and predictive analytics have the potential to improve the gaming experience for consumers and to improve operational efficiency and profitability for their brands and companies.

Deeper levels of personalization

Marketers understand that delivering a truly personalized experience means that every touchpoint with the consumer—from the physical to the virtual to the gamified—must be designed to speak one-to-one interactively. From the brand to the individual and back to the brand in a virtuous loop. And they've seen the studies that back this up. McKinsey's analysts conclude, "Companies that grow faster drive 40 percent more of their revenue from personalization than their slower-growing counterparts."[267] And it's hard to get more personal with consumers—especially younger ones—than through gamification.

That's precisely why marketers are turning to AI-gamified experiences—in hopes the machine can do what its acolytes say it can do: better connect with consumers over their core interest in games, opening new paths to purchase and brand immersion.

This level of personalization is possible because consumers essentially "hand over" a wealth of data on preferences, needs, and pain points willingly as part of the game experience. They also hand it over less intrusively than when marketers directly ask for personal information. This data is inherently more valuable since it's based on actual behavior, as opposed to the stated preferences or future intentions that come from market research—which are often skewed or unreliable.

Once handed over, the data from in-game interactions and behavioral patterns can be analyzed in real time by AI, yielding a far more sophisticated level of insight into players' motivations and feelings. At its most basic, AI delves into a player's demographic and behavioral data (browsing history, purchasing history, social media exchanges) to try to tailor (a) game activity in real time to the player's closest interests and (b) game rewards as well as associated product recommendations to match those interests. AI can then apply predictive analytics, layering in any relevant data that the AI has been trained on, giving marketers reliable datasets to use in crafting tailored experiences with stimuli that appeal to players' unique personalities—better engaging and motivating them.

For example, a fitness app is set up to track a user's progress and adjust the fitness plan from start to finish on the fly. Building in AI-driven gamification, the app then learns from the user's behavior to know when best to offer personalized product recommendations and how to offer them in an enjoyable way at the most appropriate intervals.

American Eagle CMO Craig Brommers shares this vision. "We're in the early stages of this and in six to twelve months, there is no doubt that AI applications will give our teams a better, more personalized relationship with our customers. We are going to use AI to provide a much more bespoke interaction with our brand. One customer is going to receive a very specific email or push notification or text that will be very different from the next customer on a particular day. That's where AI and gamification come into play."

Given the above, it's easy to see how AI can surely add a heightened level of personalization to gamification experiences, making them more engaging and motivational. AI can better analyze player data in real time to help marketers create better customized and more immersive experiences, delivering on the brand promise in meaningful, measurable ways.

AI provides the potential to engage with the consumer on a genuine, one-to-one basis through each touchpoint on the consumer's journey—from the initial messaging to the offer recommendations to the add-ons and follow-on messaging—all custom-crafted on the fly, as it were, to the individual. But yes, this AI layering is still in its early stages.

Real-time adaptations to difficulty and skill levels

AI is on a trajectory to actually create a game's mechanics and content based on the marketer's instructions at the prompt. And this could result in all kinds of new creative and innovative gameplay experiences—since AI can iterate as long as the marketer instructs it to.

By analyzing players' data in real time, and assessing individual preferences, performance, and behavior, AI can adapt game elements to more suitably tailor the campaign to the individual. Specifically, AI can adapt gameplay to align with a player's skill levels—adjusting upward or downward for difficulty, allowing less or more time to complete a given task, adding or subtracting elements of the storyline to improve understanding, and extending time spent in the game.

By dynamically adjusting the difficulty level of the game experience based on players' individual performances, the game can be kept challenging enough to be engaging but not so difficult as to be frustrating. This helps players improve their skills and progress toward their goals with greater confidence, which, in turn, translates into greater affinity for the brand.

Progressive rewards based on purchase history and performance

AI-driven gamifications can offer progressive rewards and incentives directly linked to the player's purchase history. So, for example, an individual player who has made purchases from a brand with some consistency could be alerted right in the game to the opportunity to win even more points based on continued purchases—locking in purchase behavior and combatting churn. AI can determine precisely which schedule of points awards is going to best increase the customer's lifetime value (LTV), adjusting on the fly as needed to always be dynamically balancing LTV.

Beyond historical purchase behavior, AI can also make the gamification experience more dynamic by setting the games' challenges and difficulty levels based on the players' performance and initial engagement levels—instead of on static, pre-programmed progression schemas. That is, AI can dynamically adjust the game's difficulty level based on the players' performance, balancing effort with reward for each player, ensuring players are given an experience attuned to their cognitive and emotional states as they are playing.

In addition to the consumer benefits of better offers and enhanced experiences, there are a number of AI-related benefits that accrue to marketers and their brands.

Increasing revenue through cross-sell and upsell

As previously discussed, AI can leverage its tremendous predictive analytics capability to forecast player behavior and needs with a high level of accuracy—even before those needs are expressed. This allows AI to alter gameplay to keep players focused longer on the game's business objectives.

Leveraging this deep learning, marketers will be able to train AI to identify, record, and categorize the actions taken on the player's journey through the gamification experience. They can then tailor rewards and incentives to meet the players' preferences and requirements, with the objective of driving more upsell/cross-sell opportunities in real time.

Automating basic functions

A number of time-consuming gamification tasks—such as tracking individual users, monitoring progress, evaluating performance, and identifying anomalies—can be automated through AI to increase efficiencies in the management of gamification.

Identifying and preventing fraud

AI can help detect fraudulent activity in ongoing gamification strategies, such as loyalty programs. AI can identify unusual patterns and behaviors that may indicate fraud (spikes in point collections, transactions in unusual locations, transactions occurring at odd hours). This can help maintain the integrity of loyalty programs, appealing to both players and the company.

Providing instantaneous feedback for improvement

During a gamification campaign and after, AI can analyze the in-game data to help inform decisions on future gamified projects, optimizing the gamified experiences and identifying areas for improvement.

SUPERCHARGED RESULTS FROM XR CAPABILITIES

AI isn't the only technology promising to accelerate gamification efforts. Some marketers feel that XR platforms may have the greatest potential for new gamification campaigns because these platforms are, by definition, games-oriented, and they can blend digital interactions with physical environments, creating all-new experiences. Gamified content that integrates physical and digital systems can improve learning outcomes and encourage players to engage with information in new, more immersive ways.

McDonald's demonstrated as much with a 2022 promotion they ran in the Metaverse tied to the Lunar New Year. As McDonald's U.S. chief marketing and customer experience officer, Tariq Hassan, explains, "We partnered with an Asian digital content Creator, Humberto Leon, to design a cultural celebration of zodiac signs inside the Spatial metaverse (and accessible on any connected device) where people could come in, have a social experience and connect with others from the culture, and learn about Lunar New Year. ... In that environment, we used gamification to engage with visitors."[268]

MOVING INTO BLOCKCHAIN-BASED GAMIFICATION

Lastly, Web3 and blockchain technologies should lead to token-based gamification campaigns where participants can gain verifiable ownership over in-game assets and rewards, potentially increasing the perceived value of those rewards and thus boosting player engagement.

Several vendors are challenging marketers to reimagine the gami-fication concept built on blockchain technology with NFTs as rewards and AI becoming a more capable extension of the company's CRM. It's a big claim, of course, and the earliest of these programs is expected to launch in late 2023. Their adoption and success can be expected to track the adoption of the blockchain itself.

As we have seen, much of technology-driven gamification is still in the product development and marketing hype cycles. But it is promising (and beginning to deliver) more dynamic in-game interactions with players and becoming an increasingly valuable utility for marketers in the years ahead.

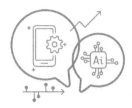

CHAPTER NINE
Influencers and Creators: The New Faces of Trust

Just a few years ago, if a world-class automotive company signaled its intention to sell cars on TikTok, roomfuls of CMOs would have snickered, "Shut the front door!" But now Jens Thiemer, senior vice president Customer & Brand BMW, is confidently saying, "I'm absolutely convinced that in the future we'll sell cars through social … because it's a snackable communication. We have younger audiences on TikTok saying, 'Wow, I want to have a car that's co-designed by a well-known Influencer!' And they can jump from TikTok or Instagram onto our website, reserve that special-edition car, book it at a monthly rate and have it!"[269]

In less than a decade, car marketing has shifted from showrooms to include online ordering and now taking reservations for special-edition cars on social media. All made possible by a new intermediary, the Influencer/Creator.

"As marketers, we went through a journey the last ten years," Thiemer recollects, "where we learned how big the impact of Influencers can be—positively as well as negatively. We saw brands becoming literally dependent on Influencer marketing in FMCG, fast-moving consumer goods, and for companies like BMW, as well."

Assessing this new impact of Influencers, Thiemer finds it "most fascinating how Influencers can shorten the access to customers so we come up faster on their awareness agenda. Less so, of course, for car makers like BMW because it's a high-investment purchase and not the most natural product for social selling. But we are going there now because digital sales for cars are on the agenda for millions of people—because it's a financed or leased transaction."

"For example, we have an impressive new SUV in our lineup. It's called the XM. We selected Naomi Campbell as an Influencer or Key Opinion Leader (KOL)—which is the term we prefer because it is more serious—for promoting that car. But we did not use her in the typical way of using supermodel personalities. Instead, we used her social power to tell stories" in social media "about strong characters having the courage of their convictions," effectively marrying the powerful personalities of Campbell and the BMW brand in the minds of those following on the social platforms.

Thiemer didn't just book Campbell for a launch campaign like he might have years ago. "Long-term is essential now, it's a commitment you have to make" to cement the relationship between the KOL and the brand.

Also evolving are the yardsticks. "In selecting KOLs, we are moving away from the awareness KPIs. The transactional potential of social selling through KOLs should be the future KPI and future use cases, even the dominant use case for many of my peers."

Transactional performance metrics involve "looking behind the curtain. Why is someone following a KOL? Do they identify authentically and intrinsically with that KOL? Are they really following the sales recommendations?" Those are the questions Thiemer is asking and attempting to quantify. "We still have our KPIs on awareness, but more and more we want to get transactional in social media because it is the transactional channel of the future."

Asked to nail down the metrics on this transactional approach, Thiemer replies, "In the merchandising of our automotive lifestyle products, we absolutely have proof that it's working. A great example is our intensive cooperation with designer and Influencer Ronnie Fieg from KITH, with whom we already realized several projects around BMW M. In the selling of the limited-edition cars, we do have every single market in my organization using KOLs, so that says a lot—since we are driven by marketing spend effectiveness. It's a proof point, but it's still on the 'believer' level."

A major Influencer like Naomi Campbell is becoming a necessary but insufficient play for major brands. At BMW, for instance, it is the so-called micro-Influencers who are proving increasingly valuable at the engagement level.

"The most powerful influence is coming from local KOLs," says Thiemer. "Our local sales organizations come up with them for us, with examples such as Caro Daur," a German fashion model and self-made digital entrepreneur "who is helping us reach a completely new group outside of our typical search field."

This combined utility of celebrity-Influencers and micro-Influencers, along with younger audiences practically living on the social platforms, is opening new opportunities for companies like BMW beyond the traditional wholesale model. "We are coming out of a system with lots of dealers and partners in between. That's happening because we are seeing consumers demanding the shortest sales journey possible. That means direct."

Today's Influencer Ecosystem

As marketers wrangle for consumers' attention amid an explosion of clutter on every channel, it's no wonder Influencers have become such important commercial facilitators. In a crowded room, in short, all eyes turn to the celebrity. Trading on their power to affect the purchasing decisions of others because of their authority, knowledge, or devotion of audiences, Influencers are turning their enthusiastic followers into essential cogs in brand marketing machinery.

The research organization Astute Analytica predicts that dollars spent on the global Influencer industry (fair to call it that) will grow from $10.5 billion in 2022 to an eye-popping $118 billion by 2031. To buttress what otherwise sounds like a "pie in the sky" projection, the analysts add that "89 percent of marketers say that ROI from Influencer marketing is comparable to or better than other marketing channels."[270]

And the Influencer Marketing Hub adds that 93 percent of marketers are using Influencers, with spending on them breaking down as follows:[271]

43 %	<$10K
36 %	$10K–$100K
21 %	>$100K

Indeed, there's so much interest in Influencer marketing that 1,360 new Influencer platforms and agencies entered the market in just the last few years.[272]

The Influencer marketing platform Linqia asked marketers what type of Influencer they *wanted* to work with.[273] The results may surprise you:

Marketers Preferences in Influencers		
Type of Influencer	Size of Following	Preference %
Celebrity-Influencers	5M+	14
No-pay-Influencers	Unknown	21
Affiliate-Influencers	Unknown	21
Nano-Influencers	5,000+	34
Mega-Influencers	500K-5M+	34
Micro-Influencers	5K-100K	90

As you can see, the lowest preference among marketers surveyed was for the celebrity-Influencers—the ones averaging 5M+ followers. Just 14 percent of marketers wanted to work with this group—even though celebrities are the highest-profile Influencers and are actively employed by major brands. Substantially more marketers, 21 percent in all, said they prefer to work with affiliate-Influencers as well as no-pay-Influencers. Next in preference was the nano-Influencers with their average 5K followers as well as mega-Influencers with 500K–5M+ followers—34 percent of marketers want to work with these very different groups. Most preferred were the micro-Influencers with their small 5K–100K followings—at 90 percent interest.

FOLLOW THE TRUST

In Nielsen's latest Global Trust in Advertising report, consumers said they trust recommendations from friends, family, and Influencers the most. A full 92 percent put these recommendations above all other forms of advertising, up from 74 percent in 2007. That's a substantial jump! As for the trustworthiness of other advertising channels, this chart shows the falloff in consumer trust:[274]

Channel	Trust Level
Recommendations from friends	**92%**
Branded websites	84%
Editorial content	78%
Ads on TV	78%
Ads in newspapers	76%

(Falling below the 75 percent trust threshold in order of declension: email pitches, TV product placements, magazine ads, radio ads, consumer opinions online, banner ads, video ads, mobile ads, social network ads, search results ads, and text ads.)

Gen Z as a cohort is most heavily inspired by Influencers. They shop through Influencers and are heavily swayed by them when it comes to forming brand perceptions. Young consumers imagine these Influencers as friends, even intimates (nobody ever accused humans of being rational), and often act on feelings they have for an Influencer. This association is strongest when the individual feels bonded to a shared community with the Influencer. Whether this bond occurs virtually or in reality, it needs to be "manufactured" authentically. That is the process of Influencers becoming Creators: actually creating a community organically around a brand promise in a community that people feel a genuine attraction to.

These Influencers/Creators come from all walks but are most commonly characterized by the medium they publish in—since, increasingly, it is the Influencer's content (over the Influencers themselves) that drives their effectiveness. So, there are, loosely categorizing, bloggers for print, YouTubers for long-form video, TikTokers, and Instagrammers for short-form video, Twitchers for gaming, podcasters for audio, and photographers for imagery. They can be celebrity personalities, of course, but also subject matter experts, employees, thought leaders, connectors, and everyday fans aiming to become superfans. They are the new faces of trust.

SOCIAL PLATFORM DYNAMICS

Instagram was the leading platform for paid Influencer promotions in 2023, with brands spending $1.96 billion on the platform. A distant second, third, and fourth in near-equal popularity were TikTok with a $990 million spend, YouTube with $962 million, and Facebook with $896 million. However, according to *Insider Intelligence*, ad spending on TikTok grew faster in 2023 than on any other social media platform.[275]

The *#TikTokMadeMeBuyIt* hashtag is an anecdotal but a powerful proof that there's great upside to working with Influencers on TikTok in both shoppable and co-created ad formats.

As well, TikTok is going all in on direct selling—opening U.S. warehouses for fulfillment and shipping in the style of—and in direct competition with—Amazon and Walmart. This development by the Chinese company is meant to (a) establish a U.S. supply chain footprint to shorten package delivery times, (b) convince more brands to join TikTok Shop and accelerate direct sales, and (c) convince lawmakers that the company is investing in—and can be trusted to compete in—the United States.

As we write, Congress has banned the TikTok app on government devices, and Montana has banned TikTok outright with other states expected to follow. TikTok has countersued, and much remains uncertain. In the meantime, Influencers are attempting to hedge their bets and diversify their content offerings across other platforms. But TikTok Influencers rarely enjoy the same reach and engagement elsewhere since each platform has a different culture from a practical engagement perspective. Brands are wise to hedge, as well, by advancing their Influencer relationships across all the popular platforms.

OUTCOMES AND BENEFITS

For most marketers, success in Influencer marketing boils down to measurable engagement. Almost eight in ten CMOs put engagement as their top priority, followed in order by conversions, impressions, product sales, quality of Influencer content, brand awareness, and lastly audience sentiment.[276] Engagement bubbles up like cream because it is the measure of the actual interaction with the Influencer's content and thus the best measure of the Influencer's value. This engagement is an aggregate measure of component priorities (some of which overlap with top-priority metrics, depending on who is doing the measuring):

- clicks (interest levels)

- likes (content appreciation)

- shares (content quality)

- reactions (a better gauge of content sentiment)

- comments (deeper context, including target market appreciation)

- brand mentions (for tracking where content is being discussed and should be amplified)

Tracking cost per engagement (CPE) using these measures is becoming a standard for assessing the brand's relationship with the Influencer.

Aligning Influencer Marketing with Business Strategy

FINDING THE RIGHT INFLUENCERS

As with any marketing tactic, working with Influencers begins with the standard questions: What are the brand or business objectives of the Influencer campaign? What will success look like for the brand, the Influencer, and the community being created? Which Influencers represent the best fit with the brand? What data will be generated to measure these objectives? With answers, marketers can begin executing by selecting the best set of Influencers based on three KPIs:

Engagement. The more engaged an Influencer's followers, the more likely they are to follow the Influencer's recommendations. A micro-Influencer with 100K truly engaged fans often delivers better results than the 3M Influencer, though big-name Influencers are indispensable to awareness campaigns.

Relevance. Is the Influencer creating and sharing content that's important to the target audience? Whether the content is funny, inspiring, or simply educational, it needs to positively impact the audience over time—for that is what builds a meaningful relationship on shared values.

Brand Fit. Does the Influencer align naturally with the brand's positioning, voice, and values? As well, does the Influencer interact with people in the domain respectfully so that their opinions and recommendations will be valued?

LETTING GO OF THE ILLUSION OF CONTROL

Control is something most marketers have a hard timing relinquishing, but doing so is absolutely vital to the success of Influencer relationships and campaigns. Among B2B marketers especially, there can be some confusion between the words *Influencer* and *Shill*. Often, contracts will state something like, "You will speak at *x* events, about which you'll blog *y* times and tweet these pre-crafted tweets *z* times." In these instances, the marketers may think they are properly managing the Influencer relationship, but more often they are handicapping the Influencer and jeopardizing the outcome of the campaign.

Good Influencers want to have creative input and a measure of control over how their content is developed and distributed because, in their view and correctly, they usually know what will best resonate with their audience to drive the results the brand seeks.

Few brands understand this notion better than **New Balance**. "We refer to all of our brand partners as brand ambassadors," says Chris Davis, CMO of the sneaker and lifestyle company. "And to us, there's a distinctive difference between a brand ambassador and an Influencer. Ambassadors are long-term strategic partners that reflect our values as an organization extended into the marketplace. Whereas Influencers, to us, are an additional channel for awareness and advocacy."[277]"

"Ambassador marketing says something about your brand, your truth, who you are, what you represent. We call it co-authoring. So, with every brand ambassador we have, we co-author the strategy, the products, and the content. It's a collaborative effort where each side has a say in the ultimate product."

New Balance doesn't focus on the size of the ambassador's following but instead on the nature of the collaboration. So even though Davis works with hundreds of brand ambassadors from well-known celebrities on down, they all serve to extend the New Balance brand positioning into the marketplace through the co-creation of content and messaging.

Most importantly, Davis explains, this investment in brand ambassadors is part of a long-term strategic plan. "When we first sign these individuals as partners, we identify individuals who are ascending, who have been lifetime fans of the brand, and we're able to grow and develop the partnership and consumer relationship with these ambassadors. So, by the time they do have a large platform and level of stardom, there's a rich heritage and authentic journey that's already occurred with the New Balance brand."

"For example, Coco Gauff recently won the US Open, but we had a signature shoe for her about a year prior to that. Whereas a lot of other brands would've waited until she won, we knew she was an individual who had a fearlessly independent mindset" that aligned with our brand's heritage positioning "and because of that, we co-authored and co-created with her far earlier than any other brand did."

Davis believes these brand ambassadors are crucial to innovating the brand and avoiding stagnation in the marketplace. "The idea of co-creating future trends is at the heart of why these partnerships exist. They could be trends in streetwear, in fashion, or in sport. But the insights that these brand ambassadors bring to coming trends is absolutely essential to not only our marketing strategy, but our business strategy."

Zeroing in on the young adult demographic through Influencers took an ironic twist for **McDonald's** recently—since the campaign featured an adult offering.

"Last year we launched the Cactus Plant Flea Market box and had the highest weekly digital transactions to date in the U.S.," says Tariq Hassan, McDonald's U.S. chief marketing and customer experience officer. [278] It came as a result of an insight from a tweet in November 2020, at the height of the pandemic. McDonald's Twitter (now X) account admin posted, "One day you wake up and you don't even realize you had your last Happy Meal."[279] And that tweet blew up.

Fans jumped into the thread. "How are you doing McDonald's?" asked one user, concerned that all was OK.

"I'm in my feels today clearly," the brand replied. "How are u?"

"You good?" asked another.

"Ignoring that I'm having an existential crisis, yes," the brand replied.

"Why did you have to do this now?" one user asked.

"I was not planning to cry today but thank you," said another.

Another said she was OK knowing she'd ordered her last Happy Meal but was upset by the realization that someday her child would order his last one.

And on it went. "So, we clearly struck a chord about the loss of childhood joy," Hassan continues, "and we wondered how to recapture the quintessential childhood experience that was a Happy Meal. Could we do it by recreating an adult version of it? And this led us to the Artist space. When we work with Influencers or in this case Artists, we work really hard to ensure they have an existing relationship with the brand before a commercial one. We ensure that they have their own experience to bring to it. So, when we discovered Cactus Plant Flea Market, an artist-owned brand and creative outlet, we told them about the joy we were trying to recapture. And Cactus poured out a flood of memories of McDonald's and how they always went there with childhood friends. Now an adult, the Cactus Plant Flea Market brand's signature icon is a little yellow character called 'Cactus Buddy!.' Cactus said, 'We want Cactus Buddy! to have friends. Let's bring McDonald's characters back alongside Cactus Buddy! and make them a friend group.' Cactus created all the merchandise, and visuals based on McDonald's beloved characters and iconography. I have no doubt that this campaign experience would've been successful. But when you overlay it with cultural relevance via Artists like Cactus Plant Flea Market, you allow yourself to lean in, and trust to take place"; then you have something magical, and in this case, tremendously successful for the business.

With Influencers, Hassan sums up, "It comes down to whether you are prepared to share the pen, to literally hand it over."

INFLUENCER PROBLEMS ARE OFTEN BRAND STRATEGY PROBLEMS

The year 2023 was a wake-up year for marketers wrestling with concerns of Influencer marketing campaigns run amuck. One blunder after another became painfully public. Influencers copy-and-pasting the brand's instructions into an actual post. Big-name personalities flouting Federal Trade Commission's (FTC) rules and trivializing highly charged social issues and misleading investors. And, of course, the all-systems-failure of **Bud Light**.

The Bud Light disaster provides context and an object lesson for marketers on strategizing more intelligently, relying on both data and creative impulses in campaign management, and aligning marketing strategy with business objectives.

Bud Light's marketing director, Alissa Heinerscheid, was tasked with reversing declining sales by targeting younger, more diverse beer drinkers. So, Bud Light created a custom can for trans-Influencer Dylan Mulvaney—with her face on the can in celebration of her gender transition. This sparked controversy and messy public boycotts. It ultimately cost parent company AB InBev $15.7 billion in losses, projected sales declines of 13 percent for the year, the dismissal of two senior marketing executives, and official statements from AB InBev retconning the narrative, which only exacerbated the issue on both sides of the culture divide.[280]

In postmortem assessments, a number of marketers wrote that Bud Light had taken a "shortcut toward trendiness" by doing an "impersonation of wokeness" that came across as inauthentic "purpose-washing."[281] Were these fair, or even accurate, assessments? The answer to this question is essentially irrelevant. Regardless of one's personal views, it was ultimately a poor marketing and business decision.

Bud Light did indeed need to act. It was being overtaken by trendier craft beers and flavored alcoholic beverages. That being the case, engaging a new Influencer or launching a creative campaign was not the solution. The only way to restore market share would have been through revisiting and addressing underlying business, brand, and marketing strategies.

For example, AB InBev could have (a) launched a new brand or sub-line, thus protecting Bud Light's valuable brand equity; (b) added a craftier flavored feel to Bud Light in hopes of extending its range; (c) more narrowly targeted younger drinkers most likely to share the attitudes of existing drinkers; and/or (d) beefed up marketing support for the company's other brands (Stella Artois, Corona, Bud Light Clamato,

Bud Light Hard Seltzer, Goose Island Brewery, Rolling Rock, Busch, etc.) that appeal more to the younger, trendier demo. No Influencer of any kind—from Dylan Mulvaney to Arnold Schwarzenegger—could have positively repositioned the brand or revived sales of Bud Light if a fundamental shift in consumer sentiment was underway.

This suggests that Bud Light's mistake may have been more of a brand and marketing strategy mistake than a broad-brush condemnation of engaging Influencers as a means for brand-building. It is imperative to consider the appropriate role of Influencer marketing (or any activation tactic for that matter) within the broader context of brand and marketing strategy in order to guard against this kind of public catastrophe.

MINIMIZING BRAND RISK ASSOCIATED WITH INFLUENCER MARKETING

Although there is no absolute, surefire way to eliminate risks associated with Influencer marketing (especially given at least some degree of control needs to be ceded to the Influencer), there are a number of steps marketers can take to mitigate risk. The following are several rules of thumb to consider.

Thoroughly research potential Influencers

before partnering with them

This one may seem obvious, but surprisingly, it isn't always a given. Marketers are in the marketing business. Personally, they can respect Dylan Mulvaney for doing what's right for her *and* respect the rights of protesters, as well, to voice their opinions. But professionally partnering with an Influencer without fully assessing that Influencer's reputational impact on the brand only invites trouble. Once again, it highlights the importance of conducting thorough research before partnering with any Influencer.

Use data to inform strategic and tactical choices

Getting feedback from actual consumers in the research phase of the campaign allows marketers to make informed decisions. This basic market research is now faster and easier to do more effectively with the help of AI tools coming to market, and it can help avoid single points of failure at key points in the development process:

- **Research phase**—when key demographics need to be consulted;

- **Creative phase**—when ad concepts need to be green-lighted based solely on audience preferences;

- **Focus group phase**—when the target audience needs to speak candidly and the production team puts aside personal preferences and listens only to the audience.

Research at each level informs a campaign properly. Whether using old-fashioned research or AI-driven analytics, it is grounded in the golden rule of marketing: understand the audience.

Be extra careful with humor and causes

Crafting an Influencer marketing campaign around humor or social causes is, as we've discussed, generally a smart move—especially when targeting younger audiences. But it's critical to be careful and sensitive to both known and potential landmines in our modern culture. Any campaign that appears indifferent to social issues can seriously damage the brand's image.

Understand management's appetite for risk

Bud Light's partnership with Dylan Mulvaney was designed to be a small tactical effort, not a big brand campaign. But in the crazy land that is social media, even an ant can distort into an elephant. Every tactic must be considered within an omnichannel view of the brand and be aligned with internal stakeholders' positions on how far the brand is willing to wade into potentially contentious social waters.

Aligning Influencers with Brands and Markets

UNDERSTAND AND EXTEND BRAND REACH

When a brand communication is misaligned with its core consumers' perceptions of the brand's values, failure is to be expected. People cannot be persuaded to buy a product that is outside their consideration set. That is, as they say, like trying to sell hamburgers to vegans. Once again, the golden rule in marketing remains: understand your target market and their perceptions.

Conversely, when executed carefully, Influencers can sometimes help extend a brand's reach and positively alter consumer perceptions. "Our brand was skewing to an older, less diverse audience with sponsorships in football and golf," says Kevin Warren, chief marketing and customer experience officer at **UPS**. "Yet you look at small- and medium-sized businesses; a lot are women-owned, younger, Asian, Latinx, African American. So, we needed to balance that out. We did a music festival with Pharrell Williams. We're underwriting two diverse filmmakers to bring out a short film. We went to New York

Fashion Week. Not exactly UPS and brown shorts, right? I had no idea if it would work."[282]

UPS sponsored a group fashion show at New York Fashion Week and released a collection of branded streetwear. The brand tapped fashion icon Christian Cody to shoot the collection and designer Ugo Mozie to style the looks. The proceeds went to "In the Blk" to support black fashion entrepreneurs. The activation was a phenomenal success. So, UPS returned to the runway for a Latinx show—again tapping fashion's top Influencer talent to call attention to "the new UPS."

Warren has results he can quantify—not only in revenue share points but also in awareness of the brand. "We're showing up in TV shows such as *Abbott Elementary*, in a Tom Hanks movie, and in a Jack Harlow song. Culturally, things are looking up. They're coming to us versus the other way around."

ENSURE INFLUENCER AUTHENTICITY

Influencer content disrupts the online experience *far less* than ads do, allowing companies to appear authentically in an environment consumers want to be in. So, the most critical challenge in Influencer marketing is getting authenticity right. Whether the Influencer is posting a single piece of sponsored content on their blog, or an entire campaign wrapped around a TikTok star, the product needs to fit the Influencer authentically with the Influencer clearly being interested in the product. That honors the basis of trust that the Influencer has built up with followers and allows that trust to be converted into credibility for the product.

"Influencers have to be credible in the space on the topic," agrees Mark Weinstein, CMO of **Hilton**, "and should genuinely use your product. So, at Hilton, ideally, an Influencer authentically travels with us before we consider the idea of a paid relationship with them.

Otherwise, we're just chasing Influencers with huge followings—but with no brand relevance or credibility—which is dangerous. It's like a sugar high. These brands might pop website visits or sales for a day or two, but it's not sustainable … because it wasn't a credible way to tell their story in the first place. In fact, the real risk is that Influencer marketing grows more commercialized than organic. Can it still fulfill its purpose when 90 percent of what an Influencer says is just brand messaging? That's why I'm confident the future of marketing will be Creators telling their own stories about brands."[283]

Echoing these sentiments, but from a very different kind of company, is Samie Barr, chief brand officer of **Kohler**. "We view Influencers and partnerships in different tiers and categories. And we evaluate them differently depending on type and benefit to the brand. Some Influencers are more what I would call product sponsors; they look to benefit from the brand and promote the product. And that's fine if that supports the objectives a brand is looking to achieve, and Influencers benefits as well. But others are what I would consider strategic partners—or co-Creators. For them, you have to start from a place of authenticity. What's their vision? What do they stand for? And how does it align with your brand? Then, how does it authentically come together to create meaningful engagement for your customers … so it doesn't look like you're just paying to play."[284]

By example, Kohler has a multiyear relationship with a well-known home designer, Shea McGee. "In the beginning, it was important to get beneath it all with Shea McGee, to understand who she is and what she believes in. For instance, she likes to combine architectural history and modern materials. She has an ability to design authentic spaces that are beautiful and gracious and make your home look phenomenal and amazing. And it was really cool as we began to unleash her creativity and relevancy" across her 3.8 million Instagram followers.[285]

"It's not just about size of their following, but also about fit and relevancy. You can choose Influencers who have 100,000 followers or fifty million. The key is to be strategic and deliberate. To ensure they fit with *our* purpose and *our* brand pillars, and to ensure a holistic point of view at the Kohler brand level." Barr's focus on holism in the company's Influencer collaborations is a commonality she shares with every CMO interviewed here.

EMBRACE SOCIAL TRENDS

Influencers are increasingly driving trends and determining what will be popular next, and brands are collaborating to play a role in that decision.

Lexus has leaned strongly into this. As discussed in chapter 6, the carmaker wanted to extend its brand position with a new generation. While long known for quality, reliability, and durability, Lexus wanted to appeal to Gen Z with the promise of performance and excitement. And Lexus executed this through an Influencer campaign. Explains CMO Vinay Shahani, "We became the official automotive partner for 100 Thieves—a lifestyle brand and gaming organization with a powerful network of Influencers. It was a great way to connect with younger consumers using our entry-level vehicle, the RC F GT3. The people at 100 Thieves brought a couple of their Influencers to the Long Beach IMSA Race. These Influencers were on their social media platforms tweeting about what they were experiencing with Lexus on the track. Ordinarily, we'd have maybe twenty thousand people engage with a typical Lexus racing post. After partnering with 100 Thieves, we saw that increase to 100,000 plus—a five fold boost." [286]

A different take on this trend-riding comes from **American Eagle**'s CMO, Craig Brommers, who has worked for a number of fashion brands in his career. "I came up with brands like Calvin Klein and Abercrombie Fitch, where we'd basically tell consumers what was cool and how to look. Now Influencers are turning that completely upside down. They're the arbiters of culture, the arbiters of what's cool. The power dynamic is shifting and marketing is going to be around the collaboration that brands have with these Influencer communities … with technology turbocharging this dynamic."[287]

The Trend toward Micro-Influencers

While big-name celebrity endorsers and Influencers get all the ink, and play a powerful role in companies' brand awareness campaigns, marketers often see the best returns from their investment in micro-Influencers.

THE TIKTOK EFFECT

"We actually have a concept called Hot on TikTok," explains Steve Lesnard, global chief brand officer of **Sephora**, "and it's working really well because that's where trends come from. Consumers come to us and say, 'I've seen that on TikTok. I've researched it and I'd like to try it.' So, when you think about how hot Influencers on TikTok are powering this, you see that they are the experts in the platforms they work on.[288]

"They're Creators on their own terms. They become artists that you commission for campaigns as well. They started by just having fun, leveraging the platform. So, it's completely changing the ecosystem. Now, if you go to runway shows, you will have Influencers, web Influencers, and TikTok Influencers sitting next to Anna Wintour in fashion shows. That's how we've seen the landscape evolve. And new platforms and new technologies and Influencers that master them are even more powerful."

INCREASING RELEVANCE

As a bank, **Wells Fargo** could have a different view on the value of Influencers to business. But Amy Bonitatibus, the company's chief communications officer, says that "using micro-Influencers is a real strategy" for the bank, as well. "Some of these people might not have recognizable names, but they have big followings on social media with the target audience. They are about relevance, not reach."

"Similarly, the idea of relevance is particularly important when trying to explain complex topics, like the mortgage process. While not micro Influencers, Drew and Jonathan Scott (HGTV's Property Brothers) may not have as many followers on their social channels as Patrick Mahomes, but what they do have is relevance in the category. That's important, especially with something as complex as home mortgages. Using someone like the Property Brothers who are engaging and have the ability to almost demystify the mortgage process in an understandable approach, given their expertise in the space is often as valuable, if not more valuable, than a top celebrity with little knowledge in the category."

FROM HI-FI TO LO-FI CONTENT

"Influencer marketing has had the single most profound impact on our marketing mix in recent years," says Craig Brommers, CMO of American Eagle. "We're transitioning from what I'll call hi-fi content (think lavishly produced TV commercials and the use of celebrity) into what I'll call lo-fi content (normal average kids posting about

American Eagle). It has turned Influencers into not just one of the most efficient content vehicles, but one of the most effective, too.[289]

"Our number-one Influencer in America is Alix Earle, a University of Miami student. Alix wore a pair of American Eagle jeans that was the 65th best-selling jean in our assortment. Overnight, it became the number one selling jean ... literally because she wore it. We did not pay her. This was something she did. And she kindly said, 'American Eagle is having a comeback, and these jeans look so great on me, you should try them too.' And of course, then it's our responsibility to fan that flame of virality and work with Alix to do that."

Brommers believes the driver behind this is simple and straightforward. "It's just normal kids in Kansas City or Salt Lake City or wherever getting their fifteen seconds of fame interacting with the brand. The brand may be reposting them, the brand may be sending them free product. But it's coming from the community and they're pushing it up."

EXTENDING THE BRAND INTO PHYSICAL COMMUNITIES

In chapter 8, **Salesforce** CMO Sarah Franklin talked about using gamification to craft their Trailblazers community of devoted fans. Trailblazers leverages an Influencer strategy, as well. "Our most influential trailblazers *are* our Influencer strategy. They're less the traditional Kardashian, McConaughey type Influencer. But you're ultimately looking for someone people trust in their daily lives, that have an affiliation or expertise that gives them credibility to promote your product. In the consumer world, brands pay a lot to get Steph Curry to eat your sandwich, or Patrick Mahomes to sell your insurance, but that's different from true Influencer marketing which is really leveraging the 'reach' of real people in your domain, letting their reach amplify your brand, your products.[290]

"Micro-Influencers are interesting because the world is becoming more global and more local at the same time. Platforms give us the ability to talk with people all around the world and to share content and experiences and endorsements everywhere. But micro-Influencers have a specific influence where they are *physically* located because they can go talk to people and meet with people in the physical world. And they can relate to the problems of people in those local communities. It's much more effective."

Salesforce has a couple hundred of these micro-Influencers who they call MVPs. Some of them may have only five thousand followers, but they're truly engaged and relevant followers, which is why they're taken very seriously by Salesforce. "We have a nomination process for our MVPs and there are expectations of them." Franklin continues, "They receive no payment but are rewarded with recognition and with special access. That's the currency that they really trade in because they're proud to promote Salesforce at their companies and in their communities."

As for proof that the MVP Influencer strategy is working, Franklin says, "We definitely see the needle move. More engagement. More revenue. It's an indirect measurement because they are not salespeople, but we know it's working because when we have Influencers in certain geos, the revenue in those geos definitely increases, the customer satisfaction score (CSAT) increases, and attrition decreases."

Another take on the Influencer-Community strategy comes from the Australian graphic design platform, **Canva**. Zach Kitschke, CMO of Canva, explains, "When we think about Influencers, we think about our communities, and it's an important distinction. Out of our global user-base of 150 million people, we now have more than 200,000 people who have joined one of our official 'communities.' It's a broad base, but this includes a teacher's community, a Creator community, and an SMB community, among others. They're helping to form a broad ecosystem of interests and needs."

Canva built these communities in Facebook groups, acting as facilitators but allowing the communities "to very much take on a life of their own. People sharing Canva tutorials or tips and tricks or classroom inspirations, lesson plan ideas, all that." Canva has then provided income opportunities to these communities, such as being able to contribute to Canva's marketplace and earn royalties from their templates and stock content.

One of those incentives, Kitschke says, "is the opportunity to speak at conferences and events all around the world. We get asked to these events all the time but can't always do it with our internal team. So, we look to offer it to folks in our community," making it a win for them and a win for the brand.

"Canva helps community members with education, with content creation—basically treating them like micro-Influencers for the brand, but with an eye to the future." Kitschke believes that "the future of Influencer marketing is all about authenticity, particularly with younger generations. People have a real filter for purpose with brands and with the authenticity of the people they follow. So, I think the days of pay-to-play—getting an Influencer to spout about your product without any depth of connection—those days are numbered."[291]

The Rise of the Virtual Influencer

The first *virtual* Influencer can probably be traced to the 1950s with musical groups such as The Archies or Alvin and the Chipmunks. Then came the GEICO Gecko as a 1990s TV icon, morphing into a brand mascot with an instructively loyal fanbase. Between 2003 and 2007, several companies internationally adopted virtual spokes-persons (or spokes-its, more accurately). Then in 2015, these virtual Influencers began really performing with an estimated two hundred of them out there today—living out their fictional lives one day at a time.

These stunningly realistic digital creations, meticulously crafted by artists and developers with unique personalities and feels-so-new storytelling abilities, are blurring the lines between fiction and reality, captivating audiences, and amassing millions of genuinely devoted followers, in turn securing lucrative brand collaborations. They are no longer the future, clearly. They are connecting with audiences on a deeply personal level, opening up new possibilities for brand storytelling and engagement.

EXAMPLES OF VIRTUAL INFLUENCERS

The biggest "Aha!" moment for marketers came in 2018 when Lil Miquela made her debut in the fashion industry, taking over Prada's Instagram account and sauntering backstage at that year's big Milan fashion show. Lil Miquela went on to become a rich virtual Influencer, as well. While the freckle-faced entertainer's earnings have fallen off since her debut years, Lil Miquela is believed to be raking in more than $1 million a year from brand collaborations with such names as **Prada**, **Samsung**, and, most notably, **Calvin Klein**, with an ad that featured a kiss with real-life supermodel Bella Hadid during the European football Super Cup.[292] Referencing a pitch-perfect voice, great fashion sense, and activist mindset, *TIME* magazine put Lil Miquela among the "25 Most Influential People on the Internet" in 2018.[293] And today, the computer-generated imagery (CGI) script boasts 2.8 million followers on Instagram and is open for business![294]

Joining in the fashion industry fun, **Amazon Fashion** partnered with Imma—a Japanese virtual Influencer with 356K Instagram followers—to promote limited-edition clothing on The Drop—where real-life Influencers' clothing brands are featured.[295]

In the nearby fragrance space, Prada "brought to life" its own virtual Influencer to promote its namesake fragrance, Candy. The campaign cleverly challenged consumers to "rethink reality," and a Prada spokesperson said of Candy, "As her own reality glitches, she begins to perceive another, expanding her existence through the power of technology. Free of constraints, her curiosity grows, new creative perspectives are opened and with them, an invitation to rethink reality."[296] It's the marketing equivalent of art imitating life imitating reality.

Also popular, though controversial, is Shudu—the first black virtual Influencer. Shudu has collaborated with name brands including **BMW, Hyundai**, and **Louis Vuitton**. Shudu was meant to showcase inclusivity and diversity in the Influencer space, with Rihanna reposting her image wearing Fenty lipstick at one point. But not everyone saw it so positively.

Author Vanessa Angélica Villarreal tweeted, "She's been 'hired' across the industry which means her Creators, white men, NOT a Black woman, are the ones paid. And companies get to say they ran Black content without having to work with or hire Black people."[297]

Then a teen magazine poll on Twitter tallied up 84 percent of respondents saying the Shudu model was a bad idea. One person commented, "We are not a 'trend' or a 'movement,'" in reference to the potential cultural appropriation of a Black woman. Another commented, "Creating a CGI Black woman and exploiting, fetishizing, and treating black skin and features as a trend instead of actually hiring and paying Black models is gross." [298]

All of these went viral, of course, blowing up in a lot of faces. And whether the commenters were trolling for clicks or genuinely aggrieved, the Shudu CGI became yet another object lesson in the difficulties of marketing in today's climate—whether using real or virtual players.

THE APPEAL OF VIRTUAL INFLUENCERS

A lot of fuzzy numbers are being put up by vendors and research firms shaking the pom-poms for this virtual Influencer future. With that caveat, it is estimated that a little more than half of U.S. adults "follow" at least one virtual Influencer.[299] Even if these numbers are inflated, they are significant. Among those following in the United States, 29 percent of them follow on YouTube, 29 percent on Instagram, and 21 percent on TikTok.[300] As for results, as many as three in ten U.S. adults report having bought a product or service promoted by a virtual Influencer.[301]

A 2023 Instagram report claimed that more than half of Gen Z plans to take fashion or beauty inspiration from virtual Influencers.[302]

The appeal of virtual Influencers to marketers is not hard to see. As the promoters at VirtualHumans.org put it, "Virtual humans epitomize sprezzatura—the art of making something highly planned seem spontaneous and casual. Studied carelessness. By creating humans in this way, brands surpass a painful dependency on conventional Influencers and, instead, unlock controlled, direct relationships with a new generation of entertainment-craving consumers. Yes, the TikTok-binging, Twitch-streaming, metaverse-exploring, vocal, fleeting Gen-Z."[303]

HUMAN VERSUS VIRTUAL INFLUENCERS

Academics have been studying the obvious question for several years now: Which is better, live or Memorex (updated)? Most studies have found that "it depends."[304] Generally speaking, human Influencers perform better when there is emotional language being used in the endorsements—because humans can more credibly convey emotional ideas than nonhumans. But when rational arguments or facts are advanced by virtual Influencers, the studies conclude that they can perform just as well as their human counterparts. This suggests, not unsurprisingly, that different kinds of Influencers are needed for different marketing objectives.

One study's co-author pointed out the limitations of using a virtual Influencer: "When it comes to an endorsement by a virtual Influencer, the followers start questioning the expertness of the Influencer on the field" and so "pretending that the Influencer has actual experience with the product backfires."[305]

THREE APPROACHES TO VIRTUAL INFLUENCERS

Brands are working with virtual Influencers in three ways—sponsoring an existing virtual Influencer to promote content for a limited time, signing a virtual Influencer to an ongoing partnership, and creating a "spokesperson" for the brand—allowing for complete control over the Influencer's story arc, personality, and brand affinity.

An effective virtual Influencer campaign requires breaking the mold of corporate social media accounts (a.k.a. hellscapes in Gen Z's eyes) by leveraging the natural storytelling abilities of virtual Influencers, artfully balancing lifestyle and branded content, and portraying a well-rounded active "human" who is going about its day just happening to interact in a delightful way with the brand. Such storytelling can captivate and engage fans when an ordinary brand presentation would put them to sleep.

Mattel turned classic Barbie into a virtual YouTuber, hosting her own channel and discussing everything from makeup to social consciousness. For decades, Mattel has fought characterizations of Barbie as sexist or anti-feminist, and Barbie's new activist platform effectively positioned the character as the role model long sought. A 2023 blockbuster movie certainly helped Mattel's most iconic character relate to a new generation.

KFC turned Colonel Sanders into a young and sexy CGI version of the crusty old Harland Sanders pitchman played for decades by actors. The virtual Colonel lived a glamorous lifestyle while mocking other virtual Influencers on social media. In "his" posts, the Colonel thought of "himself" as an actual person, and "food fans" reportedly felt conflicted about their attraction to "him." Yet, KFC's Instagram engagement reportedly doubled during the campaign's run period.[306]

VIRTUAL INFLUENCERS AND E-COMMERCE

One of the promising opportunities for virtual Influencers is in e-commerce. Shoppers can, for example, click on clothing and see it displayed on a range of different models—all of them virtual. The advantage of employing these virtual models over virtual try-on technology is that the shopper can aspire to look like the virtual model. Instead of obsessing on perceived flaws in their own figures, shoppers can opt to believe that the clothes will look better on them when they arrive by mail.

One approach to this is **Google**'s try-on feature located right in its search results. Online shoppers can see clothing on a wide range of models and use various filters to refine their options. They can see clothes on a range of skin tones and body types. Google's generative AI models can take an article of clothing and demonstrate how it drapes, folds, clings, stretches, or wrinkles on eighty different models in sizes XXS–4XL in various poses. Google's technology is available for such brands as Anthropologie, Everlane, H&M, and LOFT. Shoppers are encouraged to keep refining until they find exactly what they want and then order with confidence.[307]

Virtual Influencers Meet Emerging Technology

FOLLOWING INFLUENCERS INTO THE METAVERSE

Brands are hosting more events in the Metaverse, giving customers an opportunity to view themselves seated next to their favorite Influencer as the event unfolds. This kind of engagement can be golden.

Maybelline is using a virtual avatar named "May" who appears along with supermodel Gigi Hadid to promote a new line of mascara. The creative hook is that the mascara itself is "so surreal, only an avatar can bring it to life." [308] Maybelline sees "May" as the next step into the Metaverse. And in partnership with the game character Creator Ready Player Me, Maybelline is showing players how to apply makeup to their avatars in fun and exciting ways. Maybelline says that "May" is here to stay and will headline the release of more virtual products and services in the Metaverse.

Jon Reily of the digital transformation company Bounteous found an interesting tidbit in a study by the gaming platform Roblox. Gen Zers were asked about their fashion preferences, "Two out of five of them said that they cared more about their digital fashion than they did their real-world fashion" and "70 percent of them responded that they use their digital avatars to influence their real-world outfits. So, we're now literally at the point where rather than designing our avatars to look like ourselves in the real world, we're designing our real-world selves to look like what we would look like in the Metaverse."[309]

This is meaningful data for the fashion industry, for sure, but well beyond. The more that virtual behavior drives offline behavior, the more brands of all kinds—from CPG to B2B—need to focus on the kinds of Influencer strategies worth deploying in alternate reality environments, bridging the digital and physical divide.

USING AI TO SELECT THE IDEAL INFLUENCER SET

It's been said by the Influencer marketing network Trend.io that "trying to find effective, trustworthy Influencers is like looking for Waldo while blindfolded."[310] While true for the last decade, going forward there may not be a single Waldo that AI can't find! Agencies are beginning to use AI to automate the entire Influencer-Creator collaboration from selection criteria to campaign monitoring and reporting, payments and rights management, everything, or à la carte.

Retail brands stand to gain the most from this AI selection capability. American Eagle CMO Craig Brommers notes, "We work with about seven hundred Influencers each season. It's a lot of people, and I do think technology such as AI will allow us to be more efficient in identifying potential partners. We're dabbling, testing, and learning and then potentially scaling some of these tools. We're going to have to use data and analytics just as much as the sexy elements of Influencer marketing. It's a continuous push for modern marketing teams from art to science. The blend of those two areas is increasingly important."[311]

Navigating the Headwinds of Influencer Marketing

WORKING AROUND AD BLOCKERS

Consumers love ad blockers as a weapon against annoying ads. Since the average person is subjected to more than four thousand ads per day, it's understandable that consumers will continue to favor platforms and hardware that promises to minimize ads. Despite disliking ads, however, consumers get a dopamine hit every time they lay eyes on their favorite personalities in advertising. So, they are more likely to tune in. And they'll happily watch that favorite personality in organic content and not consider it "promotional" at all. This makes Influencers—especially celebrity personalities—a great hedge against the increase in ad blocker technologies.

STRICTER REGULATIONS ON THE USE OF INFLUENCERS

After years of consumer complaints about questionable Influencer marketing, in 2017, the FTC cracked down on online Influencers. An FTC warning letter made clear that material connections must be disclosed in the advertising.[312] In the same year, the Securities and Exchange Commission (SEC) warned that public companies were improperly using celebrity-Influencers to promote stocks.[313] And, in 2022, the SEC slapped serious fines on a number of celebrities, most notably, Kim Kardashian, for hawking crypto firms without disclosing the paid relationships.[314] The FTC and SEC, and their counterparts globally as well, are expected to continue tightening rules on the use of Influencers, requiring brands to better manage Influencer partnerships.

This is likely to impact micro-Influencers the most, and on multiple levels. For one, brands generally ask Influencer partners to hold general liability insurance. With annual premiums for a $1 million policy running above $2,000, this is not an issue for big names.[315] But for the growing legions of micro-Influencers, the math won't always add up. On another level, with such explosive growth of highly recognized Influencers appearing on behalf of highly regarded brands on highly trafficked social platforms, the potential for copyright licensing and infringement issues is likely only to expand and test the patience of marketers.

DEALING WITH IP ISSUES

As with all the new AI-based technologies, marketers could face a number of potentially thorny legal concerns with virtual Influencers.

For one, AI is being used to create these virtual models both with and without permission being granted from the original humans. Models are seeing likenesses of themselves on billboards and in the Metaverse and are bringing lawsuits. Others have willingly undergone volumetric scanning and 3D real-time design to construct strikingly realistic digital characters of themselves. Kendall Jenner's avatar, as an example, walked a virtual runway in a Burberry show.[316]

Some are claiming that the responsible use of digital rendering tools will boost creativity in commerce and that this "new thing" should be embraced. Others disagree. A number of lawsuits, including a major class action by visual artists against generative AI toolmakers, will decide how much leniency marketers have in using virtual Influencers.

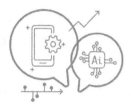

CONCLUSION
Becoming a Future-Ready Brand

We've looked at the three futurewaves of change impacting brand marketers and how today's most successful CMOs are facing these unfolding challenges. There are the societal shifts prompting brands to *position* themselves to meet the values and expectations of an emerging and newly demanding consumer base. There are the technological innovations that allow brands to *personalize* the product offer and the customer experience with near-prescient precision. And there are the brand activation trends that are rejiggering how brands *promote* themselves profitably.

Within this framework, we began **chapter 1** with a case study of Accenture taking action—at the peak of the pandemic—to reorganize its entire global staff around a new "purpose" and how superbly that plays out. With Accenture and other leading brands as well, we find their commitment to "purpose" manifesting in three ways: in exemplary corporate cultures, publicly recognized competence, or widely heralded champions of vital causes.

Numerous benefits then accrue to these purpose-driven companies, including a positive correlation between purpose and profit, outperforming the overall market, an ability to command premium pricing, and winning the war for talent.

This focus on purpose is most pronounced among industry standouts and is shown to be a driving force behind the acceptance these companies enjoy with Millennials and Gen Z, the new majority of customers.

Chapter 2 gave us a case study of Moderna navigating the pandemic and then needing to position a suddenly popular brand for continued success. The mRNA pioneer surely faces its own unique hurdles in competing in the new wellness economy. But it equally faces the same hurdles all brands face in a time when a heightened prioritization of "healthy living" is driving consumer buying behavior.

Today's overarching health trends—increased consumer awareness through easy online research, a dramatic rise in healthcare costs, a fast-aging population, the overhang of the pandemic, and technology's acceleration of everything—have forced new wellness directives on brand marketers across the spectrum.

Chief among these directives is reassessing the brand promise in terms of a total health orientation—physical, mental, and spiritual; making the brand feel as "personal" as an individual's own wellness feels; finding ways to generate healthier in-store experiences; meeting consumers "where" and "why" they are shopping for solutions; and cultivating the brand's authentic community with a "health orientation" in mind.

Chapter 3 dug into Gen Z and opened with a case study of the Coty cosmetics company. It is Coty's CMO's belief, shared by other CMOs as well, that this generation of newly/relatively affluent consumers is better named Gen Z ME *and* Gen Z WE—two very different and often opposing facets within each person.

In marketing to this generation, then, it is critical to know the Gen Z ME facet places a high value on authenticity and transparency, individualism and personalization, and connection and experience.

And the Gen Z WE facet places a high value on meaning and purpose, diversity and inclusion, and sustainability and the ESG agenda.

Aligning with these dearly held generational values requires new steps from the marketing department, specifically holding the company's public-facing actions to a higher level of accountability; pointedly meeting Gen Z where they're hanging out; integrating the brand/products in an organic way into the action on gaming sites; and raising the brand's voice in both online and offline communities where values and interests are shared.

Chapter 4 moved into the "technology section" of the book and opened on a pioneer in AI marketing, IBM. Its case study showed how marketers expect to thrive in the cookieless future ahead.

Of course, AI is on every marketer's mind as they grapple with machine learning's capabilities, super-granular predictive analytics, micro-segmentation, generative AI content, and hyper-personalization in customer engagement.

Companies set on gaining the greatest competitive advantage from AI are elevating the marketing function in the C-suite to drive business strategy, bringing any truly strategic AI functionality in-house, transitioning their teams to an AI-centric future, and putting adequate guardrails in place.

Marketers are plenty aware of the downside of AI and related technologies, as well. The challenges CMOs are facing head-on are data integrity, copyright and IP issues, brand fit and authenticity, fake ads, systemic biases, keeping the human touch alive so that creativity doesn't suffer, and regulations in the pipeline that impact every level of operation.

Chapter 5 tracked Ally Financial's "crawl, run, walk" approach to following younger audiences into the alternate realities of XR technologies. Marketers' greatest successes thus far involve XR technologies that do not require people to slap on cumbersome headgear. More user-friendly "goggles" of some kind are coming at one point, marketers agree. But, in the meantime, CMOs are tinkering with "Web 2.5"—using other XR technologies to showcase their cutting-edge brand, extend their robust omnichannel brand experience, leverage the huge popularity of gaming communities, conduct far better product sampling and market research, and build more efficiencies into in-person events and community gatherings.

As for the Metaverse, marketers are toe-dipping and trying to figure out how to turn what could become a vast entertainment complex into a brand-friendly experience for customers. Progress is being made, but the "killer app" for the Metaverse remains an elusive goal.

Chapter 6 opened on a racetrack with Lexus melding real-world racing with new Web3 technologies to extend its brand attributes to a new generation of drivers.

At this point, Web3 represents as much hype as hope, but marketers are finding novel methods for aligning their products/services with early adopters of decentralized ownership schemes based on blockchain and crypto, NFTs and token economics, and the gradually unfolding Metaverse itself.

Consumers are expected to benefit greatly from the security, transparency, and investment potential of Web3 technologies.

Brands and marketers are expected to benefit from revenue generation from the sale of digital assets, forging deeper customer relationships, and testing new products in a real-time feedback loop.

Markets and communities should come to value the alternative economies that people can participate in and the ways that societal issues can be positively impacted.

Chapter 7 opened with UScellular's innovative Super Bowl marketing campaign to demonstrate how marketers are stepping into the "sci-fi" future of content marketing where new technologies are literally transforming the interplay between brands and audiences.

New AI-driven marketing strategies and solutions are being deployed at each level of content management—in research, creation, personalization, curation, and optimization. And marketers are seeing the many *limitations* of automated systems, as well, particularly in trying to generate AI content that's creative enough to convert, obtaining good SEO, dealing with larger ethical concerns, and effectively controlling and policing messaging.

Companies are finding value in developing in-house AI tools and using off-the-shelf solutions. Whichever choice they make, there is a fast-growing list of available options (categorized at chapter's end as a reference guide).

A powerful case study from Salesforce.com opened **chapter 8** because the CRM leader is a model for applying gamification to community-building efforts, and in turn, company- and brand-building.

Companies executing superbly on gamification hold five tenets dear: at the core of a successful campaign there is always *a story*, every story features a novel *challenge*, no challenge is worthwhile without some *ownership* tendered, urgency must be layered in with time-proven *timing* techniques, and the story becomes complete in the consumer's mind with *social sharing*.

The summary value of gamification to marketers includes elevating brand awareness, improving customer satisfaction, increasing customer loyalty, accruing brand equity, and simply, driving conversions.

AI is expected to play a substantial role in future gamification campaigns and drive deeper insights via personalization, generate more profitable experiences for marketers, offer intelligent game design and recommendations, provide instant feedback and analysis, supercharge results with XR capabilities, and likely move onto the blockchain in select cases.

Finally, in **chapter 9**, the evolving influence of Influencers and Creators was explored, initially in a BMW case study.

Today's most successful marketers are adept at aligning Influencer marketing with business strategy—not just saying it but actually doing it. This requires sourcing the right Influencers, letting go of the illusion of control, and minimizing the brand risks associated with Influencer marketing—and there can be many.

While major brands use celebrity-Influencers often for awareness, CMOs are uniformly turning to and finding their greatest ROI from micro-Influencers. This shift grows out of the impact the TikTok platform is enjoying, the increasing relevance of Influencers who manage their own content creation, the shift from hi-fi to lo-fi content, and the ability to propel the brand into many smaller physical communities effectively.

There is a growing belief, still being proven out, that virtual Influencers can perform as well as or better than humans. CMOs are even starting to use AI to select the ideal Influencer sets for their campaigns.

Most marketers feel certain that the future of influence will be very different from what we see today. Fair to say that this has been the theme of this book—the future is unfolding fast for marketers, and remaining on top of it is a top priority.

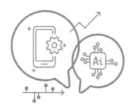

ABOUT THE AUTHOR

Mitch Duckler is founder and managing partner of FullSurge (www.fullsurge.com), a brand and marketing strategy consultancy based in Chicago, Illinois. He is also author of the bestselling book *The Indispensable Brand*. Mitch has more than thirty years of brand management and management consulting experience at Unilever, the Coca-Cola Company, and Prophet. His client base includes Fortune 500 companies and numerous world-class brands, such as ExxonMobil, Deloitte, Cox Communications, Manpower Group, Blue Cross Blue Shield, LexisNexis, Caterpillar, Abbott, and Hyatt Hotels.

Mitch is also a frequent speaker on key topics related to brand and marketing strategy. In 2021, he delivered a TEDx Talk—*Define Your Differentiator*—at the Cal State-Fullerton TEDx event in Orange County, CA. Over the past twenty years, he has spoken at dozens of high-profile events across five continents, and he is a frequent interview guest on brand and marketing related podcasts. Mitch is a faculty member of the Association of National Advertisers (ANA) Marketing Training & Development Center, where he facilitates workshops for member organizations on key topics related to brand and marketing strategy.

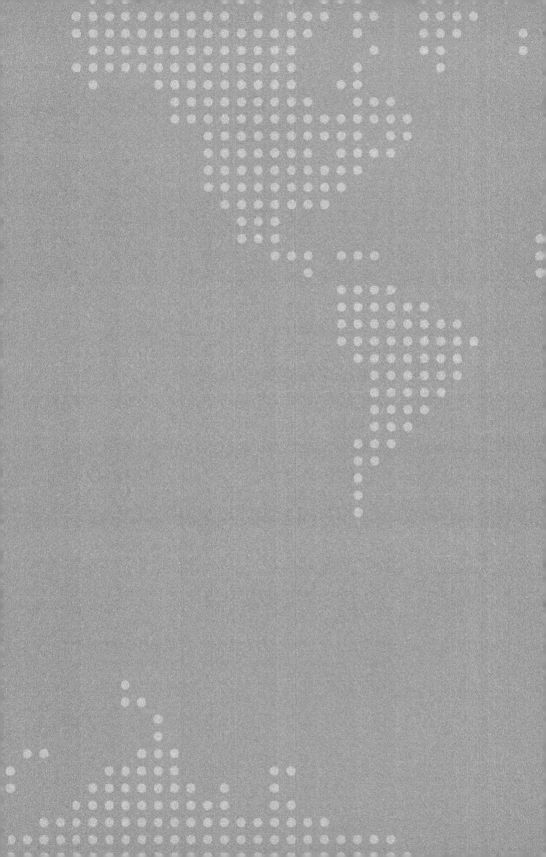

CONTACT

It has been a pleasure bringing these insights to my fellow brand marketers, and I look forward to discussing it further—should you be interested.

Mitch Duckler
mduckler@fullsurge.com
linkedin.com/in/mitchduckler/

About FullSurge

FullSurge is a brand and marketing strategy consultancy based in Chicago, IL. We are relentlessly committed to helping clients build brands the world cannot live without. We dig deep to uncover truths others cannot easily see. We believe our job as strategy consultants is to solve complex brand challenges. Only then can we begin to build a truly indispensable brand.

Our core service offerings include: brand positioning, brand architecture, brand extension and growth, digital and brand experience, naming and messaging, and research and insights.

For more information, please visit us at FullSurge.com.

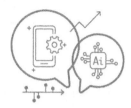

ACKNOWLEDGMENTS

I purposely set out to write a comprehensive book spanning the many different forces and trends—societal, technological, and commercial—that are impacting the world of marketing and brand-building. The broad array of topics under consideration required me to rely heavily on many subject matter experts for input. As such, there are many people to whom I owe thanks, as their encouragement, guidance, and support were invaluable throughout the writing of this book.

I would like to begin by acknowledging the talented and supportive staff at Forbes Books. Caroline Moore was particularly instrumental in guiding me through every stage of the book writing process, and she was infinitely patient with me along the way. A special thanks also to Forbes's Patti Boysen, Samantha Miller, Matthew Morse, and Jenna Panzella.

Without question, the very cornerstone of this book is the 40+ CMO and other C-level executives I interviewed over the course of ten months. Without their invaluable contributions, this book would never have been written. As such, a very special thank you to Melissa Brotz, Jill Kramer, James Temple, Andrea Brimmer, Craig Brommers, Jens Thiemer, Jeff Mirviss, Zach Kitschke, Johanna Murphy, Yvette Morrison, Stefano Curti, Michelle Peluso, Linda Bethea, Suzanne Kounkel, Ulrich Klenke, Jill Cress, Gary Kuchta, Mark Weinstein, Jonathan Adashek, Kate Ardini, Michael, Marcellin, Samie Barr, Brian Miske, Paige Guzman, Vinay Shahani, Tariq Hassan, Kate Cronin,

Chris Davis, Jim Lecinski, Todd Kaplan, Peggy Ang, Remi Kent, Antonia Wade, Sarah Franklin, Garry Wicka, Steve Lesnard, Chema Alonso, Lisa Caputo, Teresa Poggenpohl, Kevin Warren, Eric Jagher, Amy Bonitatibus, and Nick Chavez.

Thank you also to Michael Million and Nancy Wulz for the up-front research they conducted to help me develop initial hypotheses and prepare for upcoming interviews. And a very special thank you to Lee Troxler for the desk research, thought leadership, and overall guidance and counsel he provided to the project.

Finally, I would be remiss if I didn't acknowledge and thank the scores of clients over the years who gave me the opportunity to consult on some of the most esteemed and valuable brands in the world. I am truly humbled to have worked with them and their remarkable organizations, and I have benefited from the challenges and opportunities they entrusted me with.

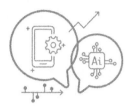

ENDNOTES

1   From author interview with Jill Kramer, Chief Marketing and Communications Officer of Accenture, April 5, 2023.

2   EY Americas, "Why business must harness the power of purpose," EY, December 15, 2020, https://www.ey.com/en_us/purpose/why-business-must-harness-the-power-of-purpose.

3   Khanyi Mlaba, "The richest 1% own almost half the world's wealth & 9 other mind-blowing facts on wealth inequality," Global Citizen, January 19, 2023, https://www.globalcitizen.org/en/content/wealth-inequality-oxfam-billionaires-elon-musk.

And

Nick Paskoski, "CEO compensation: an issue of fairness or evidence of a functioning free market?" Closeup.org, February 10, 2023, https://www.closeup.org/ceo-compensation-an-issue-of-fairness-or-evidence-of-a-functioning-free-market.

4   "Strength of purpose study," The Zeno Group, June 17, 2020, https://www.zenogroup.com/insights/2020-zeno-strength-purpose

5   Jonathan Knowles, B. Tom Hunsaker, Hannah Grove, and Alison James, "What is the purpose of your purpose?" March-April 2022, https://hbr.org/2022/03/what-is-the-purpose-of-your-purpose.

6   From author interview with Peggy Ang, President, CMO, and board member of Polar Electro, February 20, 2023.

7   Jeff Fromm, "The purpose series: Mars focuses on driving purpose," Forbes, March 12, 2019, https://www.forbes.com/sites/jefffromm/2019/03/12/the-purpose-series-mars-focuses-on-driving-purpose.

8   "Save money, live better and the full potential of Walmart," Walmart, 2008, https://corporate.walmart.com/_news_/executive-viewpoints/save-money-live-better-the-full-potential-of-walmart.

9   From author interview with Teresa Poggenpohl, SVP & Chief Marketing Officer of Unisys, June 27, 2023.

10   From author interview with Melissa Brotz, Chief Marketing and Communications Officer of Abbot, February 27, 2023.

11   From author interview with Yvette Morrison, VP, Head of Marketing and Brand of Caterpillar, February 21, 2023.

12   From author interview with Nick Chavez, CMO of KFC, April 3, 2023.

13   From author interview with Remi Kent, CMO of Progressive, June 27, 2023.

14   "IBM builds a smarter planet," IBM, n.d., https://www.ibm.com/smarterplanet/us/en/.

15   "Putting purpose to work: a study of purpose in the workplace," PWC, June 2016, https://www.pwc.com/us/en/about-us/corporate-responsibility/assets/pwc-putting-purpose-to-work-purpose-survey-report.pdf.

And

Jennifer Robison, "The future of your workplace depends on your purpose," Gallup, May 24, 2019, https://www.gallup.com/workplace/257744/future-workplace-depends-purpose.aspx.

16   "Can a purpose, beyond profit, really drive results and long-term value?," Ernst & Young, April 29, 2019, https://www.ey.com/en_us/purpose/how-purpose-has-driven-three-decades-of-award-winning-entreprene.

17   Claudine Gartenberg, Andrea Prat, and George Serafeim, "Corporate purpose and financial performance," Harvard Business Review, January-February 2019, https://www.hbs.edu/faculty/Pages/item.aspx?num=54523.

And

"The business case for purpose," EY Beacon Institute, 2015, https://assets.ey.com/content/dam/ey-sites/ey-com/en_gl/topics/digital/ey-the-business-case-for-purpose.pdf.

And

Giusy Bounfantino, "New research shows consumers more interested in brands' values than ever," Consumer Goods Technology, April 26, 2022, https://consumergoods.com/new-research-shows-consumers-more-interested-brands-values-ever.

And

Gordon L. Clark, Andreas Feiner, and Michael Viehs, "From the stockholder to the stakeholder, how corporate sustainability can drive financial outperformance," March 2015, https://arabesque.com/research/From_the_stockholder_to_the_stakeholder_web.pdf.

18   "Strength of purpose study," The Zeno Group, June 17, 2020, https://www.zenogroup.com/insights/2020-zeno-strength-purpose.

19   "Global leadership forecast 2018," DDI, The Confer-
      ence Board, EY, 2018, https://media.ddiworld.com/research/
      global-leadership-forecast-2018_ddi_tr.pdf.

And

      Diana O'Brien, Andy Main, Suzanne Kounkel, and Anthony R.
      Stephan, "Purpose is everything," Deloitte Insights, October 15, 2019,
      https://www2.deloitte.com/us/en/insights/topics/marketing-and-sales-
      operations/global-marketing-trends/2020/purpose-driven-companies.
      html.

20   "3/4 of millennials would take a pay cut to work for a socially respon-
      sible company," Sustainable Brands, 2017, https://sustainablebrands.
      com/read/organizational-change/3-4-of-millennials-would-take-a-pay-
      cut-to-work-for-a-socially-responsible-company.

21   "The science of purpose," Science of Purpose, n.d., http://scienceof-
      purpose.org.

22   Jason Mathew, "A conversation with Whirlpool about technology that
      matters," Whirlpool, May 15, 2018, https://www.whirlpoolpro.com/
      news-events/a-conversation-with-whirlpool-about-technology-that-
      matters.

23   "Whirlpool brand challenges industry marketing norms; champions the
      importance of daily tasks," Whirlpool, October 7, 2014, http://www.
      multivu.com/players/English/7318751-whirlpool-announced-launch-
      of-every-day-take-the-chore-out-of-household-responsibilities/.

24   From author interview with Linda Bethea, Head of Marketing at
      Danone, April 12, 2023.

25   "How a higher purpose drives better innovation," EY,
      April 29, 2019, https://www.ey.com/en_us/purpose/
      how-can-you-innovate-today-to-shape-tomorrow.

26 "The 2021 Axios Harris poll 100 reputation rankings," Axios, May 13, 2021, https://www.axios.com/2021/05/13/the-2021-axios-harris-poll-100-reputation-rankings.

27 From author interview with Moderna CMO Kate Cronin, April 3, 2023.

28 Karl Greenberg, "For Moderna's head of marketing ops, finessing pharma and air traffic control have something in common," FiercePharma, July 7, 2022, https://www.fiercepharma.com/marketing/modernas-head-marketing-ops-finessing-pharma-and-air-traffic-control-have-something.

29 Jack O'Brien, "Welcome to the mRNAge: Moderna launches global mRNA campaign," AdAge, April 17, 2023, https://www.mmm-online.com/home/channel/welcome-to-the-mrnage-moderna-launches-global-mrna-campaign.

30 Source references: "Health care worldwide," Statista, June 2023, https://www.statista.com/outlook/dmo/ecommerce/beauty-health-personal-household-care/health-care/worldwide.

"NHE fact sheet," CMS.GOV, 2021, https://www.cms.gov/research-statistics-data-and-systems/statistics-trends-and-reports/nationalhealthexpenddata/nhe-fact-sheet.

"2019 Move to be well: the Global Economy of Physical Activity," Global Wellness Institute, 2019, https://globalwellnessinstitute.org/industry-research/global-economy-physical-activity.

"Health and wellness market by product type, distribution channel, and Geography - forecast and analysis 2023-2027," Technavio, October 2022, https://www.technavio.com/report/health-and-wellness-market-industry-analysis.

Smiljanic Stasha, "21+ Statistics about the health and wellness industry," PolicyAdvice summary of PwC report, March 23, 2023, https://policyadvice.net/insurance/insights/health-wellness-industry.

"The wearable life 2.0—connected living in a wearable world," PwC, 2016, https://www.pwc.com/ee/et/publications/pub/pwc-cis-wearables.pdf.

"Healthy outlook for wearables as users focus on fitness and well-being," CCS Insight, n.d., https://www.ccsinsight.com/company-news/healthy-outlook-for-wearables-as-users-focus-on-fitness-and-well-being/.

"New year, new you," PwC, 2017, https://www.pwc.com/us/en/consumermarkets/assets/pwc-holiday-outlook-wrap-up-health-and-fitness.pdf.

Shaun Callaghan, Martin Lösch, Anna Pione, and Warren Teichner, "Feeling good: the future of the $1.5 trillion wellness market," McKinsey, April 8, 2021, https://www.mckinsey.com/industries/consumer-packaged-goods/our-insights/feeling-good-the-future-of-the-1-5-trillion-wellness-market.

"Meditation apps worldwide," Statista, April 2023, https://www.statista.com/outlook/dmo/digital-health/digital-fitness-well-being/digital-fitness-well-being-apps/meditation-apps/worldwide.

Peeyush Singh, "Future of wellness industry market in 2022 and beyond!," Appinventiv, July 7, 2022, https://appinventiv.com/blog/wellness-market-statistics-for-future-growth/.

31 "Consumers see health and well-being as 'essential' spend category, Accenture survey finds," Accenture, September 7, 2022, https://newsroom.accenture.com/news/consumers-see-health-and-well-being-as-essential-spend-category-accenture-survey-finds.htm.

32 Ibid.

33 Shaun Callaghan, Martin Lösch, Anna Pione, and Warren Teichner, "Feeling good: The future of the $1.5 trillion wellness market," McKinsey, April 8, 2021, https://www.mckinsey.com/industries/consumer-packaged-goods/our-insights/feeling-good-the-future-of-the-1-5-trillion-wellness-market.

34 "New state-by-state report: in 37 states, workers' health insurance premiums and deductibles take up 10 percent or more of median income," The Commonwealth Fund, January 2022, https://www.commonwealthfund.org/press-release/2022/new-state-state-report-37-states-workers-health-insurance-premiums-and.

35 Jennifer M. Ortman, Victoria A. Velkoff, and Howard Hogan, "An aging nation: the older population in the United States," The Census Bureau, May 2014, https://www.census.gov/content/dam/Census/library/publications/2014/demo/p25-1140.pdf.

36 Anastassia Gliadkovskaya, "Patients doing more of their own research online, often leaving doctor's office with questions," Fierce Pharma, October 19, 2021, https://www.fiercehealthcare.com/practices/americans-don-t-understand-provider-information-seek-help-from-internet.

37 "Beauty, health, personal & household care sales as percentage of total retail e-commerce sales in the United States from 2017 to 2025," Statista, January 2022, https://www.statista.com/forecasts/278899/health-care-as-percentage-of-total-retail-e-commerce-in-the-us.

38 Jennifer Berg, Cynthia Pelayo, Nicolas Boyon, and David Scowcroft, "What the future: wellness," Ipsos, 2022, https://www.ipsos.com/sites/default/files/What-The-Future-Wellness.pdf.

39 "New report shows over 180,000 consumer goods products reformulated," The Consumer Goods Forum, March 2107, https://www.theconsumergoodsforum.com/press_releases/health-new-report-shows-over-180000-consumer-goods-products-reformulated.

40 "2021 State of mental health in America," Mental Health America, October 20, 2020: https://mhanational.org/research-reports/covid-19-and-mental-health-growing-crisis.

And

"Adults reporting symptoms of anxiety or depressive disorder during COVID-19 pandemic," KFF (Kaiser Foundation), February 13, 2023, https://www.kff.org/other/state-indicator/adults-reporting-symptoms-of-anxiety-or-depressive-disorder-during-covid-19-pandemic.

41 "Your 2021 workplace mental health trends forecast," Lyra Health, January 6, 2021, https://www.lyrahealth.com/blog/mental-health-benefits-trends-2021.

42 "Teen depression on the rise: what to look for," Scripps, April 25, 2022, https://www.scripps.org/news_items/5319-teen-depression-on-the-rise-what-to-look-for.

And

Ashley Mowreader, "Wellness tip: using polls to get a pulse on students' mental health," Inside Higher Ed, March 7, 2023, https://www.insidehighered.com/news/2023/03/08/professor-polls-students-mental-health-check.

And

Max Margolius, Alicia Doyle Lynch, Elizabeth Pufall Jones, and Michelle Hynes, "The state of young people during COVID-19: findings from a nationally representative survey of high school youth," America's Promise Alliance, June 2020, https://eric.ed.gov/?id=ED606305.

43 "Emerging trends shaping the future of health and wellness part III: mental health," RGA, n.d., https://www.rgare.com/knowledge-center/article/emerging-trends-shaping-the-future-of-health-and-wellness-part-iii-mental-health.

And

Tori DeAngelis, "As funding cools, venture capitalists shift investments in mental health," American Psychological Association, January 1, 2023, https://www.apa.org/monitor/2023/01/trends-venture-capital-funding-shifts.

44   From author interview with Michelle Peluso, Executive Vice President and Chief Customer and Experience Officer of CVS Health, June 19, 2023.

45   From author interview with Danone CMO Linda Bethea on April 12, 2023.

46   Kristiana Lalou, "Trending in gut health: branded probiotics build consumer trust, says Kerry expert," Nutrition Insight, April 28, 2020, https://www.nutritioninsight.com/news/trending-in-gut-health-branded-probiotics-build-consumer-trust-says-kerry-expert.html.

47   "Zero to one (million)," Zero, November 28, 2018, https://zerolongevity.com/blog/zero-to-one-million/.

48   "Self-care," Exploding Topics, June 14, 2023, https://explodingtopics.com/topic/self-care.

And

Christianna Silva, "The millennial obsession with self-care," NPR, June 4, 2017, https://www.npr.org/2017/06/04/531051473/the-millennial-obsession-with-self-care.

49   From author interview with Jeff Mirviss, President of Boston Scientific, June 26, 2023.

50   Douglas Broom, "6 Trends that define the future of health and wellness," World Economic Forum, February 15, 2022, https://www.weforum.org/agenda/2022/02/megatrends-future-health-wellness-covid19.

51 "What is personalization?" McKinsey & Company, May 30, 2023, https://www.mckinsey.com/featured-insights/mckinsey-explainers/what-is-personalization.

And

Marc Brodherson, Adam Broitman, Jason Cherok, and Kelsey Robinson, "A customer-centric approach to marketing in a privacy-first world," McKinsey & Company, May 20, 2021, https://www.mckinsey.com/capabilities/growth-marketing-and-sales/our-insights/a-customer-centric-approach-to-marketing-in-a-privacy-first-world.

52 "What is personalization?", McKinsey & Company, May 30, 2023, https://www.mckinsey.com/featured-insights/mckinsey-explainers/what-is-personalization.

And

Marc Brodherson, Adam Broitman, Jason Cherok, and Kelsey Robinson, "A customer-centric approach to marketing in a privacy-first world," McKinsey & Company, May 20, 2021, https://www.mckinsey.com/capabilities/growth-marketing-and-sales/our-insights/a-customer-centric-approach-to-marketing-in-a-privacy-first-world.

53 "What is personalization?" McKinsey & Company, May 30, 2023, https://www.mckinsey.com/featured-insights/mckinsey-explainers/what-is-personalization.

And

Marc Brodherson, Adam Broitman, Jason Cherok, and Kelsey Robinson, "A customer-centric approach to marketing in a privacy-first world," McKinsey & Company, May 20, 2021, https://www.mckinsey.com/capabilities/growth-marketing-and-sales/our-insights/a-customer-centric-approach-to-marketing-in-a-privacy-first-world.

54 From author interview with Abbott CMO Melissa Brotz on February 27, 2023.

55 "Wearable healthcare devices market," MarketsAndMarkets, December 2021, https://www.marketsandmarkets.com/Market-Reports/wearable-medical-device-market-81753973.html.

56 "Big tech in healthcare," Insider Intelligence, January 24, 2023, https://www.insiderintelligence.com/insights/big-tech-in-healthcare-report/.

57 "Apple heart study launches to identify irregular heart rhythms," Apple, November 30, 2017, https://www.apple.com/newsroom/2017/11/apple-heart-study-launches-to-identify-irregular-heart-rhythms/.

58 "Amazon's new pharmacy may steal market share from CVS, Walgreens amid pandemic," S&P Global Intelligence, January 5, 2021, https://www.spglobal.com/marketintelligence/en/news-insights/latest-news-headlines/amazon-s-new-pharmacy-may-steal-market-share-from-cvs-walgreens-amid-pandemic-61558230.

And

"The latest shakeup in the prescription drug market: $5 generics via Amazon Prime," American Hospital Association, January 31, 2023, https://www.aha.org/aha-center-health-innovation-market-scan/2023-01-31-latest-shakeup-prescription-drug-market-5-generics-amazon-prime.

59 From author interview with Lagunitas CMO Paige Guzman on June 6, 2023.

60 From author interview with John Hancock CMO Kate Ardini on March 31, 2023.

61 "Under Armour wants the world's biggest connected health community," Digital Commerce 360, June 8, 2017, https://www.digi-

talcommerce360.com/2017/06/08/under-armour-wants-the-worlds-biggest-connected-health-community.

62   From author interview with Moderna's Kate Cronin on April 3, 2023.

63   From author interview with Michelle Peluso, Executive Vice President and Chief Customer and Experience Officer of CVS Health, June 19, 2023.

64   "Forget bars and malls: why wellness spaces have become *the* social hangouts of choice," Well and Good, October 16, 2018, https://www.wellandgood.com/fitness-wellness-communities.

65   Ibid.

66   "New Klarna survey finds Boomers value sustainability more than Gen Z when shopping beauty brands," Klarna, March 30, 2021, https://www.klarna.com/international/press/new-klarna-survey-finds-boomers-value-sustainability-more-than-gen-z-when-shopping-beauty-brands.

67   Comments from Stefano Curti, CMO of Coty, from author interview, June 9, 2023.

68   "Coty 2022 sustainability report: celebrating new SBTi-approved commitments and gender equity achievements," Coty, November 14, 2022, https://www.coty.com/news/coty-2022-sustainability-report.

69   Kim Parker and Ruth Igielnik, "On the cusp of adulthood and facing an uncertain future: what we know about Gen Z so far," Pew Research, May 14, 2020, https://www.pewresearch.org/social-trends/2020/05/14/on-the-cusp-of-adulthood-and-facing-an-uncertain-future-what-we-know-about-gen-z-so-far-2.

70   Tracy Francis and Fernanda Hoefel, "'True Gen': generation Z and its implications for companies," McKinsey, November 12, 2018, https://www.

mckinsey.com/industries/consumer-packaged-goods/our-insights/
true-gen-generation-z-and-its-implications-for-companies.

And

Michael Dimock, "Defining generations: where millennials end and generation Z begins," Pew Research, January 17, 2019, https://www.pewresearch.org/fact-tank/2019/01/17/where-millennials-end-and-generation-z-begins.

71　Virna Sekuj, "Generation Z: self-care is more than a hashtag," Martech Series, October 11, 2019, https://martechseries.com/mts-insights/guest-authors/generation-z-self-care-is-more-than-a-hashtag.

72　"Global gaming market size & share analysis - growth trends & forecasts (2023 - 2028)," Mordor Intelligence, 2023, https://www.mordorintelligence.com/industry-reports/global-gaming-market.

And

Anne-Lise Sharbatian, "The future of fashion and gaming: e-commerce," Forbes Technology Council, March 17, 2021, https://www.forbes.com/sites/forbestechcouncil/2021/03/17/the-future-of-fashion-and-gaming-e-commerce.

And

"How many people play video games in the world?" Bank My Cell, June 2023, https://www.bankmycell.com/blog/how-many-people-play-video-games.

And

"The immersive media obsession: Gen Z can't get enough," Yahoo Finance, February 22, 2023, https://finance.yahoo.com/news/immersive-media-obsession-gen-z-154319812.html.

73   Erika Giovanetti, "Half of millennials have a side hustle amid coronavirus pandemic," LendingTree, October 22, 2020, https://www.lendingtree.com/personal/side-hustle-survey/.

74   James Anthony, "8 Generation Z trends & predictions for 2022/2023 ⊠a look into what's next," Finances Online, May 18, 2023, https://financesonline.com/generation-z-trends/.

75   Levi Leidy, "4 Industries Gen Z might save — and 4 it might destroy," Yahoo Finance, December 7, 2022, https://finance.yahoo.com/news/4-industries-gen-z-might-210047915.html.

And

      "EY releases Gen Z survey revealing businesses must rethink their 'Plan Z'," EY, November 4, 2021: https://www.ey.com/en_us/news/2021/11/ey-releases-gen-z-survey-revealing-businesses-must-rethink-their-plan-z.

76   Jeff Fromm, "How much financial influence does Gen Z have?" Forbes, January 10, 2018, https://www.forbes.com/sites/jefffromm/2018/01/10/what-you-need-to-know-about-the-financial-impact-of-gen-z-influence.

77   "Gen Z financial habits: spending and saving stats 2022," Self, 2022, https://www.self.inc/info/gen-z-financial-habits.

78   Dimock, "Defining generations: where millennials end and Generation Z begins."

79   Ibid.

80   Ibid.

81   Brandon Doyle, "TikTok statistics—updated March 2023," Wallaroo Media, March 21, 2023, https://wallaroomedia.com/blog/social-media/tiktok-statistics.

82   Comments from Gary Kuchta, CMO of Herbalife, from author interview, June 29, 2023.

83   Comments from Jill Cress, CMO of H&R Block, from author interview, June 27, 2023.

84   "The state of Gen Z 2020," The Center for Generational Kinetics, 2020, https://genhq.com/generation-z-consumer-research-2020.

85   Tony Coray, "Marketing to Generation Z," November 21, 2022, https://www.sheerid.com/business/blog/marketing-to-generation-z.

86   Comments from Lisa Caputo, Executive Vice President and Chief Marketing, Communications, and Customer Experience Officer for The Travelers Companies, Inc., from author interview, March 15, 2023.

87   Deyan Georgiev, "Gen Z statistics – what we know about the new generation," Review42, May 20, 2023, https://review42.com/resources/gen-z-statistics.

88   Graham Vyse, "The loneliest generation," The Signal, June 10, 2022, https://www.thesgnl.com/2022/06/political-divergence-men-women-us-daniel-cox/.

89   From author interview with Brian Miske, Managing Director of KPMG, April 10, 2023.

90   Dimock, "Defining generations: where millennials end and Generation Z begins."

And

"Status of social commerce report," The Influencer Marketing Factory, 2021, https://theInfluencermarketingfactory.com/wp-content/uploads/2021/03/social-commerce-report.pdf.

And

> Kim Parker and Ruth Igielnik, "On the cusp of adulthood and facing an uncertain future: what we know about Gen Z so far," Pew Research, May 14, 2020, https://www.pewresearch.org/social-trends/2020/05/14/on-the-cusp-of-adulthood-and-facing-an-uncertain-future-what-we-know-about-gen-z-so-far-2.

91 Dimock, "Defining generations: where millennials end and Generation Z begins."

92 From author interview with Paige Guzman, CMO of Lagunitas CMO, June 6, 2023.

93 "Uniquely Generation Z," IBM Institute for Business Value in association with National Retail Federation, 2017, https://www.ibm.com/downloads/cas/9PPL5YOX.

And

> "Survey reveals Generation Z is driven by digital touchpoints to identify products, but prefers in-store experience," Euclid Analytics, March 8, 2017, https://www.globenewswire.com/news-release/2017/03/08/1212529/0/en/Survey-Reveals-Generation-Z-is-Driven-by-Digital-Touchpoints-to-Identify-Products-but-Prefers-In-store-Experience.html.

> Monica Aldea Guest Author, "New data! 18 Gen Z characteristics & stats (+how to market to them)," Creatopy Survey published in Wordstream, December 12, 2022, https://www.wordstream.com/blog/ws/2022/08/09/gen-z-stats.

94 Ellyn Briggs, "More than half of Gen Zers spend four or more hours on social media every single day," Morning Consult, December 12, 2022, https://pro.morningconsult.com/instant-intel/gen-z-social-media-usage.

95 Comments from Gary Kuchta, CMO of Herbalife, from author interview, June 29, 2023.

96 "Uniquely Generation Z."

97 Stephanie Chevalier, "Devices most frequently used for online shopping among consumers in the United States in 2019, by generation," Statista, February 16, 2023, https://www.statista.com/statistics/518925/online-shopping-device-share-age.

98 Sara Wilson, "Where brands are reaching Gen Z," Harvard Business Review, March 11, 2021, https://hbr.org/2021/03/where-brands-are-reaching-gen-z.

99 Michael Schneider, "100 Most-watched TV series of 2022-23: this season's winners and losers," Variety, May 29, 2023, https://variety.com/2023/tv/news/most-popular-tv-shows-highest-rated-2022-2023-season-yellowstone-football-1235623612.

100 Andrea Knezovic, "Gen Alpha and Gen Z gamers: how they engage with games," Udonis, February 23, 2023, https://www.blog.udonis.co/mobile-marketing/mobile-games/gen-alpha-gen-z-gamers.

101 Mack Gelbe, "Here's what you need to know about Gen Z," Monster.com, n.d., https://www.monster.com/career-advice/article/gen-z-boss-0816.

And

Kerri Anne Renzulli, "Four ways that Gen Z is changing shopping forever," Newsweek, March 2, 2022, https://www.newsweek.com/2022/03/11/four-ways-that-gen-z-changing-shopping-forever-1683745.html.

And

"The state of Gen Z 2020," The Center for Generational Kinetics, 2020, https://genhq.com/generation-z-consumer-research-2020.

102 From author interview with Jens Thiemer, senior vice president of Customer & Brand BMW, June 16, 2023

103 Comments from author interview with Jill Cress, CMO of H&R Block, June 27, 2023.

104 Mario Carrasco, "Gen Z: brands need to prioritize DEI and gender liberation," Forbes, March 1, 2022, https://www.forbes.com/sites/forbesagencycouncil/2022/03/01/gen-z-brands-need-to-prioritize-dei-and-gender-liberation.

105 Michelle Martin, "24 Gen Z statistics that matter to marketers in 2023," Hootsuite, August 30, 2022, https://blog.hootsuite.com/gen-z-statistics/.

And

"Gen Z: getting to know the 'me is we' generation," Meta Facebook IQ, October 22, 2019, https://www.facebook.com/business/news/insights/generation-z.

106 Jack Beresford, "Millennials want gender pronouns on work emails, but many in Gen Z don't," Newsweek, April 30, 2023, https://www.newsweek.com/millennials-gen-z-workplace-pronouns-emails-1797270.

107 Ibid.

108 Comments from author interview with Ulrich Klenke, Global Chief Brand Officer of Deutsche Telekom, May 22, 2023.

109 Seth Matlins, "The Forbes world's most influential CMOs list: 2022," Forbes, 2022, https://www.forbes.com/sites/sethmatlins/2022/06/23/the-forbes-worlds-most-influential-cmos-list-2022/?sh=7a3066b21b8a.

110 René Bresgen, "Deutsche Telekom is the most popular mobile communications provider among young people," YoungBrandAwards & T-Mobile, November 18, 2022, https://www.telekom.com/en/company/details/dt-is-the-most-popular-mobile-communications-provider-1021320.

111 "Brand finance global 500 2023," Brand Finance, 2023, https://brandirectory.com/rankings/global/table.

112 Mike Proulx, "Reaching Gen Z starts with understanding their truths," Forester, January 14, 2021, https://www.forrester.com/blogs/reaching-gen-z-starts-with-understanding-their-truths.

113 Kathy Gurchiek, "Survey: ESG strategies rank high with Gen Z, Millennials," SHRM, March 21, 2023, https://www.shrm.org/hr-today/news/hr-news/pages/survey-esg-strategies-rank-high-with-gen-z-millennials.aspx.

114 "Gen Z, Millennials stand out for climate change activism, social media engagement with issue," Pew Research, May 26, 2021, https://www.pewresearch.org/science/2021/05/26/gen-z-millennials-stand-out-for-climate-change-activism-social-media-engagement-with-issue/.

115 Liz Hilton Segel and Homayoun Hatami, "Mind the gap: curated readers for Gen Z and their Z-curious colleagues," McKinsey, 2022, https://www.mckinsey.com/~/media/mckinsey/email/genz/2022/12/06/2022-12-06b.html.

116 Maya Beyhan, "The key to the S&P 500 ESG index's outperformance," S&P Dow Jones Indices, January 18, 2023, https://www.indexology-blog.com/2023/01/18/the-key-to-the-sp-500-esg-indexs-outperformance-avoiding-the-worst/.

117 Claudine Gartenberg, Andrea Prat, and George Serafeim, "Corporate purpose and financial performance," Harvard Business Review, January-February 2019, https://www.hbs.edu/faculty/Pages/item.aspx?num=54523.

And

"The business case for purpose," EY Beacon Institute, 2015, https://assets.ey.com/content/dam/ey-sites/ey-com/en_gl/topics/digital/ey-the-business-case-for-purpose.pdf.

And

Giusy Bounfantino, "New research shows consumers more interested in brands' values than ever," Consumer Goods Technology, April 26, 2022, https://consumergoods.com/new-research-shows-consumers-more-interested-brands-values-ever.

And

Gordon L. Clark, Andreas Feiner, and Michael Viehs, "From the stockholder to the stakeholder, how corporate sustainability can drive financial outperformance," March 2015, https://arabesque.com/research/From_the_stockholder_to_the_stakeholder_web.pdf.

118 PwC. "Purpose and values," PricewaterhouseCoopers, https://www.pwc.com/us/en/about-us/purpose-and-values.html.

119 From author interview with Jonathan Adashek, Chief Communications Officer and SVP, Marketing and Communications at IBM, [date]

120 "The power of AI to marketers," IBM Watson Advertising, August 30, 2022, https://www.ibm.com/watson-advertising/thought-leadership/power-of-ai.

121 Ibid.

122 "What is synthetic data?," IBM, February 7, 2023, https://research.ibm.com/blog/what-is-synthetic-data.

123 David Ratajczak, Matthew Kropp, Silvio Palumbo, Nicolas de Bellefonds, Jessica Apotheker, Sarah Willersdorf, and Giorgo Paizanis,

"How CMOs are succeeding with generative AI," Boston Consulting Group, June 15, 2023, https://www.bcg.com/publications/2023/generative-ai-in-marketing.

124 Jeff Katzin, Laura Beaudin, and Max Waldron, "Ready for launch: how Gen AI is already transforming marketing," Bain, May 23, 2023, https://www.bain.com/insights/ready-for-launch-how-gen-ai-is-already-transforming-marketing/.

125 David Ratajczak, Matthew Kropp, Silvio Palumbo, Nicolas de Bellefonds, Jessica Apotheker, Sarah Willersdorf, and Giorgo Paizanis, "How CMOs are succeeding with generative AI."

126 Kipp Bodnar, "How AI will revolutionize the future of business, according to HubSpot's CMO," HubSpot, June 5, 2023, https://blog.hubspot.com/marketing/how-ai-will-change-businesses.

127 "Salesforce execs weigh in: what is generative AI?" Salesforce, April 28, 2023, https://www.salesforce.com/news/stories/what-is-generative-ai/.

128 From author interview with Jim Lecinski, Associate Professor of Marketing at Northwestern University, June 20, 2023.

129 From author interview with Brian Miske, Managing Director, KPMG, April 10, 2023.

130 From author interview with Garry Wicka, Vice President Global Strategic Marketing of SEE, February 21, 2023.

131 "The generative AI market map: 335 vendors automating content, code, design, and more," CB Insights, July 12, 2023, https://www.cbinsights.com/research/generative-ai-startups-market-map.

132 From author interview with Brian Miske, Managing Director, KPMG, April 10, 2023.

133 From author interview with Steve Lesnard, Global Chief Brand Officer of Sephora, September 20, 2023.

134 From author interview with Jim Lecinski, Associate Professor of Marketing at Northwestern University, June 20, 2023.

135 Ibid.

136 Jay Pattisall, "Generative AI revolutionizes marketing creativity," Forrester, June 1, 2023, https://www.forrester.com/blogs/generative-ai-revolutionizes-marketing-creativity.

137 Ibid.

138 From author interview with Suzanne Kounkel, Global and US Chief Marketing Officer of Deloitte, February 14, 2023.

139 From author interview with Brian Miske, Managing Director, KPMG, April 10, 2023.

140 From author interview with Jill Kramer of Accenture, April 5, 2023.

141 Tobias Härlin, Gardar Björnsson Rova, Alex Singla, Oleg Sokolov, and Alex Sukharevsky, "Exploring opportunities in the generative AI value chain," McKinsey Digital, April 26, 2023: https://www.mckinsey.com/capabilities/quantumblack/our-insights/exploring-opportunities-in-the-generative-ai-value-chain.

142 "Artificial intelligence use cases and best practices for marketing," IAB, March 2021, https://www.iab.com/wp-content/uploads/2021/03/IAB_AI_Cases_and_Best_Practices_2021-03.pdf.

143 From author interview with Brian Miske, Managing Director, KPMG, April 10, 2023.

144 Kyle Wiggers, "The week in AI: generative AI spams up the web," TecgCrunch, July 8, 2023, https://techcrunch.com/2023/07/08/the-week-in-ai-generative-ai-spams-up-the-web.

145 Natasha Lomas, "Martin Lewis warns over 'first' deepfake video scam ad circulating on Facebook," TechCrunch, July 7, 2023, https://techcrunch.com/2023/07/07/martin-lewis-deepfake-scam-ad-facebook.

146 Rhiannon Williams, "Humans may be more likely to believe disinformation generated by AI," Technology Review, June 28, 2023, https://www.technologyreview.com/2023/06/28/1075683/humans-may-be-more-likely-to-believe-disinformation-generated-by-ai/.

147 Ibid.

148 From author interview with Suzanne Kounkel, Global and US Chief Marketing Officer of Deloitte, February 14, 2023.

149 Jay Pattisall, "Generative AI revolutionizes marketing creativity," Forrester, June 1, 2023, https://www.forrester.com/blogs/generative-ai-revolutionizes-marketing-creativity.

150 Ryan Tracy, "Business and labor square off over AI's future in American workplace," The Wall Street Journal, July 19, 2023, https://www.wsj.com/articles/business-and-labor-square-off-over-ais-future-in-american-workplace.

151 From author interview with Andrea Brimmer, CMO of Ally Financial, on July 10, 2023.

152 Ben Arnold, "Do consumers still dream of the metaverse?" NPD, February 24, 2023, https://www.npd.com/news/blog/2023/do-consumers-still-dream-of-the-metaverse.

And

Josef Erl, "10.1 Million units: short-term lower demand for VR and AR headsets," Mixed News, March 22, 2023, https://mixed-news.com/en/vr-and-ar-market-growing-slower-than-expected/.

And

Thomas Alsop, "AR/VR headset shipments worldwide 2020-2023," Statista, July 3, 2023, https://www.statista.com/statistics/653390/worldwide-virtual-and-augmented-reality-headset-shipments.

153 "Augmented Reality (AR) Market," Fortune business insights," n.d., https://www.fortunebusinessinsights.com/augmented-reality-ar-market-102553.

154 "AR & VR – worldwide," Statista, June 2023, https://www.statista.com/outlook/amo/ar-vr/worldwide.

155 "Immersive technology to reimagine online shopping experience and increase consumer purchasing confidence, according to new Accenture interactive report," Accenture Press Release, September 22, 2020, https://newsroom.accenture.com/news/immersive-technology-to-rei-magine-online-shopping-experience-and-increase-consumer-purchas-ing-confidence-according-to-new-accenture-interactive-report.htm.

156 Thomas Alsop, "Frequency of AR use in the U.S. 2022," Statista, March 23, 2023, https://www.statista.com/statistics/1310579/augmented-reality-use-frequency-us/.

157 Puri, Shaan. Twitter, 27 October 2021, https://twitter.com/ShaanVP/status/1454151250216308742..

158 Sandeep R. Chandukala, Srinivas K. Reddy, and Yong-Chin Tan, "How augmented reality can — and can't — help your vrand," Harvard Business Review, March 29, 2022, https://hbr.org/2022/03/how-augmented-reality-can-and-cant-help-your-brand.

159 Chantal Tode, "Walmart embraces augmented reality to enhance in-store shopping," Retail Dive, 2023, https://www.retaildive.com/ex/mobilecommercedaily/walmart-embraces-augmented-reality-to-enhance-in-store-shopping.

160 From author interview with Antonia Wade, Global Chief Marketing Officer of PwC, on May 3, 2023.

161 From author interview with Chema Alonso, Chief Digital Officer of Telefonica, on July 18, 2023.

162 From author interview with Lisa Caputo, Executive Vice President and Chief Marketing, Communications, and Customer Experience Officer for The Travelers Companies, Inc., on March 15, 2023.

163 From author interview with James Temple, Global Metaverse Lead at Accenture, on April 5, 2023.

164 Ryan Joe, "Brands like PepsiCo, Ally, Mondelēz, and Coty reveal how they've scored big returns by advertising in video games," Business Insider, March 9, 2023, https://www.businessinsider.com/heres-how-brands-like-pepsi-and-ally-scored-big-returns-by-advertising-in-video-games-2023-3.

165 Chris Wood, "PepsiCo's strategies for marketing via online games and esports," MarTech, June 23, 2022, https://martech.org/pepsicos-strategies-for-marketing-via-online-games-and-esports.

166 Ryan Joe, "Brands like PepsiCo, Ally, Mondelēz, and Coty reveal how they've scored big returns by advertising in video games."

167 Christine Hall, "Advances in fit technology could minimize those onerous online returns," TechCrunch, October 18, 2022, https://techcrunch.com/2022/10/18/advances-in-fit-technology-could-minimize-those-onerous-online-returns.

168 Sandeep R. Chandukala, Srinivas K. Reddy, and Yong-Chin Tan, "How augmented reality can — and can't — help your brand."

169 From author interview with Steve Lesnard, Global Chief Brand Officer of Sephora, September 20, 2023.

170 Ibid.

171 Ibid.

172 From author interview with Antonia Wade, Global Chief Marketing Officer of PwC, on May 3, 2023.

173 "PwC buys virtual land NFT in the Sandbox's metaverse," Consultancy.uk, January 4, 2022, https://www.consultancy.uk/news/30011/pwc-buys-virtual-land-nft-in-the-sandboxs-metaverse.

174 Koba Molenaar, "Discover the top 12 virtual Influencers for 2023 – listed and ranked!," Influencer Marketing Hub, December 15, 2022, https://influencermarketinghub.com/virtual-influencers/.

175 https://www.instagram.com/reel/Cki4FXPJsRZ.

176 Koba Molenaar, "Discover the top 12 virtual Influencers for 2023 – listed and ranked!"

177 From author interview with James Temple, Global Metaverse Lead at Accenture, on April 5, 2023.

178 "Climate change gets real in the metaverse," Accenture, n.d., https://www.accenture.com/us-en/case-studies/technology/tuvalu#.

179 "Climate change gets real in the metaverse," Accenture, 2023, https://www.accenture.com/us-en/case-studies/technology/tuvalu.

180 From author interview with Jonathan Adashek, Chief Communications Officer of IBM, on February 9, 2023.

181 From author interview with Suzanne Kounkel, Global and US Chief Marketing Officer at Deloitte, on February 14, 2023.

182 From author interview with Chema Alonso, Chief Digital Officer of Telefonica, on July 18, 2023.

183 Thomas Stackpole, "Exploring the metaverse," Harvard Business Review, July–August 2022, https://hbr.org/2022/07/exploring-the-metaverse.

184 Justin McLaughlin, "Marketing in the metaverse," self-published, November 11, 2022.

185 Cam Thompson, "It's lonely in the metaverse," CoinDesk, October 13, 2022, https://www.coindesk.com/web3/2022/10/07/its-lonely-in-the-metaverse-decentralands-38-daily-active-users-in-a-13b-ecosystem/.

186 Yvonne Lau, "JPMorgan bets metaverse is a $1 trillion yearly opportunity as it becomes first bank to open in virtual world," Fortune, February 16, 2022, https://fortune.com/2022/02/16/jpmorgan-first-bank-join-metaverse.

187 Thomas Stackpole, "Exploring the metaverse."

188 From author interview with Ulrich Klenke, CMO of Deutsche Telekom, on May 22, 2023.

189 Verena Fulde, "Telekom electronic beats expands its virtual world on Roblox with the launch of 'Floating Forest," Deutsche Telekom, August 28, 2023, https://www.telekom.com/en/media/media-information/archive/floating-forest-on-roblox-1047770.

190 Jackie Wiles, "What is a metaverse? And should you be buying in?" Gartner, October 21, 2022, https://www.gartner.com/en/articles/what-is-a-metaverse.

191 Koen van Gelder, "Interest in augmented reality for shopping 2022, by generation," Statista, July 11, 2023, https://www.statista.com/statistics/1308187/augmented-reality-interest-shopping-generation.

192 "2020 US vehicle sales figures by brand," GoodCarBadCar, n.d., https://www.goodcarbadcar.net/2022-us-vehicle-sales-figures-by-brand/.

193 From author interview with Vinay Shahani, Vice President Marketing at Lexus, on May 2, 2023.

194 Jade Yan, "20 Brands getting Gen Z's attention (and dollars)," AdAge, March 17, 2022, https://adage.com/article/marketing-news-strategy/20-brands-getting-gen-zs-attention-and-dollars/2401866.

195 Brian Solis, "The CMO's guide to understanding the future of brands, consumers, and community in a Web3 world," August 8, 2022, https://www.briansolis.com/2022/08/the-cmos-guide-to-understanding-the-future-of-brands-consumers-and-community-in-a-web3-world/.

196 From author interview with Andrea Brimmer CMO of Ally Financial, July 10, 2023.

197 From author interview with Suzanne Kounkel, Global and US Chief Marketing Officer at Deloitte, on February 14, 2023.

198 From author interview with Chema Alonso, Chief Digital Officer of Telefonica, on July 18, 2023.

199 From author interview with Todd Kaplan, CMO of PepsiCo on October 30, 2023.

200 "NFT sales value in the art segment worldwide in the last 30 days July 2023," Statista, July 20, 2023, https://www.statista.com/statistics/1235263/nft-art-monthly-sales-value/.

Andrew Hayward, "NFT sales in 2022 nearly matched the 2021 boom, despite market crash," Yahoo Finance, January 4, 2023, https://money.yahoo.com/nft-sales-2022-nearly-matched-231149675.html#.

201 @NFTgators. "9 ethereum! Are you kidding me!." Twitter, August 16, 2022, 4:17 p.m., accessed July 9, 2023, https://twitter.com/NFTgators/status/1561630116035305474.

202 "Has Nike found playbook for winning Web3 game?" Yahoo!, October 6, 2022, https://www.yahoo.com/video/nike-found-playbook-winning-web3-224646398.html.

203 Ashi Bhat, "Web3: what does it mean for brands?," Medium, November 25, 2022, https://medium.com/geekculture/web3-what-does-it-mean-for-brands-e4cdd6863c1e.

204 From author interview with Ulrich Klenke, CMO of Deutsche Telekom, May 22, 2023.

205 Musk, Elon. Twitter, 20 December 2021, https://twitter.com/elonmusk/status/1472745072277995526..

206 Madeleine Schulz, "Web3 has a branding problem. It's not just semantics," Vogue Business, December 13, 2022, https://www.voguebusiness.com/technology/web3-has-a-branding-problem-its-not-just-semantics.

207 "Web3 is going great," Web3 Is Going Great, accessed June 30, 2023, https://web3isgoinggreat.com.

208 https://twitter.com/jack/status/1473139010197508098.

209 Daniel Konstantinovic, "Coca-Cola's message to brands: invest in AI, not Web3," Insider Intelligence, May 18, 2023, https://www.insiderintelligence.com/content/coca-cola-s-message-brands-invest-ai-not-web3.

210 Scott Galloway, "The false promise of Web3, medium, January 18, 2022, https://marker.medium.com/the-false-promise-of-web3-7e6c1a00d4be.

211 "Wireless carrier/operator subscriber share in the U.S. 2011-2023," Statista, August 8, 2023, https://www.statista.com/statistics/199359/market-share-of-wireless-carriers-in-the-us-by-subscriptions/.

212 From author interview with Eric Jagher, CMO of UScellular, August 1, 2023.

213 Phil Britt, "UScellular: many miss super bowl top moments due to phones," Telecompetitor, February 13, 2023, https://www.telecompetitor.com/uscellular-many-miss-super-bowl-top-moments-due-to-phones/.

214 Nat Ives, "JPMorgan Chase taps AI to make marketing messages more powerful," The Wall Street Journal, July 30, 2019, https://www.wsj.com/articles/jpmorgan-chase-taps-ai-to-make-marketing-messages-more-powerful-11564482606.

215 From author interview with Todd Kaplan, CMO of PepsiCo on October 30, 2023.

216 Jessica Devo, "Coke helps festival-goers drop a track with generative AI music studio," Marketing Dive, July 18, 2023, https://www.marketingdive.com/news/coca-cola-generative-ai-music-coke-studio/688206.

217 Webb Wright, "Coke launches 'create real magic' AI art contest using GPT-4 and Dall-E 2," The Drum, March 20, 2023, https://www.thedrum.com/news/2023/03/20/coke-launches-create-real-magic-ai-art-contest-using-gpt-4-and-dall-e.

218 "The Coca-Cola company announces timing of second quarter 2023 earnings release," The Coca-Cola Company, June 28, 2023, https://d1io3yog0oux5.cloudfront.net/_c4aeacfac-fa6879b9b7b146a69673f70/cocacolacompany/db/734/8024/

earnings_release/Coca-Cola+2023+Q2+Earnings+Release_
Full+Release_7.26.23+FINAL.pdf.

219 Dom Galeon, "An algorithm designed 7 million one-of-a-kind labels
for a Nutella campaign," Futurism, June 22, 2017, https://futurism.
com/an-algorithm-designed-7-million-one-of-a-kind-labels-for-a-
nutella-campaign.

220 Alain Rees, "Cyber Inc. creates training courses with its own avatar,"
Synthesia, 2023, https://www.synthesia.io/case-studies/cyber-inc.

221 Bob Fernandez, "Generative AI promises an economic revolution.
Managing the disruption will be crucial," The Wall Street Journal,
August 28, 2023, https://www.wsj.com/articles/generative-ai-prom-
ises-an-economic-revolution-managing-the-disruption-will-be-crucial-
b1c0f054.

222 "AI content marketing market to hit US$ 17.6 billion by
2032," Market.us, August 2023, https://market.us/report/
ai-content-marketing-market/.

And

"Generative AI market by offering," MarketsAndMarkets, 2023,
https://www.marketsandmarkets.com/Market-Reports/generative-ai-
market-142870584.html.

223 Jackie Wiles, "Beyond ChatGPT: the future of generative AI for
enterprises," Gartner, January 26, 2023, https://www.gartner.com/en/
articles/beyond-chatgpt-the-future-of-generative-ai-for-enterprises.

224 Petroc Taylor, "Amount of data created, consumed, and stored 2010-
2020, with forecasts to 2025," Statista, August 22, 2023, https://www.
statista.com/statistics/871513/worldwide-data-created.

225 Bergur Thormundsson, "Generative AI adoption rate at
work in the United States 2023, by industry," August

8, 2023, https://www.statista.com/statistics/1361251/generative-ai-adoption-rate-at-work-by-industry-us/.

226 Randy Swineford, "Generative AI is empowering the digital workforce," MIT Technology Review, July 25, 2023, https://www.technologyreview.com/2023/07/25/1076532/generative-ai-is-empowering-the-digital-workforce/.

227 From author interview with Jim Lecinski, Professor of Marketing at Northwestern University, on June 20, 2023.

228 From author interview with Sarah Franklin, Chief Marketing Officer of Salesforce, on April 6, 2023.

229 From author interview with Brian Miske, KPMG Managing Director, on April 10, 2023.

230 From author interview with Zach Kitschke, CMO of Canva, October 2, 2023.

231 From author interview with Jill Kramer, CMO of Accenture, on April 5, 2023.

232 From author interview with Mark Weinstein, CMO of Hilton Hotels, on February 28, 2023.

233 From author interview with Garry Wicka, Vice President of Marketing, SEE, on February 21, 2023.

234 From author interview with Jim Lecinski, Professor of Marketing at Northwestern University, on June 20, 2023.

235 From author interview with Jill Kramer, CMO of Accenture, on April 5, 2023.

236 From author interview with Mike Marcellin, CMO of Juniper Networks, on May 4, 2023.

237 From author interview with Mark Weinstein, CMO of Hilton Hotels, on February 28, 2023.

238 From author interview with Zach Kitschke, CMO of Canva, October 2, 2023.

239 From author interview with Chris Davis, CMO of New Balance, September 28, 2023.

240 From author interview with Sarah Franklin, Chief Marketing Officer of Salesforce, on April 6, 2023.

241 From author interview with Chris Davis, CMO of New Balance, September 28, 2023.

242 From author interview with Mark Weinstein, CMO of Hilton Hotels, on February 28, 2023.

243 "What Creators should know about Google's August 2022 helpful content update," Google Search Central Blog, August 18, 2022, https://developers.google.com/search/blog/2022/08/helpful-content-update.

244 Tony Ho Tran, "Scientists built an AI to give ethical advice, but it turned out super racist," October 22, 2021, https://futurism.com/delphi-ai-ethics-racist.

245 Joseph A. Wulfsohn, "ChatGPT faces mounting accusations of being 'woke,' having liberal bias," Fox News, February 16, 2023, https://www.foxnews.com/media/chatgpt-faces-mounting-accusations-woke-liberal-bias.

246 Joseph Henry, "Elon Musk says leftist programmers train AI to lie," Tech Times, April 19, 2023, https://www.techtimes.com/amp/articles/290565/20230419/elon-musk-leftist-programmers-train-ai-lie.htm.

247 Ibid.

248 Blake Brittain, "US judge finds flaws in artists' lawsuit against AI companies," Reuters, July 19, 2023, https://www.reuters.com/legal/litigation/us-judge-finds-flaws-artists-lawsuit-against-ai-companies-2023-07-19.

249 "ANA provides 'first look' at in-depth programmatic media transparency study," Association of National Advertisers, June 19, 2023, https://www.ana.net/content/show/id/pr-2023-06-programmaticstudy.

250 Patrick Coffee, "AI fuels new brand-safety worries, and would-be solutions, for marketers," The Wall Street Journal, August 29, 2023, https://www.wsj.com/articles/ai-fuels-new-brand-safety-worries-and-would-be-solutions-for-marketers-50342971.

And

Dorsey, Jack. Twitter, 20 December 2021, https://twitter.com/jack/status/1473139010197508098.

251 "Google Bard vs. ChatGPT vs. Bing AI: the ultimate AI showdown," iGeeksBlog, July 13, 2023, https://www.igeeksblog.com/google-bard-vs-chatgpt-vs-bing-ai/.

252 James Vincent, Jacob Kastrenakes, Adi Robertson, Tom Warren, Jay Peters, and Antonio G. Di Benedetto, "AI chatbots compared: Bard vs. Bing vs. ChatGPT," The Verge, March 24, 2023, https://www.theverge.com/2023/3/24/23653377/ai-chatbots-comparison-bard-bing-chatgpt-gpt-4.

And

Emily Dreibelbis, "ChatGPT vs. Google Bard vs. Bing: which AI Chatbot gives the best answers?," PC Mag, March 23, 2023, https://www.pcmag.com/news/chatgpt-vs-google-bard-vs-microsoft-bing-which-ai-chatbot-gives-best-answers.

And

Umar Shakir, "Bing, Bard, ChatGPT, and all the news on AI chatbots," The Verge, August 22, 2023, https://www.theverge.com/23610427/chatbots-chatgpt-new-bing-google-bard-conversational-ai.

And

"Google Bard vs. ChatGPT vs. Bing AI: the ultimate AI showdown," iGeeksBlog, July 13, 2023, https://www.igeeksblog.com/google-bard-vs-chatgpt-vs-bing-ai/.

253 From author interview with Sarah Franklin CMO of Salesforce.com, April 6, 2023.

254 "What I learned from completing every trailhead badge: my trailblazer story," Salesforceben, January 1, 2022, https://www.salesforceben.com/what-i-learned-from-completing-every-trailhead-badge-my-trailblazer-story.

255 Holly Rushton, "Our favorite trailblazers: Mary Tagler," AppExchange and the Salesforce Ecosystem via Medium, June 2, 2021, https://medium.com/inside-the-salesforce-ecosystem/favorite-trailblazers-mary-tagler-949777b7ee2e.

256 For information on the program, see https://trailhead.salesforce.com/mvp/.

257 Gartner Newsroom, 2012: https://www.gartner.com/en/newsroom

258 "Gamification global market report 2023," ResearchAndMarkets, 2023, https://www.researchandmarkets.com/report/gamification.

And

"Gamification market size," Fortune Business Insights, 2020, https://www.fortunebusinessinsights.com/industry-reports/gamification-market-100632.

259 Henry Bewicke, "9 Excellent examples of gamification in retail," Talon One, August 23, 2023, https://www.talon.one/blog/9-excellent-examples-gamification-retail.

260 Nike's SNKRS webpage: https://www.nike.com/launch.

261 "Nike does it again claiming title of world's most valuable apparel brand for 7th consecutive year," BrandFinance, April 8, 2021, https://brandfinance.com/press-releases/nike-does-it-again-claiming-title-of-worlds-most-valuable-apparel-brand-for-7th-consecutive-year.

262 From author interview with Zach Kitschke, CMO of Canva, October 2, 2023.

263 From author interview with Mark Weinstein, CMO of Hilton, February 28, 2023.

264 From author interview with Steve Lesnard, Global Chief Brand Officer of Sephora, September 20, 2023.

265 From author interview with Andrea Brimmer CMO of Ally Financial, July 10, 2023.

266 From author interview with Craig Brommers, CMO of America Eagle, September 15, 2023.

267 Nidhi Arora, Daniel Ensslen, Lars Fiedler, Wei Wei Liu, Kelsey Robinson, Eli Stein, and Gustavo Schüler, "The value of getting personalization right—or wrong—is multiplying," McKinsey, November 12, 2021, https://www.mckinsey.com/capabilities/growth-marketing-and-sales/our-insights/the-value-of-getting-personalization-right-or-wrong-is-multiplying.

268 From author interview with Tariq Hassan, Chief Marketing and CX Officer of McDonald's, October 10, 2023.

269 From author interview with Jens Thiemer, senior vice president of Customer & Brand BMW, June 16, 2023

270 "Global Influencer marketing platform market," Astute, Analytical, March 9, 2023, https://www.astuteanalytica.com/industry-report/ Influencer-marketing-platform-market.

271 Werner Geyser, "The state of Influencer marketing 2023: benchmark report," Influencer Marketing Hub, February 7, 2023, https://Influencermarketinghub.com/Influencer-marketing-benchmark-report/.

272 Ibid.

273 "The state of Influencer marketing 2021," Linqia, 2021, https://www. linqia.com/wp-content/uploads/2021/04/Linqia-The-State-of-Influencer-Marketing-2021.pdf.

274 "2022 media planning: why brands need to understand consumer sentiment," Nielsen, 2021, https://www.nielsen.com/ insights/2022/2022-media-planning-why-brands-need-to-understand-consumer-sentiment/.

And

"Consumer trust in online, social and mobile advertising grows," Nielsen, April 2012, https://www.nielsen.com/insights/2012/ consumer-trust-in-online-social-and-mobile-advertising-grows.

275 Sara Lebow, "5 Charts that explain the new era for social media," Insider Intelligence, September 19, 2023, https://www.insiderintelligence.com/content/5-charts-that-explain-new-era-social-media.

276 "The state of Influencer marketing 2021."

277 From author interview with Chris Davis, CMO of New Balance, September 28, 2023.

278 From author interview with Tariq Hassan, Chief Marketing and CX Officer of McDonald's, October 10, 2023.

279 "McDonald's." Twitter, 1 December 2020, https://twitter.com/McDonalds/status/1331260307772121088.

280 Matt Krantz, "Bud Light boycott already costs Anheuser-Busch $15.7 billion," Investors.com, May 24, 2023, https://www.investors.com/etfs-and-funds/sectors/bud-light-boycott-already-costs-anheuser-busch-15-7-billion/.

281 Seth Weinkranz, "How to avoid Bud Light's marketing disaster," RAD AI, June 5, 2023, https://blog.radintel.ai/avoid-bud-lights-marketing-disaster-with-data-informed-decisions-rad-ai-explains-authentic-Influencer-marketing.

282 From author interview with Kevin Warren, chief marketing and customer experience officer at UPS, March 1, 2023.

283 From author interview with Mark Weinstein, CMO of Hilton, February 28, 2023.

284 From author interview with Samie Barr, Chief Brand Officer of Kohler, July 13, 2023.

285 "Studio McGee." Instagram, https://www.instagram.com/studiomcgee, 15 September 2023.

286 From author interview with Vinay Shahani, Vice President Marketing at Lexus, on May 2, 2023.

287 From author interview with Craig Brommers, CMO of America Eagle, September 15, 2023.

288 From author interview with Steve Lesnard, Global Chief Brand Officer of Sephora, September 20, 2023.

289 From author interview with Craig Brommers, CMO of America Eagle, September 15, 2023.

290 From author interview with Sarah Franklin CMO of Salesforce.com, April 6, 2023. Influencers

291 From author interview with Zach Kitschke, CMO of Canva, October 2, 2023.

292 Jagdishh Thadhanii, "The emergence of virtual Influencers," Grandview Research, n.d., https://www.grandviewresearch.com/research-insights/emergence-of-virtual-Influencers.

293 "The 25 most influential people on the Internet," Time, June 30, 2018, https://time.com/5324130/most-influential-internet/.

294 "Lil Miquela." Instagram, https://www.instagram.com/lilmiquela/?hl=en. Accessed September 15, 2023.

295 "3 Brands that created virtual Influencers in the metaverse," Ypulse, March 1, 2022, https://www.ypulse.com/article/2022/03/01/3-brands-that-created-virtual-Influencers-in-the-metaverse/.

296 Ibid.

297 Randi Richardson, "Who is Shudu? AI model is reigniting debate around technology, beauty and race," Yahoo!, December 13, 2022, https://www.yahoo.com/now/shudu-ai-model-reigniting-debate-234517271.html.

298 "The Affinity Magazine." Twitter, 25 February 2018, https://twitter.com/TheAffinityMag/status/968572456767287302.

299 "Virtual Influencers Survey + INFOGRAPHIC," Influencer Marketing Factory, 2022, https://theInfluencermarketingfactory.com/virtual-Influencers-survey-infographic.

300 Valentina Dencheva, "Platforms where consumers follow virtual Influencers in the U.S. 2022," Statista, May 30, 2023, https://www.statista.com/statistics/1303988/top-platforms-consumers-follow-virtual-Influencers-us/.

301 Nick Baklanov, "The top virtual Instagram Influencers in 2021," Hype-Journal, December 6, 2021, https://hypeauditor.com/blog/the-top-instagram-virtual-Influencers-in-2021/.

302 "Instagram trend report 2023," WGSN Field Survey, December 2022, https://about.instagram.com/en-us/file/1276350079639305/TRENDREPORT_2022_fin-2.pdf/.

303 Christopher, "These brands are creating humans—you can, too," VirtualHumans.org, July 7, 2020, https://www.virtualhumans.org/article/these-brands-are-creating-humans-you-can-too.

304 Ozan Ozdemir, Bora Kolfal, Paul R. Messinger, and Shaheer Rizvi, "Human or virtual: how Influencer type shapes brand attitudes," Science Direct, August 2023, https://www.sciencedirect.com/science/article/pii/S074756322300122X.

305 Lisa Ward, "Influencers don't have to be human to be believable," The Wall Street Journal, June 17, 2023, https://www.wsj.com/articles/virtual-Influencers-social-media-advertising-9cabecd2.

306 Christopher, "These brands are creating humans—you can, too."

307 Lilian Rincon, "Virtually try on clothes with a new AI shopping feature," Google, June 14, 2023, https://blog.google/products/shopping/ai-virtual-try-on-google-shopping.

308 "Maybelline New York launches the falsies surreal extensions mascara featuring its first-ever avatar," Maybelline, February 27, 2023, https://www.prnewswire.com/news-releases/maybelline-new-york-launches-the-falsies-surreal-extensions-mascara-featuring-its-first-ever-avatar-301756669.html.

309 Gabrielle Bar, "Metaverse marketing: Influencer avatars open up retailers to a target generation of consumers," MarketScale, March 22, 2023, https://marketscale.com/industries/retail/metaverse-marketing-Influencer-avatars-in-virtual-realities-open-a-target-generation-of-consumers-for-retailers/.

310 "The complete guide to Influencer networks," Trend.io, n.d., https://www.trend.io/blog/what-is-Influencer-network.

311 From author interview with Craig Brommers, CMO of America Eagle, September 15, 2023.

312 Lesley Fair, "Three FTC actions of interest to Influencers," Federal trade Commission, September 7, 2017, https://www.ftc.gov/business-guidance/blog/2017/09/three-ftc-actions-interest-Influencers.

313 "SEC statement urging caution around celebrity backed ICOs," SEC Division of Enforcement and SEC Office of Compliance Inspections and Examinations, November 1, 2017, https://www.sec.gov/news/public-statement/statement-potentially-unlawful-promotion-icos.

314 Matthew Goldstein, "Kim Kardashian to pay $1.26 million to settle S.E.C. charges over crypto promotion," The New York Times, October 3, 2022, https://www.nytimes.com/2022/10/03/business/kim-kardashian-sec-crypto.html.

315 Daphne Zhang, "TikTok, YouTube Influencers pressured by brands to buy insurance," TechCrunch, August 1, 2023, https://news.bloomberglaw.com/insurance/tiktok-youtube-Influencers-pressured-by-brands-to-buy-insurance.

316 "Katharine K. Zarrella, Is that a model or AI?," The Wall Street Journal, September 14, 2023, https://www.wsj.com/style/fashion/ai-models-levis-nars-Influencers-8cab8ba5.

Printed in the USA
CPSIA information can be obtained
at www.ICGtesting.com
JSHW082104210524
63565JS00002B/66